BELFAST DIARY

BELFAST DIARY

War as a Way of Life

JOHN CONROY

BEACON PRESS · BOSTON

Beacon Press
25 Beacon Street
Boston, Massachusetts 02108

Beacon Press books
are published under the auspices of
the Unitarian Universalist Association of Congregations.

96 95 94 93 92 91 90 89   8 7 6 5 4 3

Text design by Linda Koegel
Map design and illustration by Lea Cyr

Library of Congress Cataloging-in-Publication Data
Conroy, John, 1951–
    Belfast diary.
    1. Belfast (Northern Ireland)—Social life and
customs.   2. Violence—Northern Ireland—Belfast.
3. Conroy, John, 1951–   —Journeys—Northern Ireland—
Belfast.   I. Title.
DA995.B5C66   1987   941.6'70824   87-47539
ISBN 0-8070-0204-6
ISBN 0-8070-0205-4

CONTENTS

Preface   vii

O N E   The Lay of the Land   1

T W O   The Neighborhood   11

T H R E E   The Rules of the Game   67

F O U R   The Wall and the People Beyond It   107

F I V E   The Neighborhood in Flames   135

Epilogue   205

Map of Belfast   220

PREFACE

I FIRST WENT to Northern Ireland in 1972. I had signed up for a summer course at Oxford University, and before it began I traveled around Britain and Ireland for a few weeks. I took the ferry to the North from Scotland and arrived at Belfast early in the morning. I was so unsettled by what I saw that I left the city by noon.

I went back in 1977 as a journalist, stayed for three weeks, and filed three stories for the *Chicago Daily News*. I was surprised to learn that no American newspaper had a bureau in the North, and when I returned to Chicago later that year I began to realize how limited the press coverage was. Most of the stories from the North were two- or three-paragraph casualty reports taken from wire copy, or combat stories and accounts of personal tragedy filed by reporters who had toured as briefly as I had. Americans I spoke to found the conflict incomprehensible and thought the participants irrational.

In 1979, I submitted a proposal to the Alicia Patterson Foundation, a foundation that annually awards five journalists a year's salary to work on a single project. I proposed to write about how ordinary life had changed in Northern Ireland as a result of the violence, how people had adapted to living with the war. I intended to write no combat stories and no political speculation. After some debate, the judges backed my proposal. I arrived in the North in February 1980, and returned to Chicago a week before Christmas. I returned to Belfast in 1981, 1982, 1984, and 1985, writing magazine and newspaper articles and gathering material for this book.

My intention in writing this manuscript was to offer a street-level view of the war from the streets most affected by the turmoil, to provide a context for the casualty reports, to explain the war in terms of ordinary human beings and the pressures placed upon them. I never intended to be subject to those pressures myself and never wanted to be more than an observer. In the end, however, I did not have that luxury.

I have changed the names of a few of the people who appear in this book; those instances are clearly indicated in the text. I would like to thank my agent, Wendy Weil, and her aide, Noirin Lucas, for their hard labor on my behalf, and the Alicia Patterson Foundation, particularly Maria Casale and Alice Arlen, for their support in 1980. I am also indebted to many friends and relatives, who lent me money when mine ran out, and to Derek Alcorn, Patrick Clinton, Colette Davison, and Michael Lenehan, who read my manuscript with a critical eye. Finally I would like to thank my friends and neighbors in Belfast, who accepted me, a complete stranger, often at considerable risk.

O N E

THE LAY OF THE LAND

IN NORTHERN IRELAND, I lived in a Catholic district called Clonard, one of many pockets inside the larger ghetto of west Belfast. Clonard is a tight neighborhood of 2,000 people, fifteen streets, and sixteen trees. The streets are lined with rowhouses, one family up against the next, twenty to a row, mother, father, and four children in two bedrooms with the toilet out the back. It is a neighborhood in which, until recent times, hot water and bathtubs were luxuries.

Rising above the district is a dark brick monastery, constructed at the turn of the century. The Redemptorists, an order dedicated to the service of "the most abandoned souls," built the French Gothic structure to serve west Belfast's impoverished linen mill workers, and soon came to regret their location. "I doubt if ever a more troublesome piece of property was acquired," the monastery's founder wrote. The Redemptorists' plot is on the border between Catholic Clonard and the Protestant neighborhood known as the Shankill, a border where Catholics and Protestants have skirmished periodically since the 1870s. By that time, Belfast's rapid industrialization had brought rural Catholics to what had been essentially a Protestant city, and the resulting competition for jobs, coupled with the poverty, disease, poor housing, and unemployment faced by both communities, had produced riots in 1835, 1843, 1857, and 1864. The generations that followed continued to express their political dissatisfaction in the streets, and there were riots and disturbances in almost every decade for the next 100 years. In August 1969, a Protestant mob, believing the fabric of their society under attack, crossed into Clonard from the Shankill and burned half the houses in Bombay Street; each side threw up barricades afterward, and in September, the army constructed a wall of corrugated iron between the two districts, much to the relief of everyone within a stone's throw of its path.

Every day in Clonard was an anxious one for me. I anticipated confrontation with four separate armed forces, all of which regarded me— an American stranger—with suspicion. There were the police, who patrolled Clonard in armored Land Rovers, afraid to leave their vehicles. The police were backed up by British soldiers, many of them teenagers from industrial cities in England, Scotland, and Wales, looking constantly for snipers and afraid they might find them. Lined up on the other side were the Provisional Irish Republican Army (the IRA), indistinguishable from the rest of my neighbors, and the Irish National Liberation Army (the INLA), a second, smaller group of Catholic guerrillas, considered reckless amateurs compared to the Provos. All four armies were sworn to the neighborhood's protection. No one felt safe.

I could never tell where the next attack would take place, as the war has no front. I could never guess who would be arrested next, as one need not have committed a crime to end up in jail. I couldn't tell when the guerrillas might knock at the door, informing me at gunpoint that the house was being requisitioned for an ambush, or when the army or police might knock to ask questions or search our rooms. In the worst of times, the most normal errands were laden with horrible possibility.

Many of my neighbors feel they have little control over their lives, and they believe in charms and talismans and spirits. The ghost of an informer, shot almost fifty years ago, is believed to walk Clonard's back streets. Relics, sold in the Holy Shop opposite the monastery, are called on to ward off illness, malignant growths, and violent death; in the early years of the troubles, a few IRA men carried the St. Joseph medal or the card that comes with it: "Whoever shall read this prayer or hear it or keep it about themselves shall never die a sudden death or be drowned nor shall poison take effect on them. Neither shall they fall into the hands of the enemy or shall be burned in any fire or be overpowered in battle."

My neighbors are haunted by the living, haunted by the dead, haunted by myths and legends and history. The conflict defines their lives. Men and women say they are Catholic, describing not their churchgoing habits but their political beliefs: they are Irish, not British. And their lot grows worse each year. More go to jail. More are killed or maimed, and others are ruined by alcohol, unemployment, and despair. Yet many believe they are winning, that they are far closer now to a united Ireland than they were when the latest round of fighting began eighteen years ago. "The contest on our side is not one of rivalry or vengeance but of endurance," said Terence McSwiney, an IRA man who died on hunger strike in 1920. "It is not those who can inflict the most, but those who can suffer the most who will conquer."

And in suffering, my neighbors have had a lot of practice.

———

At the end of May 1980, three months after I moved to Northern Ireland, sixty angry citizens gathered at the town hall in Newtownabbey, a suburb about six miles from Clonard. When the councilmen of the village arrived for their scheduled meeting, the demonstrators took up a chant, calling the men "murderers."

The accusation had nothing to do with the political violence in Northern Ireland. The demonstrators hoped that their protest would persuade the Newtownabbey councilmen to refuse Abbey Meats, a local meat packer, a license to carry out the ritual slaughter of some cattle. The meat company had negotiated a £4 million contract to provide beef to Libya, and the agreement required the company to slaughter the animals according to Islamic tradition. The process involved penning the animals in a confined space and, while they were still fully conscious, lifting their heads and slitting their throats. A Newtownabbey councilman who witnessed the method claimed it took the animal fifteen minutes to die.

Those who objected to the killing thought the method was too brutal, and felt that the animal should be stunned first. At the council meeting, the town fathers decided to grant Abbey Meats the required license, but agreed they would revoke it if, after inspection, they found that the method caused unnecessary suffering. The protestors' leader rose to his feet after the vote. "May God forgive you all," he said.

A week later, a small boy came to my door in Clonard selling the *Andersonstown News,* a community newspaper serving the Catholic ghetto in Belfast. I bought the paper, opened it to the editorial page, and found that the editors had chosen to comment on the Newtownabbey protest. They noted that the residents of Newtownabbey had shown far more concern about the slaughter of cattle than they had about the recent killings of teenagers in joyriding incidents. "Joyriders" was the label applied to teenagers in Catholic west Belfast who steal cars and drive them through army checkpoints, refusing to stop. The kids consider this great sport. The soldiers manning the checkpoints are not sure if the car bearing down on them is a teenager out for kicks or a terrorist out to kill them, and around the time of the Abbey Meats protest, the troops had a tendency to shoot first and ask questions later; several Catholic teenagers had been wounded, some fatally, in joyriding incidents.

I cite the slaughterhouse protest and the *Andersonstown News* coverage to warn you to avoid the notion that life in Clonard's grim streets is typical of life in Northern Ireland. The province is by no means consumed by war. Many of the 1.5 million people in the North are, like the residents of Newtownabbey, unconcerned—at least on the surface— with the eighteen-year-old conflict. The middle and the upper classes go about their business much like their counterparts in Dublin, London, Manchester, and Glasgow. They are active in no peace groups, they make few demands on their elected representatives to end the conflict, and when they take to the streets in protest it is more likely to be about the bloodletting at their local slaughterhouse than it is to be about the war.

Many middle- and upper-class Catholics and Protestants resent news coverage that depicts Northern Ireland as a country at war, and they object or smile condescendingly when the word "war" is used. They encourage reporters to write about the good things in the country, the normal things. To them there is no war, there is just sporadic violence, ritual killing in a part of the city they simply avoid, much as whites in New York avoid Harlem and parts of the Bronx.

In the early 1970s, the war was more intense and its ramifications were not as predictable. Since then, however, the war has become less random and, for many, easily adapted to. W. A. Galbraith, the manager of an extermination business ("Anything that walks or crawls and shouldn't, I'm your man"), told me in 1980 that he had made his adjustments. "About ten years ago, I used to sit here and worry," he said. "I'd think, 'So-and-so got blown up today, that means we lost a contract.' Well, over the years we lost some business, but it's not like that now. There's not so many bombs. And we've learned to live with the thing, which is a terrible thing to say, but it's a fact."

After about ten months in Clonard, I found that I too had become fairly accustomed to the troubles. I caught myself saying "thank you" to the men who frisked me when I went through the gates around the city center. Murders faded quickly, and the ones I remembered were the ones that occurred in and around my usual haunts, the deaths of children, and the deaths laced with some particularly tragic detail: "He was going to emigrate to Canada in June." "He was buried on the day he was to retire from the force."

The possibility that this war could become a normal way of life was foreseen back in 1971. Reginald Maulding, the British Home Secretary and the Cabinet minister responsible for Northern Ireland's affairs, told the press on December 15 of that year that he could see the day when the IRA would "not be defeated, not completely eliminated, but have their violence reduced to an acceptable level." The term "acceptable level of violence" became a standard refrain in the North after Maulding's statement. Today, many think that level has been reached.

Gordon Mawhinney is one. Mawhinney is the province's leading authority on property damage compensation, a man who works with businessmen immediately after their establishments have been destroyed by bombs and fires. "There is an unhealthy disregard for bomb scares in Belfast now," he told me in 1980. "At the beginning of the troubles, if there was a bomb scare at the city center, the whole area would empty. Now, it's hard to keep people away from an area that has been blocked off because of a scare."

By the time I met Mawhinney, his office, located just outside the security gates in the city center, had been damaged in eight different explosions. He told me the story of a coworker who was talking on the phone to a client when a car bomb went off just up the street. All of the windows in the room were blown out, but the man never left his chair and never interrupted his phone conversation.

The IRA bombs businesses as part of its economic campaign; the British Treasury pays compensation to shopkeepers who suffer as a result of terrorist activity. The owner of a shop in downtown Dungannon admitted in 1978, after his store was bombed for the eighteenth time, that he had a special bomb account at his bank, separate from his trading returns, so the bank could more easily verify his rebuilding costs when he entered his claims for compensation.

Compensation claims have become a minor industry in the years since 1969. At the outset of the conflict, the destruction from riots, gun battles, and bombings was astronomical. The government established a compensation scheme for both personal injury and property damage, but during the first eight years of the conflict, merchants and businessmen exploited various flaws in the system. Some people collected from both the government and their insurance company, making a handsome profit in the process. Compensation officers accepted claims of shopkeepers and businessmen without much question, and the police certified almost any fire as the work of a proscribed organization. Mawhinney told me that some businessmen bought old buildings, insured them for full replacement value, burned them down, collected their compensation, and never replaced the structure. "I have personal knowledge of people who made hundreds of thousands of pounds before the law was changed," Mawhinney said.

He went on to say that in 1980, cases of compensation fraud were small in proportion to the number of claims, but large in relation to the amount of money involved. He also suspected that most of the people attempting fraud were getting away with it. Of every ten cases that the compensation authorities referred to the prosecutor's office, Mawhinney said, only one resulted in criminal charges.

And conviction on those criminal charges did not necessarily result in jail terms for the accused. On May 15, 1982, for example, the *Irish News* reported that the director of a firm that sold office supplies had been convicted of trying to cheat the government out of £80,000 following a burglary and fire in the mid-1970s. The judge imposed a £27,500 fine, saying, "This is intended to hit you hard, as I believe you to be a worshipper of the Golden Calf." He went on to say, however, that he would not sentence the worshipper to jail as he was afraid that doing so would jeopardize the jobs of the defendant's sixty employees. With one out of four men unemployed in the North, sixty jobs were not to be sneezed at.

Andy Tyrie, the commander of the Ulster Defense Association (UDA), the largest group of Protestant paramilitaries, believes that the compensation scheme has preserved the character of the war as working class against working class. "If there was no compensation," Tyrie told me in 1980, "businessmen would be demanding that all IRA men should be bound and tortured and hung at the end of the street. The compensation keeps the business community off the government's back. It keeps them out of the conflict."

Tyrie told me that "more than a few" businessmen had torched their own establishments in order to claim compensation, and that others had asked the UDA to arrange fires. Tyrie insisted that he refused all requests. "Just two months ago," he said, "we had a man up the Newtownards Road, he tried to burn himself out. He didn't do such a good job, so he tried it again. The police smelled a rat and took him to court. His lawyer argued that the man had asked the UDA to burn it down. That was a load of shit. I know it was a load of shit. I got on the phone and I called the television and newspapers and I said we would like the police to go back to this man and found out who the UDA men were and then take them to court and prosecute them. It was just a ploy in court to blame it on us, hoping for a lighter sentence."

"Business people are rotten. We are called thugs and gangsters, but I'll tell you that between me and the Provies [the Provisional IRA, Tyrie's bitter enemies], we are more honest than most of the businessmen around here, and that's not a load of shit."

As the business community has adjusted to the political upheaval, so has much of the rest of Belfast, and visitors to the city often come away impressed by how normal the place seems. The papers carry ads for sun tanning parlors. The bookies run an annual beauty pageant. The bus drivers make change for passengers. A public relations man who worked at the DeLorean plant once told me that he took particular delight in driving American executives from the airport to downtown Belfast, knowing their expectations. Once he got past the airport checkpoint, he could often get all the way to the city center without passing a soldier or a policeman in flak jacket, much to the surprise of his passengers.

A change of tactics by the IRA in the late 1970s has contributed to this image of normality. The Provisionals now fight a very selective war, shooting and bombing soldiers, policemen, and members of the national guard, but leaving most of the rest of society unharmed.

The strategy of the British Army, however, has had an even greater effect in isolating normal society from the conflict. The army has severely altered the geography of Belfast. My neighbors have been walled in. Streets are blocked by walls of corrugated iron, steel gates, and huge chunks of cement called dragon's teeth.

The fine details of the military's role in urban planning were exposed in late 1981 by David Beresford, Belfast correspondent for the *Guardian* (formerly known as the *Manchester Guardian*). Beresford revealed that in one Catholic housing project, the footpaths had been laid not merely for pedestrians, but with the foundations and width necessary to support the army's fourteen-ton personnel carriers. In another Catholic district, the army insisted that a planned group of houses threatened the troops' security, and although the neighborhood suffered from an acute housing shortage, the houses in question were removed from the plans. In other Catholic areas, the army had imposed cul de sac arrangements for the streets and had stipulated that houses constructed near a police station have no windows facing the station.

All of this is done to hamper IRA operations, but the army's role in urban planning has had two dangerous side effects: it has encouraged the feeling among those living outside the ghetto that the current level of violence is acceptable, and it has institutionalized the conflict. Life in Belfast is now based upon the notion that working-class Catholics need to be isolated, but isolating them, treating them as a separate and dangerous race, insures that they will indeed continue to revolt.

West Belfast has become an incubator for a counterculture that a whole generation now accepts as the norm. No child in west Belfast knows the words to the national anthem; not a school in the district sings "God Save the Queen." The Union Jack flies only above the police barracks and the army forts, while Irish tricolors—the flag of the Republic of Ireland—fly everywhere else. Families proudly advertise that their kin have done time in prison, decorating their walls and window sills with prison crafts—Celtic crosses made of popsicle sticks, carved wooden harps, handkerchiefs painted with portraits of the fathers of the Irish revolution. IRA veterans drink in a club called the Felons Association and proudly march in parades behind signs identifying them as ex-cons, banners identifying the Lower Falls Former Prisoners of War, the Andersonstown Ex-Prisoners Association, or any of a half dozen similar groups. The pop music includes "The Sniper's Promise," the story of a volunteer's guilt after an ambush, recognizing that the shooting was necessary. "Jesus and Jesse James," a country and western song, tells of the Savior and the bandit riding through Belfast. Jesus, eyeing the burned houses and the barbed wire, says "I never thought I'd see the like of Calvary again." He raises his hand to bless the bleak site and is grazed by a bullet, which prompts the remark, "I guess that old stigmata is infectious in this land." And, in the final verse, "A multitude assembled and a spokesman up and said, 'Just give us back our country and to hell with the fish and bread.'"

There is little to dilute this counterculture; segregation is worse now than it was twenty years ago, and the government has given up all thought of housing working-class Protestants and Catholics in the same neighborhood. Catholics and Protestants, I hasten to add, are not clamoring to live side by side. In fact the residents of west Belfast don't object at all to being walled in; the walls not only keep Catholics in, they also keep Protestants out. There is no reason to fear sectarian attacks by your neighbors in west Belfast, as they are Catholic too.

And so dilapidated homes, some without bathtubs, some with toilets in the backyard, were in great demand when I moved to west Belfast, while nice homes in other areas were unacceptable because their location was considered risky. Young married couples competed for miserable houses in treeless avenues where the streetlights had not been lit for years. One such competition occurred in August 1980, when an old man died in a rowhouse in Spinner Street, about a half mile from my lodgings in Clonard. On the day of his funeral, two couples took up rival positions at the dead man's door, waiting for his relatives to return from the cemetery, knowing that the first couple inside would have the stronger claim on the house. An official of Sinn Fein, the political wing of the IRA, had to be called upon to determine which of the two families was more needy, and to install them as the rightful squatters.

T W O

THE NEIGHBORHOOD

WHEN I ARRIVED in Belfast in 1980, I had no intention of living in the Catholic ghetto. I intended to rent a furnished flat near Queen's University, a neutral area that was about a ten-minute walk from the city center. There have been sporadic incidents in the university district over the past fifteen years, but by 1980, they were few and far between, and most of the shops no longer bothered to employ security men to search handbags and frisk customers. Many of the buildings in the district are divided into small flats for students, but housing is in short supply, and I had to join the queue. I put down a deposit with a rental agency and went about my business, content to stay in a bed and breakfast establishment in the neighborhood in the meantime.

I met my future landlady, a woman named Bridgit Barbour, entirely by accident. I was working on a story about businessmen who had made and lost fortunes as a result of the troubles, and I was looking for a small shopkeeper in west Belfast who could tell me of his or her personal experiences with the IRA, the army, the Protestant terrorists, the compensation office, the neighborhood hooligans—the powers that, since 1969, had changed many a small shopkeeper's life. A fellow I'd met on a brief trip to Belfast in 1977 suggested I contact a woman named Barbour who lived on the Springfield Road in Clonard; he was certain she would know someone who could help me.

I called Mrs. Barbour and made an appointment for that afternoon. I started the trip from the city center, and, finding that the buses which normally went up the Springfield Road were not running because of a bomb scare, I took a black taxi from Castle Street up the Falls Road.

Belfast's black taxis are secondhand London cabs, big, lumbering Austins which seem so friendly in the British capital but somehow acquire a sinister air once moved to Belfast. They have been used by the IRA as getaway cars and to take alleged miscreants away for punishment shootings. A group of Protestant paramilitaries, known as the Shankill Butchers because they mutilated the bodies of the twenty Catholics they murdered, also used a black taxi to cart off their victims.

Those taxis are also, however, one of the most efficient forms of public transportation in western Europe. The fleet that serves west Belfast, known as the Falls Taxi Association (FTA), runs a jitney service on fixed routes that is faster, cheaper, and far more regular than the city bus service. There are no scheduled stops between beginning and end: people simply flag down a cab from any point on the route, join the passengers already inside, and upon reaching their destination, tap the plastic shield that separates the front seat from the back. The government has opposed the Falls Taxi Association for years, in part because the fleet costs the bus company an estimated £2 million a year, and in part because the FTA is closely linked to the IRA. The cabs offer free transportation to Republican funerals and demonstrations, and the police have charged that FTA drivers give a share of their take to the Provisionals. "The police have tried every trick in the book to discredit us," Joe Edwards, the FTA's press spokesman, told me in a 1981 interview. "And since an overwhelming number of people in west Belfast prefer our taxis to the bus, you can conclude that either the majority of the people of the area don't believe what the police say, or that the overwhelming majority of the people do believe what the police say and support the IRA. Take your pick. We don't care."

When I left the black taxi that day, I stood at the junction of the Falls and Springfield Roads, a site dominated by the Royal Victoria Hospital, called "the Royal" or "RVH" by locals and known for having one of the finest trauma units in Europe. I walked up the Springfield, past Healey's and O'Kane's, two undertakers who compete for the Catholic trade, and then past the local headquarters of the Royal Ulster Constabulary (RUC), the Northern Ireland police force. The Springfield Road police station is a remarkable structure, surrounded by fencing three stories high that serves as protection against incoming grenades and petrol bombs. On an antenna above the building is a surveillance camera that can scan the whole district, one of several such cameras perched above west Belfast. At the front gate is a sentry post made of cement blocks and called a sangar (*sangar* is a Hindi word that originally was applied to a small breastwork or rifle pit constructed of boulders). The sangar on the Springfield Road is painted black and is surrounded by camouflage netting. The soldier inside peers through slits at passersby, comparing the faces he sees with those on wanted posters. The double doors next to the sangar, through which army and police vehicles come and go, are pierced by bullet holes. The holes on the back side of those doors are circled with yellow paint; the paint reduces confusion after sniper attacks, allowing an investigator to determine which holes are fresh and which ones are not.

I felt very foreign as I walked up the road that day. I was certain that I stuck out as a stranger, and that I was being noticed, perhaps by the police and army, perhaps by the guerillas and their supporters, perhaps by them all. Mrs. Barbour's house is a few hundred yards past the RUC station, and I knocked at the door with some relief. I expected to be greeted by a wiry, wizened woman who had spent all of her life in a few streets. I was instead greeted by a lively, sturdy woman, sixty-three years old, grey haired but full of energy, born and raised not in those mean streets but in Dublin.

In the course of the next three hours, I heard a bit of her background, and over the course of the next few years I heard a good bit more. She was born in Dublin in 1916 during the Easter Rising, the week of violence that led to war and independence for the south of Ireland. "I was born in trouble," she used to tell me, "and I've never been out of it."

She was baptized Bridgit O'Dwyer and grew to be a popular young woman. She was engaged twice to different men, rejecting both suitors before settling with Jack Barbour, whom she met at a dance in Dublin after World War II. Jack lived in Belfast, where he worked as a liquor wholesaler, and he happened to be down in Dublin on holiday. There were two blacks at the ball, perhaps the only two blacks in the city, perhaps the only two in the whole country, and they approached Bridgit O'Dwyer and her girlfriend to ask for a dance. "Jack and his friend spotted this happening," Mrs. Barbour recalls, "and they just got in first and asked us."

In some ways it was an ironic competition, as Northern Catholics in Belfast had a position in society equivalent to blacks in the United States at that time—they were subject to the same discrimination and put down with the same stereotypes. Even today, the stereotype of the ghetto Catholic in the North is that they do not want to work (they're interested only in collecting welfare); that they breed like rabbits; that they drink too much; and that they are dirty. The *Protestant Telegraph,* a newsletter published by followers of Reverend Ian Paisley, has referred to Catholics as "Irish negroes." "I treat them like animals," one Protestant told me in 1982, "because that's what they are." The attitude is not a new one. A hundred and twenty years ago, the humor magazine *Punch* suggested that scientists looking for the intermediate animal to fill the evolutionary gap between "the Gorilla and the Negro" would find it in the Irish race. "The Irish Yahoo generally confines itself within the limits of its own colony," *Punch* proclaimed in October 1862, "except when it goes out of them to get its living. Sometimes, however, it sallies forth in states of excitement and attacks civilized human beings that have provoked its fury." A hundred years later, in 1982, Michael Cummings, the cartoonist for the *Daily Express,* a British tabloid, defended his depiction of the Irish with vaguely simian features: The IRA's violence, Cummings told the *Irish Times,* "makes them look rather like apes, though that's rather hard luck on the apes."

Jack Barbour and Bridgit O'Dwyer were married in June 1947, and so Miss O'Dwyer from Dublin came to run the Barbour household on the Springfield Road. She was different from her neighbors. She was from the Free State, where the citizenry had won their war with England. The land was theirs, they made the rules, and they carried no sense of defeat. While politically Mrs. Barbour is a pacifist, personally she is a fighter, a woman who knows what she wants and goes out to get it.

Her husband was a gambler. Mrs. Barbour is fond of saying that Jack "would bet on two flies goin' up a wall." In Belfast, a two-fly bet is almost possible. Bookmakers take wagers, as small as ten pence, on horses, dogs, soccer, golf, tennis, and boxing. I have heard of bets placed or odds offered on the weather (one bookmaker gave odds on a white Christmas), on which country would be the first to land on the moon, and on the outcome of the Miss Universe contest.

In the early years of his marriage, Jack left his job with the wholesalers and gambled on a pub in the city center. (Catholics, unable to get jobs in the big factories or with the city, except as garbagemen, came to dominate the restaurant and catering trades and the roofing and construction businesses.) As the son of a publican, he felt he knew the liquor business well enough to make a go of it, but the pub proved to be a bad investment. Eventually, he lost the enterprise.

Jack then went to England for a few years. It was not unusual for a Northern Catholic to go "across the water" to find work, but Jack could probably have found a job in a pub in Belfast. He was, however, a stubborn and proud man, and he did not want to work for one of his friends. In England, he worked as a barman until he contracted tuberculosis, which landed him in a hospital for almost a year. In the meantime, Mrs. Barbour was struggling to raise the four Barbour daughters on her own back on the Springfield Road, and one Christmas she didn't have the money to put a turkey on the table.

And so she began to take in boarders, a practice she continued when Jack returned and took a job as a barman in Daley's pub on the Falls Road. There were times when twelve people were fed and housed in the Barbour home. The boarders ate in the dining room, the family ate in the kitchen, and Mrs. Barbour ate when everyone else had been fed. In time, Mrs. Barbour got referrals from business and industry. She housed Italian engineers who were brought in by a textile firm, Thais who came to be trained at a nearby foundry, and a Chinese Jamaican woman who studied physiotherapy at the Royal Victoria Hospital.

That routine was altered considerably in the late 1960s and early 1970s, when riots, barricades, hijackings, explosions, random death, and incarceration without trial became standard fare. Many people fled the North. Two of the Barbour daughters went off to universities in England. The other two, studying at Queen's University at Belfast, decided to move out of the house into a flat near the college, in part because crossing the city at night was sometimes a death-defying feat. The number of boarders at the Barbour house dropped to two.

Jack Barbour continued to work at Daley's pub. On March 9, 1972, he was on his way to Daley's at the same time that three IRA volunteers were assembling a bomb in number 30 Clonard Street. The bomb exploded.

The three volunteers were killed instantly. Bits of the house blew in all directions, and three other houses on the block were severely damaged. Jack was passing Ross's mill at that instant, and he was shielded from the debris and the blast by a large truck parked on the street. "All he saw was arms and legs," Mrs. Barbour says. "He came home at lunchtime and got sick and I thought he had taken spirits or something, and he said nothing to me. That evening I got the telephone message from Daley's to say that he had taken a heart attack. He took a stroke that night in the hospital."

Jack never worked after that. He came home with a walker, and didn't leave the house much afterward. He later had a second stroke, and his speech became slurred, interpretable only by those close to him. He was often in great pain. On May 31, 1975, he had a brain hemorrhage while watching a war film on television and died.

Mrs. Barbour decided to have Jack cremated, although the Irish church still frowned on the practice. "I wouldn't have him buried in Milltown cemetery," she told me. "It is dreadful. I mean you have the army running in with Saracens and cowboys and Indians flying around among the tombstones, hiding guns and what have you. I mean what kind of peace is that?"

That first afternoon with Mrs. Barbour was both sad and funny. She told me of the Clonard Street bombing and Jack's death; she was near tears and I was moved. She also told me with great humor and relish of the night that thirteen nail bombs were thrown at the security forces between 9:30 and 3:30, all in the Clonard enclave; she recalled that she was "throwing down the Valium like Dolly Mixtures." (Dolly Mixtures are small bits of candy.) I heard about the great bomb damage sales, when you could get crystal or clothes or good china at bargain rates, when people went into stores and bought clothes that didn't fit, knowing they'd find somebody in the family or neighborhood who could wear them.

(Crowds were so great at one such sale that an army band set up on the sidewalk outside to entertain those who were waiting to get in.) I also saw Mrs. Barbour's collection of spent shells, found on the street, and nuts, bolts, and small pieces of machinery that had been fired at local Catholics by Protestants, who were armed with slingshots and standing on the roof of James Mackie & Sons, a foundry and machine-building firm located directly across the road from Mrs. Barbour's.

Many Clonard residents are not enamored with Mackie's, as the firm, although located in an ocean of Catholics, is known as a major employer of Protestants. Mrs. Barbour told me she was not particularly fond of the firm because in the years before the troubles started, the foundry workers often leaned against her front gate during their lunch hour, making comments about the women passing by and throwing the remains of their meals into her tiny garden. After the troubles began, however, the workers thought it unwise and potentially unhealthy to aggravate a population that was armed and itching to shoot, and so they stopped congregating on Mrs. Barbour's side of the road. Mrs. Barbour told me she didn't miss the lunchtime crowd at all. "Ever since the troubles," she said half jokingly, "we have had peace."

By the end of the afternoon, I didn't know what to make of this woman. Here was an outsider, a woman who knew and liked fine things, a woman who simply knew better, who nonetheless had settled and even thrived in this godforsaken district. I asked why she stayed, why she didn't simply move to a safer area, maybe even go back to Dublin, where her brothers and sisters lived. She explained that she had been on the Springfield Road for thirty-three years. The church was nearby, the post office was just up the street, and the bus stop was a thirty-second walk from the front door. Her bridge partners lived within a few hundred yards, and it was a short drive to the homes of two of her daughters. If she sold the house, she would probably receive only half of its value, and she would then have to move to a new neighborhood, full of strangers, or down to Dublin, where she would seldom see her children and grandchildren.

"I'm like in the middle of everything," she said, "and yet I'm not. What could be more quiet than this room? I'm happy, and it's a way of life."

Mrs. Barbour then asked where I was staying, and when she heard that I had not yet secured a flat, she suggested that I board with her. I thought that was a tremendously bad idea; the district's routine and atmosphere might be Mrs. Barbour's idea of "a way of life," but it was not mine. I don't mind being scared once in a while, but I didn't want to be scared twenty-four hours a day for the rest of the year. I also thought that the police, the army, and the Protestant community would not be enamored of the address; I thought they might assume I was not a neutral observer simply because I lived in a district which was usually hostile to the security forces, sort of like covering the Vietnam war from Hanoi. I also knew that it was going to be very hard to live anywhere in Belfast; I knew no one, and if there was any comfort to be had—and I thought I saw some in and around the university—I reasoned that I should not have to go far to find it. I told Mrs. Barbour that I would think about her offer, expecting to call her in a few days and decline the invitation.

A few days later, I moved in. I intended it to be a brief experiment. I had been offered a flat near the university that would not be vacant for another two weeks, and I thought I'd spend that time in Clonard, quickly learn as much as I could, and then get out. I found, however, that Protestants I interviewed either never asked where I lived, or were satisfied by the combination of my American accent and my answer that I lived across the street from Mackie's; the foundry is such a great employer of Protestants that mere mention of the company name evokes a favorable response in the loyalist community, much like the words "Queen" and "shipyard." The army and police also seemed to pay me no more attention. Mrs. Barbour's cooking and personality were winning, and she let me take over her sitting room as a sort of office. When it came time to move into the flat near the university, I decided I would learn a lot more if I stayed where I was, so I forfeited my deposit, and, with considerable trepidation, stayed put.

I can't say that I felt at home. While my surname is Irish, my family did not discuss or celebrate our Irish heritage. I did feel sorry for Catholics in Belfast, but I felt sorry for Protestants as well. So when I moved into the house on the Springfield Road, I can't say I was among my own, and I did not expect any welcome.

"It's a way of life," Mrs. Barbour's summation of her individual situation, is an attitude by no means peculiar to that household on the Springfield

Road. "The troubles" have been a way of life for millions of people for hundreds of years.

I will not attempt to cover those hundreds of years here, but I would like to pause briefly and touch on five key periods: the seventeenth-century plantation of Ulster and the upheaval that followed; the formation of the Orange Order in the 1790s; the 1916 Easter Rising and the partition of Ireland; the growth of the civil rights movement in the late 1960s; and the state's slide into violence after August 1969.

In the early 1600s, Ireland was a very rebellious British colony. The native Gaels spoke a different language and practiced a different religion from their rulers, and they fought fiercely British attempts to impose firm control. In an attempt to secure the island once and for all, and to protect the British mainland from invasion from the west, Parliament passed the Articles of Plantation in 1610.

Plantation was a tested method of securing territory (it is mentioned by Machiavelli in his advice to the princes). The technique involved "planting" loyal citizens on land confiscated from natives; such settlements were cheaper than maintaining a huge garrison. A prince who adopts this technique, Machiavelli wrote, "injures only those from whom he takes land and houses to give to the new inhabitants, and these victims . . . can never do any harm since they remain poor and scattered." The Articles of Plantation were designed to displace the rebellious Irish by confiscating their land, giving it to loyal Englishmen and Scots, and confining the native Irish to less fertile lands. In his book, *Ireland; A History* (Weidenfeld & Nicolson, 1980), Robert Kee reports that the percentage of land owned by Catholics in all of Ireland declined steadily over the course of the seventeenth century, and by 1714, Catholics owned only 7 percent of the island.

Ulster, which had been the most rebellious, the most Catholic, and the most Gaelic of the four Irish provinces, was profoundly altered by plantation. The planters who arrived from the British mainland were mostly Scottish Presbyterians—due in large part to Ulster's proximity to Scotland. They did not settle easy, fearing the natives' wrath, and so they armed themselves and built towns protected by walls and earthen banks. And the natives, not a mild-tempered bunch to begin with, did not take easily to the confiscation of their land.

In 1641, the fears of the newcomers proved justified. The Gaels rose in bloody revolt, some of them proclaiming allegiance to the Crown while

crying for return of their land. Twelve thousand Protestants were slaughtered. Some were tortured. Robert Kee reports that at Portadown, a
city about thirty miles from Belfast, 100 Protestant men, women, and
children were robbed, stripped naked, and forced onto a bridge; they
were then thrown into the waters below, where they were drowned or
clubbed to death if they reached the shore.

One atrocity bred another. Oliver Cromwell arrived in 1649, and in
Drogheda killed 2,000 Catholic men, women, and children, and in Wex-
ford 2,000 more. The few survivors were transported to the West In-
dies, and thereafter, Cromwell confiscated more land, dispatching the
Gaels to the bleak and impoverished west of the island.

The natives rose again later in the century, casting their lot with
James II, the Catholic monarch of England who had been deposed by the
Dutchman William of Orange in 1688. James, supported by French troops
and the native Gaels, made a stand in Ireland culminating on July 1, 1690,
in the Battle of the Boyne. William triumphed. James fled to France, and
he was followed a year later by thousands of Irishmen who had been part
of the resistance. The conquest of Ireland seemed complete.

Penal laws, designed to persecute the Catholic Church and thereby
the majority of the population, were introduced in 1695. Catholics were
banned from public office, the legal profession, the army, and the navy.
They could not vote, teach, maintain schools, buy land, or own a horse
worth more than five pounds. Masses were said in secret. Catholics came
to distrust the laws of the state, as they do today, while Protestants lived
in fear of another rising, just as they do today.

In the late 1700s, violence broke out in rural areas of the north. Land-
lords who had usually rented to Protestants found Catholics more attractive as tenants, as Catholics were more desperate for land and would pay
higher rents. In 1795, a group of rural Protestants formed the Orange
Order, a society named for William of Orange and dedicated to preserv-
ing the Protestants' privileged position in society. Today, the Orange
Order is the largest Protestant organization in the North. It claims
80,000 to 100,000 members and holds a parade every twelfth of July to
celebrate King William's victory at the Boyne in 1690. Although the
charter of the Order calls for civil and religious liberty, in practice the
Orangemen pay no attention to those principles. The Catholic drive for
civil rights in the 1960s was denounced as Communist inspired, and proposals to form a government in which Protestants would share power
with Catholics have been denounced as undemocratic (in this line of rea-

soning, democracies are governed by majority rule, and since Protestants are the majority in the North, their will should be done; giving Catholics an equal say in the North's affairs would amount to giving Catholics a more powerful vote than Protestants).

With the start of the Industrial Revolution and the onset of the potato famine of the 1840s, many of those starving and doing battle in the countryside flocked to the cities—particularly to Belfast, where the linen industry and the shipbuilding firms were hiring thousands of workers. Both Catholic and Protestant immigrants lived in miserable conditions and worked long hours for low wages. They brought with them the agrarian tradition of the violent battles for land, and as competition for jobs increased, so did animosity between the two groups. There were riots in Belfast as early as 1835, and the streetfighting was repeated in almost every decade that followed for the next 150 years.

Catholics continued to conspire to win independence from Britain throughout the nineteenth century, but their efforts came to naught until 1916. In Dublin on Easter Monday of that year, a group of about 1,000 men took over several strategically placed buildings, including the General Post Office, and proclaimed a Provisional Government of the Irish Republic. They were considered ill-armed fanatics with no mandate from the people they claimed to represent. In less than a week of fighting, 300 civilians, 60 rebels, and 130 British soldiers were killed. Dubliners jeered the rebels after their arrest. Robert Kee reports that some of the teenagers who had participated in the rising were sent home with a reprimand: "You are thoughtless youths. . . . You've been led by madmen. . . . Go home and get your mothers to wipe your noses."

The leaders of the movement, however, were tried in secret, and ninety men—some of questionable importance—were sentenced to death. The executions began on May 3, with the shooting of the poet Padraig Pearse, and continued until May 12, when James Connolly was shot while tied to a chair (he had been wounded in the leg during the rising and could not stand). Public outrage over the trials and sentences finally put a halt to the proceedings, but not before fifteen men had been killed. The fanatics jeered at the end of Easter week were folk heroes by mid-May. Their movement for independence from Britain, which was not at all popular in 1916, was registered as the overwhelming national sentiment two years later. In the general election of 1918, the political party Sinn Fein (the words, pronounced "Shin Fane," mean "ourselves alone") won 73 of 105 Irish seats in the British parliament. (Today, Sinn

Fein is considered the political wing of the IRA; at that point in history, the party was considered the most militant among the nationalist groups.) The 73 Sinn Feiners refused to take their seats at Westminster and instead established their own parliament in Dublin. Thirty-six of the elected representatives could not attend because they were in jail.

From 1919 to the end of 1921, a fierce and bloody war was fought in the cities and the countryside between the IRA and the forces of the state, which consisted of the British Army, the Royal Irish Constabulary, and two groups of police recruits—the Black and Tans (made up of out-of-work British World War I veterans) and the Auxiliaries (made up of former British army officers). "The cruelty of these assistant police has never been denied, still less (except officially) condoned," historian George Dangerfield wrote in his book *The Damnable Question*, (Little, Brown & Co., 1976) "but it only serves to emphasize the fact that cruelty is inseparable from guerrilla warfare; and that the invading or occupying force is, in this respect, merely more extreme than the indigenous one. The IRA used methods of terrorism all over the country during the bleak years of 1920 and 1921; but, given a choice of terrorists, the Irish preferred their own, supported them, hid them, and suffered both from and for them. "Suffered" is no exaggeration, for when it came to reprisals, the invading forces always exacted the greater price. Sniped at and bombed by the IRA in civilian clothes, which, having done its worst, melted back into the landscape, they tended to believe that all civilians were enemies."

In Belfast between July 1920 and July 1922, 453 people were killed (257 Catholics, 157 Protestants, 2 people of unknown religion, and 37 members of the security forces); Protestant mobs drove 10,000 Catholics from their jobs in Belfast shipyards, foundries, mills, and factories; 500 Catholic-owned shops were burned, looted, and wrecked; country mansions, railway stations, and local mills were burned by the IRA, while Protestant forces torched hundreds of Catholic homes.

In July 1921, the exhausted IRA agreed to a truce with the British, and in December the Anglo-Irish Treaty was signed. The new Irish Free State would have its own parliament, though the nation would remain part of the empire and Irish MPs would have to swear allegiance to the British Crown. To appease the northern Protestants, who were threatening violence if Britain abandoned them, a new state was created called Northern Ireland. It was to include six of Ulster's nine counties—the largest area that could be ceded to the Protestants in which they would remain a majority. Many Catholics refused to recognize the new state as permanent; a Boundary Commission had been appointed to study and adjust the haphazard and artificially created border, and Republicans believed that if local preference was taken into account by the Commission, large parts of the North would be ceded to the Free State (two of the North's six counties had Catholic majorities), and the Northern Ireland that remained would be so small that it would prove economically unviable. In the end, however, the Boundary Commission changed nothing, and a bitter civil war was fought in the south between the Republicans who had agreed to the partition of the island and those who believed the agreement was a terrible sellout.

The northern state was born with severe economic problems, but its governors were far more concerned with political questions. According to Thames Television's history, *The Troubles* (MacDonald Futura Publishers, 1980), the new government was "parochial, part-time, and amateur," "a government of businessmen and landowners," all of them Protestant, all of them afraid of Catholicism and socialism. The first Catholic member of the Cabinet was not appointed until 1969.

It is easy to understand why the Unionists who formed the government saw the Catholic community as a threat. Town and city councils where Catholics were in the majority voted their allegiance to the Dail, the new Dublin parliament. Catholics elected to the Northern Irish parliament at Stormont refused to take their seats. Those offered positions in the new government refused to serve.

The border that separated Northern Ireland from Ireland was based on county boundaries that had been drawn between the twelfth and seventeenth centuries, and for those who live alongside it even today, the line is absurd. It randomly follows minor streams, hillsides, and hilltops, and runs through farms, lakes, barns, and houses. The village of Pettigo was split in two when the border became official, so that during World War II, when Ireland was neutral and the North was part of the British war effort, half of the old town was rationed, and half was not. For years, the border was not even fully demarcated. Smuggling became a way of life and a tradition in some border families. Horses, greyhounds, petrol, bananas, grain, pigs, cattle, CB radios, cigarettes, alcohol, meat, televisions, and furniture have all been imported or exported illegally at different times. The North's Customs and Excise Department lists sixteen approved border crossings, but there are more than 300 unapproved roads that cross the state line. Many of the roads are about as wide as a tractor, unmarked, twisted, and lined with overgrown brush. They provide excellent cover for IRA men who set out to ambush soldiers on patrol.

The border was one of many factors that contributed to Catholics' resentment. The Northern Irish government gerrymandered election districts and altered voting procedures to ensure that Catholics would not be represented in proportion to their numbers, and so even in areas where Catholics were the majority population, they were the minority on elected councils. These councils allocated housing and jobs, and so the discrimination against Catholics was institutionalized in those sectors also. In his book, *Northern Ireland: The Orange State* (Pluto Press, 1980), Michael Farrell records Basil Brooke, Parliamentary Secretary in the Northern government and later its Prime Minister, boasting to an assembly of Orangemen that he did not have a single Catholic in his employ. Farrell notes that on the same occasion, Minister for Labour J. J. Andrews reported that he had investigated allegations that twenty-eight of thirty-one porters at Stormont were Catholic; he assured the crowd with the news that there were thirty Protestants and only one Catholic, and that the Catholic was there only temporarily.

To deal directly with the threat of Catholic dissatisfaction, the government created a sectarian auxiliary police force called the B-Specials and in April 1922 passed the Special Powers Act. The act allowed the Minister of Home Affairs to arrest and search without warrant; to detain people without charge or trial; to prohibit inquests; and to suspend the circulation of any newspaper. It was forbidden to produce any play or film "or commit any act which is intended or likely to cause any disaffection, interference, or prejudice." One section of the law provided for the whipping of men who were convicted of certain crimes; that section was only repealed in 1968.

The London-based National Council for Civil Liberties examined the use of the Special Powers Act in the wake of riots in Belfast in 1935 and concluded that the government used the legislation "towards securing the domination of one particular political faction, and at the same time, towards curtailing the lawful activities of its opponents. The driving of legitimate movements underground into illegality, the intimidating or branding as law breakers of their adherents, however innocent of crime, has tended to encourage violence and bigotry on the part of the Government's supporters as well as to beget in its opponents an intolerance of the 'law and order' thus maintained. The Government's policy is thus driving its opponents into the ways of extremists."

The report did not spur reform, and the Special Powers Act stayed on the books for another thirty-seven years. The "Catholic threat" was the dragon that held the state together. The Northern Ireland government provided little in social benefits for the Protestant workers who supported the ruling Unionist party, but the party leaders were able to prevent revolt by identifying cries for reform with Republicanism, a united Ireland, and "Rome rule," a technique known as "playing the Orange card" or "beating the Orange drum." The Protestant working class was well mired in prejudice, and exploiting their fears was a relatively easy task. Unemployment averaged 25 percent through most of the 1920s and 1930s. In 1940, most homes still had no running water and tuberculosis was rampant. In the face of such poverty, Protestant workers were happy to have the few bones that were tossed their way, and they were loyal to those who tossed them.

As the decades passed, the British paid little attention to the province; the Treasury wrote checks, the Northern Ireland government passed laws and spent money. In London, no senior civil servant worked full time on the North. Until October 1968, the General Department of the Home Office held responsibility for Northern Irish affairs; the office also regulated London taxicabs, liquor licensing, the protection of animals, and the British version of daylight savings time. The media were no better. Up to 1948, the BBC, the government-owned broadcasting company, would not allow mention of partition, as this would suggest disunity; the BBC governors believed that it was their duty to emphasize reconciliation and the common ground between the two communities. Under the laws for broadcasting and the BBC charter, broadcasters were forbidden to transmit anything which would incite violence, which added to reporters' difficulties when tension mounted in the North in the mid-1960s. In their book *The Troubles,* published in 1980, reporters from Thames Television wrote that as far as they could establish, the political situation in the North was covered on national television on only two occasions in the years before 1968, "while amongst the national newspapers, effective coverage of the situation . . . was rare."

When the 1960s began, the North had achieved a strange peace in spite of the state's obvious flaws. In 1963, there were no murders at all in the province—no husband killed a wife, no policeman shot a suspect, no armed robber took the life of his victim. In 1964, there was one killing, and one more in 1965. Anyone who looked only at the surface might well have concluded that these Northerners were a peaceful, complacent lot.

Under the surface, however, the old tensions were still present. They surfaced briefly in 1964, when the militant Reverend Ian Paisley forced the police to remove a tricolor (the flag of the Irish Republic) from the window of Sinn Fein headquarters; a riot followed, but it was over and done in twenty-four hours. In 1966, events were slightly more serious, but still far from overwhelming; five Catholics were shot dead by Protestant paramilitaries; a riot occurred when Paisley paraded to a Catholic district to protest against the growing ecumenical trend in Christian churches; and a concrete block was thrown at a car bearing Queen Elizabeth.

In 1967, a fledgling civil rights movement became a major political force. Students, professionals, liberal Protestants, and Catholics of all political leanings joined the movement, which was patterned on the civil rights movement in the United States. The leaders preached nonviolence, activists organized protest parades, and marchers sang "We Shall Overcome."

The demonstrators' demands were not radical. They wanted an end to gerrymandering. They asked for "one man, one vote"; many poor Catholics, (and, in lesser number, poor Protestants) were denied the right to vote in local elections, while those who owned businesses were allocated up to six votes. The movement's leaders asked that public housing be allocated on a points system so that houses would go to the neediest, not to Protestants first and Catholics second, and they asked for legislation against discrimination and a system for dealing with complaints. Finally, they wanted the government to repeal the Special Powers Act and to disband the B-Specials, the sectarian auxiliary police force.

At that stage in the North's history, the IRA was a dormant organization. It had mounted campaigns in the 1930s, during World War II, and in the late 1950s, when IRA men staged battles along the border that resulted in the deaths of six policemen and the wounding of thirty-two other members of the security forces. In 1962, the IRA called off its border campaign, admitting it had failed because it did not have the support of Catholics north or south. Some IRA men who had been active in the forties and interned in the fifties then drifted away from the organization as its leadership abandoned violence, agitated for social reform, and sold its weapons to Welsh nationalists. In *Northern Ireland: A Report on the Conflict* (Penguin, 1972), the London Sunday Times Insight Team quoted Cathal Goulding, former IRA Chief of Staff, saying, "In August, 1967, we called a meeting of local leadership throughout the country to assess the strength of the movement. We discovered that we had no movement."

The Protestant establishment, however, was not so quick to forget the organization's violent history, and when the government saw the Catholic community rising in protest with some IRA men among them, Unionist politicians took the group's demands not as legitimate requests for reform, but as the seeds of revolution. Although the civil rights marchers never carried the tricolor, Unionists assumed that what the group really had in mind was a United Ireland, and accused the movement of being Communist inspired.

The government invoked the Special Powers Act and banned some civil rights marches. In October 1968, police set upon demonstrators in Londonderry and smashed heads in front of television cameras, sending one Catholic Member of Parliament to the hospital with blood running down his face. In January 1969, at Burntollet Bridge outside Derry, a march was ambushed by followers of Reverend Paisley (100 of them later identified as members of the B-Specials). Uniformed constables stood by as the marchers were clubbed. In Derry on April 19, 1969, a sit-down protest was attacked, and a riot followed. The police chased Catholics back into Derry's Bogside district and pursued one band of stone throwers into the house of a man named Sam Devenny. The lads ran in the front and out the back. The policemen ran in the front and beat up the Devenny family, women and children, the sick and the healthy alike, without mercy. Mr. Devenny died three months later.

The government and the constabulary shared the perception that a dangerous rebellion was in the works. A series of bomb attacks in March and April, one causing £2 million damage to an electricity station, seemed to be the work of a reborn IRA. (The bombings were in fact done by a Protestant group whose aim was to embarrass and discredit Prime Minister Terence O'Neill, who wanted to grant the civil rights protestors their demands.) The government was further alarmed when Catholics in mid-Ulster united and sent a twenty-two-year-old protestor to Parliament, the fiery and outspoken Bernadette Devlin.

Everyone looked to Derry in August 1969, when an annual parade by Protestants seemed sure to bring trouble. In view of the fact that Stormont had seen fit to ban civil rights marches, many Catholics thought it was about time that a Protestant march was prohibited. The new prime minister let the parade go on, and, as predicted, there were riots. Police again chased Catholics back into the Bogside, but this time the Catholics threw up barricades, fearing another police invasion like the one that had sent the Devennys to the hospital. The people of the Bogside then organized "Free Derry," with their own fire brigade and first aid depots. The police fired tear gas for the first time in the history of the United Kingdom, but still the Bogsiders held their own, keeping the police out.

Catholics throughout the North organized to support the people of the Bogside, and riots spread. In Dublin, Jack Lynch, the Taoiseach (prime minister) of the Republic of Ireland, appeared on television on August 13, the day after "Free Derry" was born. The Northern government, Lynch said, had lost control, and the Republic could not stand by and see Northern Catholics "injured and perhaps worse." Lynch ordered the Irish Army to the border to establish field hospitals and refugee centers for those fleeing the North; with the Irish Army poised on the border, there was always the danger that they would cross it, that they would invade to protect Northern Catholics, a threat that inflamed Protestants.

———

In the timeline of the current troubles, there is no Pearl Harbor, no assassination of the archduke, no precise date for which one can say, "This is the moment when it all began." When Mrs. Barbour or my Clonard neighbors speak of the start of the troubles, however, they talk of August 14 and 15, 1969, but particularly the latter, which is usually referred to as "the night they burned Bombay Street."

On Thursday, August 14, 1969, British Prime Minister Harold Wilson and Home Secretary James Callaghan, threatened by impending civil war and invasion, decided they had no choice but to order the British Army onto the streets. At five o'clock that afternoon, British soldiers marched into Derry.

Catholics were jubilant. The soldiers were greeted as a liberating army, an army that had deposed the Unionist government at Stormont and had pushed aside the Northern constabulary. The Bogsiders believed their lives would surely be better from that day forward. The British government, however, was not so thrilled with the new command. It had provided only 400 soldiers and had no intention of sending in reinforcements. A government spokesman told the press that the troops would be back in their barracks by the weekend.

Belfast, however, was about to explode.* There had been riots on Wednesday night, August 13, but no casualties. At 1:30 on Thursday afternoon, an anonymous phone caller told the Redemptorists at Clonard monastery to evacuate, indicating that Protestants were going to torch the building. Father McLaughlin, the acting Superior, called the police at Springfield Road barracks and told them of the threat. The police were already in bad shape: they anticipated in Belfast what they saw in television coverage of Derry; they were stretched by riot duty the night before; and they felt a very tangible lack of welcome in Catholic districts. The RUC told the priest to do whatever was necessary to protect his property, and Father McLaughlin said he would organize vigilantes, unarmed men from the neighborhood who would be wearing white armbands. That night, two men with guns showed up along with the other guards. Father McLaughlin let them stay, advising them to fire only in defense and then only into the air.

There was no attack on the monastery that night. There was, however, mayhem in nearby Conway Street and in Divis Flats. In Conway Street, Catholics and Protestants confronted each other. Missiles flew back and forth. There was gunfire from the Catholic side, but Catholics never left their territory. By the end of the night, forty-eight Catholic families had been burned out; police had been present during some of the burnings. In Divis Street, there may or may not have been a Catholic gunman. What is certain is that B-Specials in armored cars opened up on Divis Flats with Browning machine guns, raking the side of one block of flats, killing a nine-year-old boy asleep in his bed and a British soldier, home on leave, who was sitting on his balcony.

Panic set in the next afternoon, Friday, August 15, 1969. "Everybody was flying," Mrs. Barbour recalls. "There was furniture being shifted in vans, and nobody had time for anything. And they said to me, 'You ought to block up your windows and your door.' And so I flew up the road and I got hardboard cut to size, and at Campbell's I picked up a piece of plywood which I thought would cover the leaded lights [stained glass] on the door, and while I was hammerin' it on, the shooting started down at the

---

*A government tribunal headed by Justice Scarman later investigated the causes of the violence in the North in the summer of 1969. The Scarman report provides an almost hourly breakdown of the events at some flashpoints, and I am indebted to it for much of what follows.

end of the Kashmir Road. And I was busy hammering the thing on, and nobody would help me because everybody was flying, and nobody would stand and tell you what was going to happen or what.

"Then my daughter Carmel came home and she was terrified. She had been told at her office at lunchtime that she would be well advised to go home because of trouble, and she thought everybody was crazy, and instead of comin' home, she went out and bought herself a new blouse. Then she went to the bus stop and there were no buses. So she went to the Falls Road bus stop, and there were no buses there either. And she walked up the Falls Road and the shooting from the mill was terrible onto the people on the Falls, and she ran for her life. And she was running into Clonard monastery to say a prayer that she got home safe when a shot rang out and knocked a man, and she ran into the church and the nuns came out to help the man, and apparently he was taken to hospital. Then she flew down home and it got really bad after that.

"The people all got out of their houses. That was when the hijacking started. I remember a lovely bakery van, a new one, and it had come along and the man was held up with a big pick axe. And he said, 'I've only got the money here, and it's not my money.' And they said, 'We don't want your money, we want your van.'"

The van was needed to move people and valuables out of the neighborhood, and later to act as a barricade. The evacuation had started that morning in Cupar Street. Cupar is the border of the district. Clonard is on one side, the Shankill on the other. On that day in 1969, Cupar was "mixed" (i.e., integrated); by nightfall it was integrated no more. Catholics in Cupar believed they were going to be burned out, as Catholics in nearby Conway Street had been the night before. They started pulling out on the morning of August 15, taking their furniture with them; some broke the windows of their own houses as they pulled away, knowing the next occupiers would not be Catholic. In the meantime, rumors began to circulate among Protestants that there had been IRA gunmen in the monastery the night before. Kids began throwing stones at each other from the opposing sides. One of the Redemptorists and a Protestant minister tried to form a "peace corps" of both religions, but their attempt failed after a Unionist politician arrived at the recruitment meeting on the Shankill and said that there was no need for any mixed patrols, that the law was all that people needed as their guide.

Sometime after 1:00 that afternoon, Finnegan's pub, a Catholic-owned tavern in Cupar Street, was looted and torched. It was destroyed completely by the time a fire truck arrived at 1:40. By midafternoon, barricades were up on both sides of Cupar, and the loot from Finnegan's was being consumed by those on the Shankill side.

The management at Mackie's, the foundry on the Springfield Road opposite Mrs. Barbour's, decided that in view of the trouble brewing, they would let their workers out early. The Mackie's men armed themselves with iron bars and other assorted makeshift weapons, and they walked the dogleg of Cupar Street toward the Shankill, either attacking Catholics along the way or defending themselves from stone throwers or both, depending upon whom you believe.

Shortly before 4:00 P.M., Protestants threw some petrol bombs and the shoemaker's shop on the corner of the Kashmir Road and Bombay Street caught fire. By this time there were about thirty Catholics at the barricades. Most of the people in the back streets seemed to have fled. Those who were left were nearly hysterical. Father McLaughlin called the police and reported the escalation of the fighting. The older Redemptorists were evacuated, and the Eucharist was moved to a place of safety. Shooting began. In Bombay Street, fifteen-year-old Gerald McAuley was shot dead by a sniper from the Shankill, and two Protestants in Sugarfield Street were wounded by shotgun fire from Clonard. Petrol bombing continued along Cupar, and Catholic homes caught fire one after another.

The police were not to be seen, and no firemen arrived to cope with the flames. Father McLaughlin again called the Springfield Road barracks. "I was terribly agitated and worked up and terribly afraid there was going to be a holocaust and that the whole area was going to be wiped out," he later told the Scarman Tribunal. "I was absolutely convinced that this was an attempt not merely to wipe out the Monastery but the whole area. I was really in desperation for help, and I said to the man, whoever answered the phone, 'Why are you not coming up to help us?' Then I said, 'Is it because your own side are doing the attacking?' And he got a bit annoyed at that and he said, 'What do you mean?' and I said, 'You know very well,' I said, 'the people of Cupar Street.' So I put down the phone and that ended the conversation."

Protestants were also calling the police, but still none came. At five o'clock, Bombay Street was black with smoke. A crowd gathered at the monastery and urged the priests to summon help by ringing the church bell. The priests thought that would only spread panic and perhaps raise more opposition on the Shankill. A young boy, however, took matters into his own hands. "Really he was mad," a priest told the investigating tribunal. "His eyes were bulging and he had lost all self control." The boy ran into the belltower and rang the bell.

Jack Barbour came home from Daley's pub in the early evening; the tavern had closed early, as Charlie Daley expected more trouble on the Falls. Bombay Street still burned. Houses on the Kashmir Road, Clonard Gardens, and Cupar Street would also go up in flames, some from petrol bombs, some from sparks leaping from one house to the next. "The burning of the houses took place all night," Mrs. Barbour recalls. "I stood up at the back attic window watchin' each house exploding from the gas. I called to Jack. I said, 'Jack, for God's sake, this place is going on fire. We're going to be burned out." He says, 'Get the blazes out of it and give my head peace. When they come up to our house you can tell me and I'll get out.'

"I was very frightened, really. You see Jack had been used to all this before, whereas I have never experienced anything like it. Growing up in Belfast, Jack and his family had to get out of a house on the Ormeau Road when he was a child. So he had seen so much of it that he wasn't worried, and he wasn't going to worry until it got to the last pitch."

At about 7:00, Mrs. Barbour saw the troops come in. They had been ordered to Belfast a few hours earlier, but had taken some time to get there. Two companies of the First Battalion of the Royal Regiment of Wales set up headquarters in the Springfield Road RUC station, under the command of a Colonel Napier. Their arrival certainly cheered many Catholics, but few were delighted in Clonard, as the Colonel sent no one to Cupar Street.

Colonel Napier was convinced that the Falls Road was the boundary line between the two communities, and he was determined to maintain a secure beachhead there. This would be roughly equivalent to defending the island of Manhattan from invasion by positioning troops on Fifth Avenue. It was not that Colonel Napier was particularly ignorant. Ignorance was the norm throughout Britain when it came to the North.

So on the night of August 15, 1969, Colonel Napier's Welshmen, their helmets covered with camouflage webbing designed for jungle warfare, took to the Falls Road. Their maps were inadequate. One street lined with rowhouses looked much like the next. At half past seven they erected barricades on the Falls to prevent movement across it, thereby separating the Catholics of the Lower Falls from the Catholics of the Springfield.

No doubt they were reassured by the lack of hostility between the two sides.

One of the Redemptorists went down to the Falls and begged the army for help. At about 8:00 P.M., Colonel Napier took a patrol to the monastery, where he was taken upstairs, and shown Bombay Street, ablaze, and Cupar. The Colonel also saw the only gunman in Clonard, a man with a shotgun stationed in the monastery.

Colonel Napier returned to the Falls about ten minutes later. He gathered a group of twenty-five soldiers, and for a short time they were posted at the monastery, but then they were sent back to the main contingent on the Falls. Napier then dispatched 2nd Lieutenant Adams and eight footsoldiers to Clonard to determine if Cupar Street was in fact the border between the two communities. Adams reported back at 9:35, and was quickly sent back to Clonard to make sure that St. Galls, the primary school next to the monastery, had not been destroyed.

The school was ablaze when Adams arrived. He could see men from the Shankill torching other houses, but could do little about the situation because his men were outnumbered. One soldier was shot near the ruins of the shoemaker's. Adams ordered his men to fire tear gas. Over the course of the next few hours, his patrol fired fifty gas grenades and cartridges.

As parts of the mob dispersed, Catholics ran out into Cupar and reeled in a fire engine that had been abandoned there in midafternoon. They turned the hoses on St. Galls and on houses in Bombay Street. Soldiers helped them when they could. After midnight, Adams's patrol received reinforcements, and he deployed his men at each of the intersections on Cupar, thereby sealing off Clonard. There were still substantial numbers of Protestants in each of the side streets to the north, and according to later testimony, some of them were drunk. A relative peace settled in, and sometime in the early hours of the morning, a fire truck arrived to supplement the efforts of the civilians manning the other appliance.

The British government later appointed a three-man tribunal, headed by Justice Scarman, to study the causes of the violence in the North. The Scarman Tribunal heard testimony from 400 witnesses and submitted its report in April 1972. The judges concluded that Protestants on the Shankill had been motivated by a feeling "of communal anger against what they believed to have been a Catholic assault on . . . the established order of the province" and that they "were retaliating against what they believed was Catholic aggression in neighbouring areas on the previous two nights."

"The Protestants began the fighting and were responsible for most of the destruction," the Tribunal concluded, adding that there was "no evidence of any military style planning in the attack."

"Both sides suffered casualties in roughly equal number, [but] the same is not true of damage to property, the brunt of which was borne by Catholics. Three-fifths of the houses in Bombay Street, which was almost exclusively occupied by Catholics, were destroyed by fire. Houses were also damaged—many so seriously that they had to be demolished—in Cupar Street, Kane Street, Kashmir Road, and Clonard Gardens. The property was overwhelmingly Catholic. . . . The Tribunal finds that almost all the burnings in the Clonard area were caused by Protestants."

From the ashes of that awful night rose a tremendous hatred of the police, who had appeared in the district once, in token force, at 9:30 P.M., six hours after the first entry in the police log of disturbances in Clonard. The police told the tribunal that their numbers were insufficient to send a force into the area; that many policemen were exhausted after a sustained period of duty; that some had been injured on previous nights; and that trouble had not been expected in the afternoon, and so many constables had been stood down and did not report until the evening. The police also said that they thought their stations were going to be attacked by the IRA, and so they were reluctant to disperse their forces.

The Scarman Tribunal, however, noted that there had been no general order for police to remain in stations. "Police tactics this day [August 15] were clearly dictated by their interpretation of the previous night's events which they saw in terms of an IRA-led uprising. The Tribunal does not question the sincerity of this belief, but it was quite mistaken."

Most Catholics were skeptical of the constabulary's defense. The fact remained that Protestants in several areas of the city had burned Catholic homes without hindrance from the police. And while most Catholics were glad that the troops had been sent in, some felt that the soldiers had also failed them. In Clonard, for instance, no one doubted that the Welshmen had saved the whole area from destruction, but the soldiers, armed with tear gas and firearms, had not been able to stop the Protestant attackers before they had wreaked considerable havoc. And the protection the troops provided was to be short term: the government was saying the men would be back in their barracks in a few days.

There was a similarly mixed attitude about the IRA. The fabled protectors of the Catholic community had been a joke that night. In this book, *The IRA* (Fontana Books, 1980), Irish Press editor Tim Pat Coogan reports that the movement had a total of ten guns in the whole North of Ireland at that time. Many Catholics were bitter, and in west Belfast graffiti appeared, smearing the old heroes, equating the letters IRA with "I Ran Away."

When the dust settled, however, many ghetto residents assessed the situation differently, concluding that if they wanted protection, they had better provide their own. Old IRA militants came out of retirement and began organizing their neighborhood defenses and accumulating weapons. Volunteers were plentiful, some from the 200 families who had been burned out in the summer riots, some from families who had been forced to leave mixed districts. (Of 1,820 families who fled their homes in July, August, and September, 82.7 percent were Catholic, and in those three months alone, 5 percent of all Catholic families in Belfast were displaced.)

On the whole, however, the Catholic attitude was one of defense, not offense. Soldiers were welcome in Catholic homes. The priests at Clonard even allowed the troops to set up an observation post on the roof of the monastery (later removed at the Redemptorists' request). In London, the Labour Government of Harold Wilson seemed sympathetic to the Catholic plight. Parliament set up committees to reorganize the police and to investigate the causes of the riots. Wilson declared that the dreaded B-Specials would be phased out. James Callaghan, the Home Secretary, walked the scarred streets of Belfast and Derry.

The Protestant community was not pleased with the London intervention, and it was particularly riled by two government reports that documented the system of discrimination and gerrymandering employed against Catholics, suggested the police should be disarmed, and described the B-Specials as "a partisan and paramilitary force recruited exclusively from Protestants." Protestants took to the streets in response. The first policeman killed during the troubles was shot on October 11; he was killed by Loyalists who were protesting about the lack of support being given to their police.

As time passed, the relationship between the Catholic community and the British troops began to sour. For fifty years the people of mainland Britain had let a Protestant state develop in the North, and when troops arrived to restore order, they were in essence shoring up an anti-

Catholic state. The same people were in power after the August riots as
had been before, and the well-meaning statements of Westminster politicians could not change the houses the Catholics lived in, the unemployment they were sentenced to, the discrimination they faced in the job
market, or their fear of the police force. Nor could those statements
change the essential nature of the constabulary: when Scotland Yard was
brought in to investigate the savage beating of Sam Devenny and his family, the investigators met with a wall of silence from the RUC. Some of
the culprits were identified; no one was prosecuted. Yet Catholics noted
how easy it was for the government to prosecute Bernadette Devlin, the
twenty-two-year-old M.P. from mid-Ulster, for her role in what Catholics
saw as the defense of the Bogside against police attack during the August upheaval. The Scarman Tribunal noted that the M.P. "was seen in
the afternoon to be actively defending the Rossville Street barricades,
taking missiles up to its defenders, and shouting encouragement to
them." Devlin was sentenced to six months imprisonment for incitement
to riot and disorderly behavior.

In the spring and summer of 1970, many Catholics who had assumed
the troops would provide a new order began to question that assumption,
gradually coming to see the army as just another armed force acting in
the Unionist interest. In the meantime, the IRA moved from a defensive
to an offensive role, bombing banks, electricity stations, and the homes
of judges. On February 6, 1971, the Provisionals killed their first British
soldier, and the war began in earnest. It escalated further after August
9, when the British Army began Operation Demetrius, arresting hundreds of men and imprisoning them indefinitely without trial, a policy
known as internment.

Initially, only Catholics were arrested. The army's intelligence was
poor, and it is estimated that only 20 percent of the men interned had
anything to do with the IRA. Fourteeen detainees were subjected to dis-
orientation procedures known as "the five techniques": they were kept
hooded at all times, except during periods of interrogation, for up to six
days; they were forced to stand against a wall in a spreadeagled position,
their bodies forming the hypotenuse of a triangle, for hours at a stretch
(one man spent forty-three hours in that position); they were bombarded
with "white noise," a continuous high-pitched throb; they were deprived
of sleep; and they were fed only one round of bread and a pint of water at
six-hour intervals. Some internees told the London *Sunday Times* and

the *Irish Press* that they had been forced to run barefoot over broken glass; that they were beaten ("My privates were the size of a football," said one man from Clonard); and that they had been pushed out of helicopters not knowing they were only a few feet off the ground. The Republic of Ireland took the case of those fourteen men to the European Commission of Human Rights. In 1976, the Commission found Britain guilty of torture and inhuman and degrading treatment. The British appealed the decision, and in 1978, the European Court of Human Rights upheld the inhuman and degrading treatment charge but dropped the torture count. In the meantime, Britain had paid a half million pounds in compensation to the victims for injuries received.

The internment policy lasted four years, and some men were interned on several occasions. Once released, many found it difficult to find work, though they had never been convicted of any crime. Some employers felt that if the men weren't IRA volunteers when they went into the internment camp, they would be by the time they came out.

Catholics were furious with the government's policy. Catholic politicians organized a massive civil disobedience campaign and refused to partake in any talks with the British or Northern Irish government until internment was ended. Many young men joined the Provisionals. By the end of the year, forty-three soldiers had been killed and there had been an average of three explosions, five shootings, and forty-seven houses searched each day. And it got worse: the 1,700 shootings in 1971 were matched by 10,000 in 1972.

On January 30, 1972, Catholics scheduled a march in Derry to protest internment; all marchers and parades had been banned after internment was introduced. Soldiers from the Parachute Regiment opened fire on the marchers, killing thirteen Catholic men. The soldiers later claimed they shot at civilians aiming bombs or weapons at them, a charge which forensic tests could not substantiate; a government tribunal had a hard time sorting out the evidence, and in the end concluded that four of the dead men might have been armed. At the end of the inquest, Londonderry City Coroner Major Hubert O'Neill, came to an entirely different conclusion, "It strikes me that the army ran amok that day. . . . They were shooting innocent people. . . . I say it without reservation—it was sheer, unadulterated murder."

In the Northern ghettos, Catholics rioted in response to the killings, and in Dublin a mob set fire to the British Embassy. On the floor of the

House of Commons, Bernadette Devlin punched Home Secretary Reginald Maulding, the man who had earlier spoken of "an acceptable level of violence." The IRA laid bombs and ambushes, killing civilians, policemen, and soldiers. By March 20, fifty-six soldiers were dead. On March 24, Prime Minister Edward Heath suspended the Northern Irish government, and direct rule of the province from London began. Today, responsibility for the North is vested in the Secretary of State for Northern Ireland and the Northern Ireland Office (NIO).

Americans might jump to the conclusion that with the assumption of direct rule, the British would be driven into a political frenzy, that while they had always been responsible for the North, the fact that they were now governing the minute daily affairs of the province would force the issue into the public's living rooms. That full-scale living room invasion, however, has never occurred.

First there is the problem of censorship. Television network internal guidelines and rulings by the Independent Broadcasting Authority dictate what can and cannot be shown on British television. By the end of 1985, more than fifty television programs on Northern Ireland had been cancelled, censored, withdrawn, or delayed. The programs ranged from contemporary news coverage to a documentary on the life of Irish patriot and guerrilla leader Michael Collins, which was banned although Collins, who had signed the treaty that created Northern Ireland, had been dead for more than fifty years. The Collins film, directed by Kenneth Griffith, was designed to end with the death of the guerrilla leader in 1922. "I wasn't saying what I think in 1978–79," Griffith wrote after his film was locked up in a safe. "I was saying what had happened 50 or 100 years ago. . . . I thought, 'I am totally protected by history.' I have invented no dialogue. It was quote, unquote, statistics, facts. But of course I always knew that history was lethal."

British television reporters have also faced restrictions imposed by the army, which means that only the barest information on incidents is released. Peter Gill, a correspondent with Thames Television, said in December 1980 that he had worked with the armies of Iran and Pakistan that year, and that both were more cooperative with British television reporters than the army of the United Kingdon. "The outlook seems to be," he wrote in a letter to the *Times* of London, "that an absence of press, particularly TV coverage, may help in the winding down of the conflict."

It has therefore been relatively easy for the British to accommodate the war in the North. They have been spared some of the disturbing television images and analysis which assaulted Americans night after night during the Vietnam war. Furthermore, the killing does not take place on the British mainland, but for an incident or two a year, which cause great fury but little long-term concern. Also adding to the mainland's complacency is the relatively low death toll: between 1971 and the end of 1985, an average of twenty-five British soldiers were killed annually in Northern Ireland. On the mainland, the deaths of policemen and members of the Ulster Defense Regiment don't count, as they are perceived as Irish, not British.

Furthermore, it is possible to look at the casualty figures—467 killed in political violence in the North in 1972 and 56 killed in 1985—and believe that each year will be more normal than the next, that the tiresome conflict will eventually peter out, that the current situation is not the problem, but the solution. In reality, however, those casualty figures do not reflect the state of the conflict; they reflect instead the refinement of killing methods, the growing precision in hitting targets, and the political mood of the men with guns. When the IRA is so popular that it can put its chief spokesman in Parliament, as happened in 1983, they don't need to shoot many soldiers in order to be heard.

Another factor contributing to the British apathy is the size of Northern Ireland. The North is a very small place—an area the size of Connecticut with a population of 1.5 million and a single telephone book for the entire province. The entire population of the North could be housed in the cities of Manchester and Birmingham.

So while the troubles have enormous scale to many of the people in the North (2,400 dead as a percentage of population would be equivalent to 88,000 dead on the British mainland or 385,000 dead in the United States), to the politicians at Westminster, the conflict in the North is a minor problem. According to Tony Benn, a member of the Cabinet during the last Labour government, the Cabinet discussed Northern Ireland only once between 1974 and 1979. Conservative, Liberal, and Labour party annual conventions passed with nary a mention of the troubles in the North. The British public was told repeatedly that the IRA was near collapse, that it was "finished," "reeling," and playing "its last card."

While the optimistic proclamations of officials and the censorship of television news are partly to blame for the public's lack of concern, there is also a sort of willing blindness. "It's not that they seem to be just bored by it," Anne McHardy, a veteran reporter for the *Guardian,* told me in 1980. "It seems most people have a will not to know about it. They refuse to read about Northern Ireland, and when you talk to them about it, they greet you with stares of total disbelief. They take the attitude that you're being paranoid, or that you're making it up."

McHardy worked in Belfast for seven of the worst years of the troubles. At one point in her tenure she was invited to a Northern Ireland Office banquet and was seated across from a very drunk NIO press officer. As the meal began, he questioned her politics, saying she was awfully friendly with some Republican chaps. He went on to remark that her husband had certainly been short tempered lately. As her husband was then living in London, she asked the press officer how he knew of the McHardy family arguments. "I listen to the tapes," he said, and he went on to relate the details of the reporter's recent phone conversations.

The NIO did not deny that the *Guardian* correspondent's phone had been tapped. One official later told her that an investigation was being conducted to determine how the press officer had received the tapes, as he was not on the authorized list.

McHardy says that when she tells that story in London, there is no outrage in the reaction of her listeners. "They'd rather not know what's happening," she says, "and when they do, they make excuses for the government's nasty behavior. 'Of course that happens,' they say. 'It's Northern Ireland. It had to happen.'"

McHardy was not the only reporter spied upon. In March 1975, the London *Times* reported that the army kept files "almost certainly gathered from tapped telephone calls" on reporters from the *Irish Independent,* the *Observer,* the *Daily Telegraph,* and the *Times*. The *Times* correspondent said his dossier included a description of a picture that he had on the wall of his home and the names of every contact and friend the army suspected he had made in the previous twelve months.

———

I found it very hard to be a reporter in west Belfast. I felt I looked suspicious—an American employed not by some well-known magazine or newspaper, but by a foundation no one had ever heard of, living not in a pleasant hotel like the rest of the American journalists, but in a boarding-house in a grim neighborhood. I would have been suspicious of such a stranger myself. I decided the best course was to move slowly and with caution, attracting as little attention as possible.

Among my first acquaintances in the district was a fellow tenant named Frank, a quiet man, nearing forty, who lived in Mrs. Barbour's back attic room. Frank worked in the newsagent's shop two doors down the road. The newsagency drew some trade from Mackie's workers, who crossed the street at noon to buy sandwiches and cigarettes, and so it sold the Protestant daily, the *Belfast Newsletter*, right alongside the Catholic *Irish News*. I visited the shop at least twice a day to buy the morning and evening papers. Other customers included neighborhood women who came in to buy cheese, sweets, and paperbacks to put in a weekly parcel for their sons in the Maze prison. The IRA gave mothers (or wives in the case of married prisoners) a weekly contribution, and many women used the cash to send a parcel to the prison. Frank told me that he had seen some women putting together parcels for their sons for years, and that one or two have told him they are glad their sons are inside, that at least in prison they are safe, unlikely to be killed or wounded.

The shop is owned by Joe Early, a thin, blond haired man in his early fifties who lives in the flat above the store. Early is a latecomer to the newsagent trade. He was trained as a tailor, but in the mid-1960s gave up that profession when he realized he could make more money and have more freedom in the taxi business. He started his own firm, Able Taxis, in 1969, and eight years later had forty drivers in his fleet.

The troubles made the taxi business dangerous but lucrative, as people were unable to rely on the buses and unwilling to walk through certain areas. Early's depot was blown up eight times, never as a target, but as an accompanying casualty when bombs went off nearby. Some of his drivers carried two licenses. "One license would be in their real name," Early says. "Say it was Seamus O'Neill. Then on the other they had a Protestant sounding name, say Billy Thompson, with an address in a Protestant district." The second license was protection in the event that a driver was stopped by paramilitaries in a Protestant zone.

Hijackings of taxis were more common than traffic accidents; Early calls them "tiddlywinks" and estimates that it happened to him ten times and to his drivers by the score. The cabs would be used by the Provos and other groups to carry out jobs or to move weapons or explosives, and the drivers would usually be held until the job was completed, then given back their vehicle. Sometimes they were held in Republican drinking clubs and were given drinks on the house. I have been told of one man who was so frightened when his car was hijacked that he drank himself silly. When the car was returned, the IRA volunteer realized the man was in no condition to drive, and so took the man home himself; he dragged the fellow to the front door, put the car keys in his pocket, rang the doorbell, and then beat the hastiest of retreats, fearing the wrath of the man's spouse. I know another man whose van was hijacked by the IRA; when the volunteers returned the vehicle, they gave him directions to the nearest police station.

Early says he gave up the taxi business on his wife's insistence after he narrowly escaped assassination when his cab was hijacked by Protestant paramilitaries. In 1979, he bought the newsagency on the Springfield Road. It's small potatoes, he says, compared to his taxi firm, and although he has been robbed three times and pistol whipped once, I sense that Early feels confined there, that he misses the action.

About a hundred yards past Early's shop, on the opposite side of the road, was Meli's fish and chip shop. Meli's had a ten-item menu. The air inside reeked of frying oil. A steady crowd of teenagers patronized the pinball machines just inside the door. Once I ducked into the shop for protection in the middle of a riot and found a teenager, bored by the shooting outside, playing a video game called "Cosmic Guerrilla."

In my early days in the neighborhood, I heard that the Meli family had suffered considerably in the course of the troubles. I learned that a grandfather and an aunt had been killed, that an uncle had had his business wrecked in a sectarian clash in 1974, and that another uncle was doing time in the Maze for IRA activity. Neighbors also told me of an incident in the chip shop in 1975, when a customer walked in at dinner time, ate, and left a transistor radio behind. Mr. Meli, expecting that the man would be back to claim the item, put it underneath the counter. The next morning, while Mr. and Mrs. Meli were still asleep, their four sons, age six to ten, found the transistor and began fighting over it. Tony, the ten year old, touched the volume knob, and the set exploded.

The radio was just the casing for a nail bomb. Mrs. Meli thought that a car bomb had gone off in the street until she heard her children screaming. She found her sons strewn and bloody around the living room. Tony was hit the hardest. He lost part of his right arm, half his left hand, and his left eye.

Compensation awards, particularly those resulting from the most gruesome incidents, are often reported in the daily newspapers and on the evening news. The amount awarded in personal injury cases varies with the degree of injury, the financial position of the victim, and the way the injury is likely to affect his future. A professional soccer player, for instance, would get more for a minor wound to the leg than a factory worker. The widow of an executive killed in an explosion would get an award that reflected her husband's earning power; a widow of a man on the dole would get very little, as the assumption in the law is that the man was not worth much to the family anyway. Anyone who is or has been a member of a proscribed organization is automatically ineligible for compensation, though he may have left that organization eight or ten years before.

Tony was awarded £85,000. From the tone of a few conversations I have heard among my neighbors about the incident, I think he lost some sympathy in the district when the award was announced.

I used to run into him every few weeks on the Springfield Road, a hook where his hand once was, his face scarred from the shrapnel. When we first met, Tony was just a few months shy of the age at which he could legally leave school. He attended a special school for the handicapped, one of the few integrated schools in Belfast. Tony didn't mind his classes, but he was looking forward to leaving because he thought there was more to a life than he knew at that point. He hoped that someday he might be a carpenter or mechanic.

No one was ever charged with the Meli bombing, but a Protestant worker was jailed for possession of a bomb much like the one that blew up in Tony's face. The Melis had been chosen as targets simply because they were Catholics.

Some of Tony's aunts, uncles, and cousins have married non-Catholics, and as a result, the bombing did not turn him to blind hatred of Protestants, nor did it radicalize him or bring him to embrace the Republican movement. When I met him in 1980, five years after the explosion, the only group he embraced was the mods, teenagers who were fond of pointed shoes, thin lapels, white shirts, and motor scooters.

Other local acquaintances included tenants who were less constant than Frank, the newsagent's assistant, and I. One was an Argentine who stayed for a few days not long after I arrived, a sculptor active in his homeland in the campaign for information on the thousands of people who disappeared during the junta's regime. Mrs. Barbour held some documents for him for a short time, storing them in the dining room cabinet with the silverware and the war souvenirs. The sculptor's name was Adolfo Perez Esquivel, and a few months after he stayed with us, he won the Nobel Peace Prize.

When I came back to Mrs. Barbour's after a nine-month absence in 1982, a twenty-two-year-old woman had moved into my old room, and I moved up to the attic. The woman, whom I will call Ann, had been shot by the army outside Fort MacRory in the mid-1970s. It was August 9, a sort of resistance holiday in west Belfast, a night when Catholics light bonfires and throw up an occasional barricade to mark the anniversary of the night in 1971 when the army swooped into the ghettos for the first wave of internment arrests. On that particular anniversary, Ann was just a high school kid, and she went off with other women and girls from the neighborhood to bang bin lids outside the entrance to the fort. A soldier shot her in the head with a rubber bullet. When she regained consciousness, she was in the hospital.

She suffered brain damage, and half her body was paralyzed. Today she limps, and she talks like someone who has had a stroke. Her right hand is permanently coiled and she rarely uses it. She can no longer read; she can make out the big words, but she can't distinguish the short ones: "a" and "at," "the" and "that," "in" and "is" all look the same to her.

People who have never seen a rubber bullet often picture it as an innocent and lightweight projectile about half the size of their baby finger. A rubber bullet is not innocent. It is deadly, 5¾ inches long, 1½ inches wide, and cone shaped on one end. It weighs 5¼ ounces, the weight of a major league baseball, and it travels at 160 miles per hour.

The rubber bullet was removed from the army's arsenal after 1975, having killed three people and maimed countless others. It was replaced by the plastic bullet, 3⅜ inches long, 1½ inches wide, the consistency of a hockey puck but three-fourths of an ounce lighter. Plastic bullets are cylinders, flat at both ends. They have greater speed, range, and accuracy than the rubber versions, which because of their length tended to wobble over long distances. The muzzle velocity of the plastic bullet is estimated at 180 to 200 miles per hour, a speed which enables the projectile to smash skulls. Between 1975 and the spring of 1982, eleven people were killed by the bullets, six of them children between the ages of ten and fifteen. The security forces justify the use of the weapon to disperse rioters by arguing that tear gas falls on the just and the unjust, alienating whole neighborhoods, and water cannon are not feasible in many of Belfast's narrow streets.

In 1980, Ann was given a large sum of money from the compensation office on the claim she filed after she was shot, and that award proved to be the second tragedy of her life. The sudden wealth divided her from her family, all of whom wanted a piece of it, and after more than a year of generosity and conflict, she moved from her mother's house to Mrs. Barbour's. She was unable to read, afraid to go to the movies because she did not like to sit alone in the dark, and afraid to go to a pub because she could not handle drink. Without friends from her old neighborhood, and divided from her family, Ann's only pastime was to spend money. Her bedroom, jammed with clothes that she never wore, came to resemble a huge closet in which a bed and a sink were stored. I doubt that she will have any money left by the time she is thirty, but I am not sure if that will be good or bad for her. The buying gave her some pleasure, and denying her that outlet would leave her with no pastimes at all. And when her money is gone, she may well be welcomed back by her family, like some prodigal daughter returning from abroad.

When I first moved into Clonard, I didn't know who or what should be feared. I had to learn to watch for unattended packages and to steer clear of cars parked in certain places. In the beginning, a visit to any of the shops in the district was a challenge, and I could feel people acting differently when they realized a stranger was in their midst. It took me some time to figure out who was a threat and who was not.

The most visible threats in the district were the British troops, who work in mysterious ways in west Belfast. Even the IRA admits that the British are very good at undercover work. One of the army's first undercover operations—and one of the few that have been uncovered—involved a cleaning service called the Four Square Laundry, established in 1972. Two soldiers—one male, one female—traveled in and out of Catholic districts dressed as civilians, picking up dirty clothes in a green laundry van. At the time, much of west Belfast was barricaded, and the laundry operation gave the army access to homes and districts it did not have access to in uniform. According to the *Belfast Telegraph,* the afternoon newspaper, the laundry's prices were much lower than those of other firms, and word spread of the bargain service.

On October 2, 1972, the van called at Twinbrook, a Catholic housing estate on the outskirts of west Belfast. While the driver's partner was calling at a customer's house, three men in a blue Ford Cortina fired twelve to fifteen shots at the van. The driver was dead on arrival at Lagan Valley hospital, and the IRA claimed the killing. The Four Square Laundry service was terminated immediately.

Incidents like those, in combination with the cameras that film street activity, the army's computer and data banks (which hold information on everyone in west Belfast and on half the citizens of Northern Ireland), the searches without warrant, the arrests at dawn, and the helicopters that hover over west Belfast, have engendered an infectious paranoia among my neighbors in Clonard. There are times when they suspect not only strangers, but people whom they have known for years or even decades.

I also took little time learning to fear the Royal Ulster Constabulary (RUC), the Northern Irish police. No policeman walked the streets of Clonard without a flak jacket, a partner, and four soldiers close behind. They were clearly outsiders in the district, unwelcome and scared.

Catholics have never been fond of the RUC. In 1969, Catholics made up about 11 percent of the force, but after the troubles escalated, some Catholic constables were intimidated by the IRA and resigned. Others left the force because it was perceived as sectarian, a perception so widespread that even the British government picked it up; after the 1969 upheaval, the government decided that a more credible constabulary was needed, and it ordered that the B-Specials be disbanded (the B-Specials were the auxiliary police who had provoked much of the hard feeling in the Catholic community toward the police force in general). Today, RUC press spokesmen claim that they have no precise figures on the percentage of Catholics on the force but estimate that it is about 10 percent; others outside the force, however, put the figure at about half the official estimate.

The Northern Irish police are an incredibly young force; in 1981, an RUC press officer told me it was the youngest in western Europe, that two-thirds of the force was under twenty-four-years old. Many of those who join do so because there are not many other jobs to be had; traditional Protestant employers like the shipyard and Mackie's have cut back on their work force, and it is often said that the police force and the prison service are the only growth industries in the North. The stress of a policeman's life is extremely high; the times when he would normally feel most safe—when surrounded by family and familiar things—are just as fraught with potential violence and assassination as the hours on the job. Every time a policeman opens a package, answers his door, or starts his car, it might well be his last effort. While a soldier has a finite tour of duty and a home in England, Scotland, or Wales to retreat to, a policeman has no escape. The RUC claims that its men run the highest risk of being killed of any police force in the world, and I do not doubt that claim.

Frightened men are capable of frightening things, and the RUC performed some horrible acts in the mid to late 1970s, acts for which they are still remembered and condemned in the Catholic community. Under increased pressure from the government to produce results in the war against terrorism, the police regularly beat and tortured suspects in interrogation centers. The Police Surgeons Association (a group of doctors affiliated with the force), the media, and Amnesty International all documented the brutal treatment. The seventy-eight former prisoners interviewed for the Amnesty International report, published in June 1978, mentioned the following treatment administered by the police: general beating and kicking; bending the wrist backward; forcing the suspect to run in place or stand for hours; pulling the hairs on a prisoner's chest or lifting him by his moustache; pouring a cola liquid into a suspect's ears; banging the prisoner's head against the wall; holding his head under water; kicking and squeezing the testicles; placing a plastic bag, a hood, or a pair of soiled underpants over the suspect's head; making the prisoner behave in a bizarre manner (one man was ridden like a horse by an interrogator, was forced to eat mucus from a policeman's nose, was ordered to count holes in the wall, and was spun around and around); burning a prisoner's hand against radiator pipes; ordering a man to stand with his underpants around his knees while interrogators made insulting remarks about his genitals. Women interviewed by the Amnesty mission reported that they had been threatened with rape. Three of the seventy-eight prisoners interviewed by Amnesty said they had attempted suicide during detention, four were under psychiatric care after they were released, and several showed signs of organic brain damage or having had "an acute psychotic episode." Jack Hassard, a member of the Police Authority, the board of civilians that advises the RUC, said in June 1978 that both the Chief Constable and the Secretary of State for Northern Ireland (the cabinet minister who oversees the province) knew all along what was happening in the RUC's lockups.

Thousands of complaints were filed against the police in those years, but no policeman was ever sent to jail for those crimes. The government did not deny that the crimes had been committed (the evidence in many cases was irrefutable), and paid some of the victims compensation. The perpetrators of those crimes, however, could not be identified, ostensibly because the police presented a wall of silence to anyone who asked. Yet Catholics wonder how hard the government tried to pierce that wall, and the knowledge that the men who did those beatings are still on the police force wins the RUC no friends in the Catholic ghetto.

The last uniformed gunmen I learned about during those first weeks in Clonard were the members of the Ulster Defense Regiment (UDR), a local militia that an American might find vaguely similar to a state unit of the national guard. The UDR is a regiment of the British Army recruited and used only in Northern Ireland, and many members serve only part time. The regiment was created in 1970 and was intended as a nonsectarian replacement for the B-Specials. While initial enrollment included a fair number of Catholics, by the time the regiment celebrated its tenth anniversary, Catholic enrollment was about 2 percent and Catholic sentiment was adamantly against the regiment, whose members have participated in various murders and attempted murders over the course of the current troubles. In 1985, Garret Fitzgerald, the leader of the government of the Irish Republic, called the regiment "a dangerous force, as their loyalty does not lie with the British Crown," a force that "Catholics must and do fear." When I moved into the district in 1980, however, the UDR was among the least of my worries; the regiment was deployed mostly in rural areas and almost never in west Belfast. I don't think I actually realized the nature of the force until one evening in 1982, when I went out to dinner with a priest at a restaurant in a seaside town. When we returned to Belfast we ran into an unexpected check-point on the outskirts of east Belfast, and my companion made a remark on the order of "God save us, it's the UDR."

Aside from learning to watch my step with the army, the police, and the national guard, I also had to be on my guard with the gunmen out of uniform. On the Catholic side, my two main worries were the Provisional IRA and the INLA (Irish National Liberation Army). The latter, also known as the Irps (a nickname derived by jumbling the initials of the group's political wing—the Irish Revolutionary Socialist Party), were terrifying in their carelessness, and their operations often involved civilian casualties.

Down the road a bit, in the Lower Falls, I was warned about a third armed Catholic group, remnants of the Official IRA. The IRA split into two in 1970, the armed militants forming the Provos, the armed liberals forming the Officials. The Official's political wing, now called the Workers Party, claims that its membership laid down its weapons in 1972. Remnants of the old military wing, however, have continued to carry out armed robberies, kneecappings, and murders. The Officials are commonly known as the Stickies: after the split with the Provos, the Officials held their own Republican parade at Easter, and one could tell an Official from a Provisional by the way he wore his paper Easter Lily (the symbol of the rising)—the Officials used an adhesive (hence Stickie), while the Provos used pins.

In some neighborhoods, people worried about all three sets of armed Catholics—the Provos, the Irps, and the Stickies—and about feuds between various factions, which took lives in 1971 and 1975. Not often armed, but still to be watched out for, were the neighborhood hooligans, the delinquents who broke into homes and shops and occasionally did an armed robbery.

I also worried about the Protestant paramilitaries—Andy Tyrie's UDA (Ulster Defense Association), the UVF (Ulster Volunteer Force), the UFF (Ulster Freedom Fighters), the Red Hand Commandos, and the Protestant Action Force—who have assassinated random and specific Catholics. Protestant paramilitaries killed 569 civilians up to the end of 1984 (Catholic paramilitaries killed 496 civilians during the same period, but far more members of the security force—705 to the Protestant paramilitaries 90). While the IRA and other Republican paramilitaries have killed policemen in front of their wives and children, loyalist paramilitaries have managed another sort of cruelty—torture and dismemberment. In October 1982, for example, loyalists tied a Catholic to a chair and sawed his hand off with a hacksaw, and later that month they chopped up a Catholic with an axe after pulling his teeth and slitting his throat; newspapers reported that the dead man was identified by his wristwatch.

Ken Heskin, Fullbright scholar and lecturer in psychology at Trinity College in Dublin, has studied the methods of both Catholic and Protestant paramilitaries, and in his book, *Northern Ireland: A Psychological Analysis* (Cambridge University Press, 1980), he points out that although there is a traditional respect for the force of arms among Northern Protestants, there is no widespread tradition of guerrilla warfare. He argues that Protestant paramilitary groups have indulged in bizarre and grisly murders because that sort of psychopathic behavior "can flourish somewhat more easily in organizations which lack the cultural traditions and historical respectability of the IRA and hence do not tend so readily to attract the stabilizing element nurtured on these traditions and conscious, to some extent, at least, of the ideals behind the conflict."

The government fears the loyalist paramilitaries not because of their lunatic fringe, but because of their numbers. The UDA claims 15,000 members, and is far more capable of making the province ungovernable than the IRA is. In 1974, for example, when Britain tried to establish a government in the North in which power would be shared between Protestants and Catholics, the loyalists resisted. Reverend Ian Paisley and other hardline Unionist politicians joined with the UDA and other loyalist paramilitary groups in an effort to topple the new government. The coalition of gunmen and politicians established barricades and roadblocks and forced shops to close. Armed men visited factories and ordered the workers out. Laborers at the power stations cut electricity, and petrol supplies were cut off to all but the chosen few. The UDA planted three car bombs in the Republic and thirty-three people were killed. Through all the upheaval in the North, police and soldiers stood by, sometimes chatting with the masked men at the barricades. When London finally ordered the troops to do something, soldiers took over twenty-seven gas stations, an act which hardly made a dent in the show. Catholics were sure they were going to be slaughtered, as the police and army would not stand up to the loyalists, who were threatening to close the water and sewage plants next. On the fourteenth day of the strike, the moderate Unionists who had joined the power-sharing government gave in to the pressure and resigned, and so the government fell.

The UDA remains a legal organization, although it advocates and carries out selective murder, while the IRA is proscribed. (On British television, it is permissible to interview a member of the UDA, but interviews of the IRA are forbidden.) Banning the UDA might not serve much purpose; proscription hasn't stopped the IRA, and it might be argued that if the UDA were banned, it could well surface under a new name with the same leadership. Catholics, however, see the refusal to proscribe the organization as blatantly unfair. Periodically, the Secretary of State for Northern Ireland announces that he is considering such a ban, but it never happens.

Having learned those fears so well, I found myself wondering if I was the only person in the neighborhood who entertained them full time. In my first four months in the district, I heard no shootings, saw no riots, and felt no explosions. There were two murders, one of them in the street just behind us, but I heard about them hours after they occurred, and they seemed to pass from neighborhood conversation even before the funerals. I found myself wary most of the time, though I was performing only the most ordinary tasks. I would get up in the morning, buy the papers, make some phone calls, perhaps do an interview or some research at the library, swim at the Falls Road public baths or at one of the city's Leisure Centers, buy the evening paper, eat dinner with Mrs. Barbour, and then work some more, read, perhaps go for a walk. In those early days I had no social life, as I knew no one.

I worked on a card table in Mrs. Barbour's sitting room, a few feet from a bay window that looked out on the street. Mrs. Barbour liked to keep the blinds partially drawn so no one could see in, but we could see out. I spent a lot of time looking out the window. I watched children go back and forth in their school uniforms. Sturdy women in old coats went past lugging groceries. The postman came up the footpath twice a day. The normality of it all nearly drove me crazy. I was slightly reassured when I discovered that Mrs. Barbour was also uneasy. "It's too quiet," she said to me one day in April. "The Provos are planning something. They must be away, training for something big."

When I moved into west Belfast, I did not know much about the Provos, nor did I intend to make any effort to become intimate with them. I intended to write stories on the noncombatants and on the consequences of the combat, not on the people doing the fighting. I assumed that an American in Clonard would not go unnoticed, that the Provos in the neighborhood would size me up, ask my neighbors who I was and what I was doing, and check my story with their political wing's press officer. I probably assumed too much, or I may have been wrong to think that if the local commander knew who I was, he would inform all his foot-soldiers to leave me alone.

And so on August 9, 1980, I had my first meeting with the Provisional's military wing, an unscheduled appointment. August 9 is a resistance holiday in the Catholic community, an unofficial day of remembrance held on the anniversary of August 9, 1971, the day the government's internment arrests began. Each year on the night of the eighth and early in the morning of the ninth, bonfires are lit all over west Belfast and other Catholic areas. I spent the night of August 8, 1980 moving from fire to fire. Toward the end of the night, I settled in to watch a tremendous conflagration, two stories high, fueled in part by a stolen car, at the dead end of Clonard Gardens. The dead end had once been an intersection—Clonard Gardens ran into the dogleg of Cupar Street—but today a fence, twenty feet high, blocks the intersection, part of the walling in of the district. Pedestrians can cross from one street to another through a gate, but cars cannot get through. The bonfire that night was set up against that fence. The crowd around the fire was peaceful, full of families with children, pensioners, and young people drinking beer.

Suddenly, two policemen came from behind the flames and burst into the street through the pedestrian gate. They began shooting, firing indiscriminately at the crowd. People screamed. I stumbled. I ran toward an open door and into a stranger's house, joining a dozen other fleeing spectators, all of us jammed into a hallway three feet wide. We stayed put for a few minutes, and then, after seeing teenagers on the street throwing stones over the fence at the retreating policemen, I apologized for barging into the house and went back outside.

A man was writhing on the pavement and an ambulance arrived a few minutes later to take him away. It was only then that I learned that the police had been firing plastic bullets, not lead. There was no reason for the police to shoot. No one's life or health was endangered by the flames. No traffic was diverted, no Union Jack was torched, no provocative songs were sung, no revolutionary speeches were made. Furthermore, the police are well accustomed to bonfires, as Protestants light their own on the eve of the Twelfth of July. The difference between a Protestant fire and a Catholic one is that the former is a show of allegiance to the state, while the latter is a show of resistance.

I hung around the Clonard fire for a short time longer, taking a few photographs, but my heart wasn't in it. Just as I was preparing to leave, a kid about nineteen years old, with the build and appearance of a high school halfback, came up and started a conversation. When I left for home, he tagged along. As we approached Oranmore Street, near the convent, he asked who I worked for. The answer was complicated, as no one in the North had ever heard of the Alicia Patterson Foundation or of such an arrangement for a journalist. I had explained it a few hundred times already, and I was tired and still uneasy about the police shooting. My answer was curt. "No one you've ever heard of," I told him.

He then asked if I had any identification. I had my Chicago press card ready, as I had expected that the army might stop me that night, and I held it out to him and asked why he wanted to see it. He didn't answer. He took the card from my hand and crossed the street. I followed, anxious to get the card back. Suddenly, out of the doorway of the bingo hall, another man appeared. The halfback handed him my credentials, reached behind his back and under his sweater, and pulled out a gun. He aimed it at my head and said, "Provisional IRA. Put your hands up."

The whole matter was over in a minute, but I remember it as a long one. My press card was issued by the Cook County Sheriff's Department. That seemed odd to the man from the doorway, and he asked if I was with the police, a most deadly question. I explained, not with any great sense of calm, that in the United States, most press cards are issued by the police. The interrogator then frisked me, and when he turned his attention to the pack containing my cameras and film, the gunman told me to raise my hands higher. His partner, however, feared that the silhouette of a man with his hands high in the air might attract some attention, so he told me to lower them, and so for a second my arms were shooting up and down like a weightlifter doing repetitions.

After my pack yielded nothing suspicious, the two men were satisfied. The halfback stepped forward, flipped open the gun so I could see that it was loaded, and by way of apology explained that they had just wanted to be sure that I wasn't with British intelligence. He shook my hand and invited me back to the bonfire, but I declined.

A few days later, I went down to Sinn Fein headquarters on the Falls Road to clear up the matter. Sinn Fein is the political wing of the IRA;

while the IRA is illegal, Sinn Fein is not. I talked to a press officer, explained what had happened, and asked him to tell his contacts in Clonard that I was a journalist. He seemed slightly surprised, saying that usually the men checked with his office before they approached anyone who claimed to be a member of the press.

I was on my way out of a local pub about a month later when, just as I opened the side door, the Provisionals' halfback passed by. I was so surprised that I had the urge to shout a greeting. Not long thereafter, I began to see him regularly. There were a group of young men who hung out on the Kashmir Road, opposite the laundromat, and he was among them. Eventually I came to know two of the others, and when I walked past I would stop and talk about whatever was happening in the district. I'd nod to the gunman. He'd nod back. Neither of us ever mentioned that he had once sighted my head.

The Provisionals are not easily understood, and I feel obliged to step outside this neighborhood account to fill in some background on their membership, tactics, ethics, and political development.

While the British call the Provos thugs, criminals, mindless psychopaths, the unemployed and unemployable, and Protestants see them as sectarian assassins, Catholics see the IRA as something else entirely. To a Catholic, an IRA man is not some outsider causing violence and death, but Sean down the street, or Mickey, whose father was interned, or Mrs. Sands' son Bobby. There is a definite ambivalence in the Catholic community; most Catholics support the IRA's goal of a united Ireland, but condemn the IRA's means.

The only evaluation of the IRA by disinterested observers, based on statistics and hard data, that I am familiar with can be found in the book *Ten Years on in Northern Ireland,* a 1980 report written by three academics, published by the Cobden Trust, a London-based civil liberties foundation. The authors—Kevin Boyle, Tom Hadden, and Paddy Hillyard—analyzed 300 terrorist trials and concluded that "the bulk of Republican offenders are young men and women without criminal records in the ordinary sense." The authors went on to say that those Catholic men and women who were tried for terrorist offenses were "reasonably representative of the working class community of which they form a sub-

stantial part. . . . They do not fit the stereotype of criminality which the
authorities have from time to time attempted to attach them. . . . The
pattern of recruitment demonstrates the essentially communal nature of
the movement and its close relationship to the political aspirations of the
Catholic community and the continuing deprivation and discrimination
which it experiences."

A cold assessment of the Provisionals contained in a British intelligence report written by Brigadier General James Glover also strips
away some of the common assumptions about the organization. (The secret report, "Northern Ireland: Future Terrorist Trends," written in
1978, became public after one copy was stolen from a mail bag in England.) "PIRA is essentially a working class organization based in ghetto
areas of the cities and in the poorer rural areas," Glover wrote. "There is
a strata of intelligent, astute, and experienced terrorists who provide
the backbone of the organization. . . . Our evidence of rank and file terrorists does not support the view that they are merely mindless hooligans drawn from the unemployed and unemployable."

The Provisionals' military tactics consist mostly of hit-and-run assassination. They ambush and bomb British soldiers, members of the
RUC, and national guardsmen. Policemen and national guardsmen are
often shot while off duty, sometimes in front of their families. The Provos
have also killed businessmen accused of doing business with the security
forces, several Protestant politicians, Lord Mountbatten (a cousin of
Queen Elizabeth and a war hero), and, in an unsuccessful attempt to assassinate Prime Minister Margaret Thatcher, two Conservative Party
officials and the wives of three others.

The Provisionals fight a war of attrition, not a war of body counts. A
spokesman interviewed in 1980 said the organization was "prepared for
the long haul, thirty, forty, fifty years if necessary." The Provos know
they cannot kill enough soldiers, policemen, and members of the national
guard to bring a military surrender. They believe, however, that if they
kill just enough to keep the war going, the toll in lives and money will
bring a political surrender and the British will relinquish their sover-
eignty over the North. So the number of casualties inflicted by the IRA is
not impressive. From 1977 through 1985, for example, an average of
thirteen soldiers, nine members of the UDR, and fourteen policemen
were killed annually (some by the INLA, but most by the Provos).

To help wear down the will of the British public, the Provos also run an
economic campaign. They bomb businesses (Catholic and Protestant)

because those bombings drain the British treasury. An Irish government study published in May 1984, found that since 1969, the British Exchequer had paid approximately $6,501 million in compensation for deaths, injuries, and property damage. After figuring in the cost to the British economy of depressed investment, damaged tourist potential, and lost output, the report added another $4,728 million to the cost of the violence.

Since 1969, the IRA has grown from an ill-armed, ill-disciplined group of amateurs to an army of considerable sophistication. In the early years, the Provos fought with Thompsons, submachine guns of great romance but no great accuracy. Today, rocket launchers are a standard part of their arsenal, silicon chips show up in their incendiaries, and surface-to-air missiles are on their shopping list. They pick their targets with precision and their discipline is much improved. In 1980, the British army estimated that the IRA's political and military expenses were running at more than £2 million a year. The Provos' income comes from bank robberies, rackets of various sorts, and contributions from sympathizers at home and abroad. British government spokesmen told me in 1984 that contributions from the United States were important for morale ("It's nice to know someone out there supports what you're doing") but not a major portion of the IRA's income. In 1978, General Glover estimated overseas contributions at about 12.6 percent of the Provos' income.

The Provisionals took a vital turn in 1977. The physical interrogation in the police stations was netting results: IRA men were "vomiting confessions," according to a senior police officer cited in Peter Taylor's book, *Beating the Terrorists?* (Penguin Books, 1980). The movement's ranks were being depleted at an alarming rate. The Provisionals decided a reorganization was in order, and they moved from a battalion structure to a classic cell organization. In the old format, one volunteer who cracked under interrogation could give away ten or more men and his commander. With the reorganization, active service units of four well-trained men could be assembled from different parts of the city for a single operation. They need never know each other's full names, and if arrested, each man would have very little to heave up about his comrades. At the same time, the IRA's intelligence efforts were beefed up and discipline was tightened.

With the new structure, the Provos needed only a fifth of the men they had formerly deployed. In 1980, police estimated that the IRA had a hard core of 300 to 500 active soldiers. By 1985, an RUC spokesman told me he thought the Provos could run their military campaign with just fifty men.

"A safe method of escape is the dominant feature in PIRA tactics," Glover wrote in his report. "PIRA seldom plan operations that involve high risk, and if in doubt, they abort the mission." The IRA claimed in 1980 that they were aborting five out of six operations, often because of the intelligence they had been able to gather about the army and the police. "If an IRA volunteer goes out to do a job," a Provisional spokesman told me in 1982, "he expects to get back from it. IRA men are not interested in suicide. They're committed, yes. Fanatics, no."

The IRA's improved security, discipline, and intelligence are reflected in the casualty figures. In 1972, seventy IRA men were killed. In 1982, they lost only four.

Ethics have also been refined. General Glover noted that up to 1973, the IRA's activity was often indiscriminate. Car bombs, for example, were left in crowded pedestrian areas. Since then, Glover wrote, the Provos have clung to a certain military code of ethics: they shoot policemen and soldiers, for instance, but they are careful not to shoot their target's families. A Provisional press officer argued to me in 1980 that the IRA's campaign was far more humane than campaigns waged by conventional armies, that guerrilla war, at least the way the Provos fought it, was selective, where the war fought by the United States in Vietnam, for example, was indiscriminate: cities were bombed from the air, whole villages were burned, forests were defoliated.

The Provisionals, however, do make some horrendous mistakes. The bombing at Harrod's department store in London in 1983 was one of them; the IRA unit gave an inadequate warning, the store and surrounding area were not evacuated, and five civilians were killed. The February 1978 bombing of the La Mon restaurant outside Belfast had even worse results. A warning was phoned in once the bomb was in place, but the Provos had underestimated the amount of time it would take to clear the restaurant, and the building was engulfed in flames before many diners found the exits. Twelve people were burned to death, and twenty-three others were badly injured.

The IRA claims it has no quarrel with working-class Protestants and insists that it would like to walk arm-in-arm with them toward the creation of a nonsectarian united Ireland. In the IRA textbook, the fight is with the British, who created and maintain the miserable Northern state, and targets are limited to the security forces who uphold that state. Occasionally the IRA also kills a politician or public official (Catholic or Protestant) whom the movement identifies as a pillar of the state, or a member of a loyalist paramilitary group who has been responsible for the murders of innocent Catholics.

For a working-class Protestant, however, it is very hard to see any codes in the IRA's behavior, very hard to buy the line that the Provos have no quarrel with the Protestant working class. The loyalist community is also afflicted with high unemployment, and many workers have joined the police force, the prison service, and the national guard not to do their patriotic duty or to oppress Catholics, but because those are the few growth industries in the North and jobs are hard to come by. To a man from the Shankill, a cop shot dead by the IRA is a dead worker, not a dead oppressor, and the killing looks sectarian. The IRA would just as soon shoot a Catholic cop or national guardsman—and has done so—but because Protestants are in the majority in the security forces, they are also the overwhelming majority of targets.

It is not only the Provisional leadership's code of ethics that dictates and limits the IRA's activity. The Provisionals are well aware that they need the passive support of large portions of the Catholic community, and that therefore they must abide by the community's sense of what is legitimate resistance and what is not. After the La Mon restaurant bombing, the police took the unusual measure of issuing photographs of the charcoaled bodies; the Catholic community was horrified, and for months afterward the Provos refrained from commercial bombing.

"The Provisionals' campaign of violence is likely to continue while the British remain in Northern Ireland," General Glover concluded in his report. "PIRA will probably continue to recruit the men that it needs. They will still be able to attract enough people with leadership talent, good education, and manual skills to continue to enhance their all round professionalism. The movement will retain popular support sufficient to maintain secure bases in the traditional Republican areas."

In essence Glover was saying that the Provisionals cannot be defeated. That does not necessarily mean that they can win, only that they cannot lose. The IRA knows it cannot beat the British Army, and the British Army knows it cannot beat the IRA. The military campaign is a stalemate.

The IRA's primary failing has been on the political front. Through the early years of the troubles, the Provos depended on the worship of martyrs and the oppression of the state to generate support, and its political thinking was muddled. It was not until the 1977 reorganization that some leaders who favored politicization of the movement really made their voices heard, and even then it was only in the wake of the hunger strike in 1981 that the IRA stopped concentrating exclusively on a military program.

Because they stood in no elections until 1982, the Provisionals left the field to the Social Democratic and Labor Party (SDLP), a party of moderate, middle-class Catholics that advocates a united Ireland achieved through peaceful means. John Hume, the party leader, was raised in Derry's Bogside, the oldest of seven children, the son of a man unemployed for twenty years. Hume is known and respected internationally. But while his party decried the plight of the working class, it had few working-class members. Until 1982, many Catholics in west Belfast voted SDLP by default, not out of great passion. In my years in Mrs. Barbour's house, no one from the SDLP ever knocked on our door.

While working at my table in Mrs. Barbour's front room, I felt pulled to the window whenever a group of soldiers passed by. Four-man patrols passed day and night at different hours. Sometimes they paused in front of the house and set up a checkpoint, stopping cars and asking questions of the passengers. Often they stopped pedestrians, usually young men from the district; the soldiers would frisk them, and ask who they were, when they were born, where they lived, and where they were going. Sometimes one of the members of the patrol assigned to provide cover for the the point man would use our railing to support his rifle, and he would aim his weapon at passing pedestrians. When I was on the street, and the weapon was aimed at me, I always had a hard time thinking of the man behind it as my protector.

At the same time, I understood that it was equally difficult for that soldier to see me or my neighbors as anything but the enemy. Everywhere he looked was a cold face that did not acknowledge his presence, and a smile was so rare that it was remembered, perhaps even recorded.

As the IRA wears no uniforms, the soldier could not tell the combatants from the noncombatants. When he treated us all as suspects, we could not respond as his friend.

Although I originally wanted to avoid writing stories about the army and the IRA, I still felt the need to try to understand what each party was up to, and so I did periodic interviews with both. In recent years, it is the police who have been conducting press briefings, but back in 1980 the army was handling press inquiries and allowing journalists to go out on patrols. I went to several briefings at army headquarters in Lisburn, and over the course of my first eight months in the North, I had tours with army personnel in Belfast, Armagh, and the border post in Middletown.

In my first visit to the barracks in Armagh in March, I talked with a major on his third tour of duty of the North. "In 1972," he told me, "the army was very aware that the people to get at were the children, not the terrorists, to separate the kids from the terrorism. But it didn't happen." He pointed to a "Wanted" poster on the wall. "They were all just ten-year-old stone throwers when this thing started."

"I see it continuing at its present level indefinitely," he said. "It's a war of attrition. All we can do is wear them down until they're too weak to carry on. There is no such thing as a military victory. If the military crushed the terrorists we'd have a military state and we'd have alienated the population. The only way this will end is if we can alienate the terrorist from the Catholic population. The way to do that is to make the law apply equally to both sides and be seen to apply equally to both sides."

The major had seen a great shift in the government's attitude toward paramilitaries. In the first years of the troubles, all paramilitaries, Catholic and Protestant, were treated as prisoners of war. They were housed in barracks, not prison cells, and in 1972, Secretary of State William Whitelaw even flew IRA leaders to London for talks which resulted in a short-lived cease-fire. In 1975 and 1976, however, all that changed. A strategy of Ulsterization was implemented: in an attempt to make life in the province seem more normal, the police were to be gradually moved to the front line and the army to the rear. The government also began to pursue a policy of criminalization: paramilitary officers were no longer community leaders with whom one negotiated; they were "godfathers of violence" who were to be treated as criminals. A member of a paramilitary group was not simply picked up and interned indefinitely; he was to be tried for specific offenses in special courts.

The major indicated that his men found these restrictions frustrating. "We know who all the players are," he said. "We're on Christian name terms with some of them." He explained that the "players" could not be arrested, however, because there was no hard evidence against them.

He went on to say that he thought many of his men sympathized with the Catholics in the North, recognizing that they had been discriminated against, but said none of his men had any sympathy for terrorists. He took me into the shop of a Republican whom the army had interrogated on several occasions; the major and the shopkeeper exchanged a bit of barbed banter while four soldiers kept watch, two inside the shop and two on the street. As we left, the major told me that he got his copy of the *Republican News,* the Provisionals' newspaper, in that shop, that he enjoyed the shopkeeper's wit and humor, and that he thought the man was capable of shooting him in the back some day.

Seven months later, I visited the same fort while working on an article for the *Atlanta Constitution*'s Sunday magazine and heard an entirely different view from the commanding officer, Lieutenant Colonel Robin Thornburn. I remarked that the North seemed to be relatively quiet just then. "I think it's quiet," Thornburn said, "because we're winning the war." Later that day, a sergeant at the border post in Middletown told me that the army could put an end to the conflict in a few months if the politicians would just let them "take off the gloves." He complained that he also knew who the players were, but he was not allowed to go out and shoot them.

One of the blackest views of the North I ever heard from a soldier came from a major stationed at Fort MacRory in west Belfast. It was a cold day in early October 1980; I was waiting to go out with a patrol, and I got to talking with the major, a handsome man in his mid-thirties, just to pass the time. He told me that he was soon to leave the army, that he was going to get married and take up stock brokering. He too believed that the war was winding down—he said that it had become nothing more than "police work"—but he was pessimistic about the prospects for lasting peace. "What have we changed here in the last ten years?" he asked. "The people are more segregated than they were before the troubles. Children are still being taught the same things they were taught when the troubles started, and in ten years a new generation of bigots will be on the street and new riots will break out. The only answer is to do everything possible to locate industry in west Belfast so Catholics can get jobs and middle-class aspirations, so when the next troubles break out, they have something to lose." (As the major spoke, workers were being hired for just such an industrial project located on the outskirts of west Belfast. While it was not going to solve the massive unemployment problem, it was a showcase project that cost the government $160 million in grants, loans, and loan guarantees, and it was expected to show investors what could be achieved. When the project failed a few years later—its director, John DeLorean, was charged with smuggling cocaine—a lot more than the auto plant's 2,000 jobs was lost.)

In addition to interviewing soldiers on duty, I also talked to Michael Biggs, an ex-officer who had served in the North and later became prominent in the "Troops Out" campaign on the British mainland. Biggs, about thirty years old when I met him in London in the spring of 1980, was a graduate of Sandhurst, the British West Point, and had served in the North in 1973. He was stationed in Newry, about forty miles south of Belfast, and during the course of his tour he came to believe that the troops were "an occupying force, not a peacekeeping one." After he left the North, he filed for, and eventually won, conscientious objector status.

The legal ins and outs of his case interested me less than his stories of ordinary life in the barracks. "You have four guys in a small room, and there's personality clashes because of the living conditions, not because of the personalities," he said. "We had a volleyball court, but that was it. You couldn't go out and run or anything. So we had a canteen and showed a lot of films and each soldier was allowed two pints of beer a day. Back then we had dances arranged. It was very secretive. It just happened in one place and it was arranged for women to go there. This is in safe areas. Apart from that, there's bugger-all to do. And patrols in a place like Newry are difficult, because for so long nothing happens. There's a danger that a soldier will switch off, and then, out of the blue, there will be contact.

"It's easier when the enemy is in the trenches. He fires at you, you fire back, but you don't see him. In the North, you're often dealing with a soldier who has no real experience, a young kid, and it's quite a frightening thing for him. I think a lot of the aggression of the soldiers there has a lot to do with the fear that they feel. It comes as a bit of a jolt. They're up against people who talk the same language, and soldiers can in many ways identify with them. They're patrolling in socially deprived communities, and many of them come from socially deprived communities. They may have joined the army because the pay was better than being on the dole. They get women and children throwing abuse and stones at them and it's a bit of a shock."

My first street confrontation with the army occurred not long after I made my decision to stay at Mrs. Barbour's. I went out to the airport one afternoon to pick up two boxes that I'd had shipped from Chicago. I took the bus back to Belfast's city center, and there I asked a cab driver to take me the mile and a half up to my house. He agreed, but only reluctantly; his taxi was the same model as the ones that ran up and down the Falls Road, but he was Protestant, and he was afraid that with no Falls Taxi Association sticker on his windshield, his new taxi might get hijacked.

When we reached the corner of the Springfield and Kashmir Roads, an army patrol was passing the intersection. They were aroused by the sight of a man getting out of a black taxi with two large boxes, and they were upon me in no time. I was ordered up against the wall of a defunct chip shop while the poor taximan had his car searched. When the soldiers finished that task, they let the driver leave and turned their attention to me.

They asked what was in the boxes. I told them I wasn't entirely sure, as I hadn't packed them, but that they certainly included clothing and files. I was told to open them, which was no small task, as they had been taped to survive an ocean crossing. Once the boxes were open, I was told to stand aside. Two soldiers held their weapons in my direction, and two others went through my belongings. It is one thing to have your belongings examined by a customs agent in an airport line when everyone around you is also having their bags examined. It is quite another thing to have your belongings poked through while you are at the wrong end of two rifles, standing in a street in the middle of the afternoon with all your neighbors passing by.

One of the soldiers pulled out some photographs of my girlfriend in Chicago, and after examining them, asked me who the lady was. The other lad thought he'd found something much hotter—a file marked "IRA," full of newspaper clippings. I told him there were other files with articles on the army, the police, and the government, but the armed teenager didn't like the look of things, and the leader of the patrol radioed for help.

By this time I was angry, scared, and feeling like I had been violated. A jeep full of military police in red berets arrived. I was surrounded by eight soldiers. I explained to the second patrol that the files were for my work, and that the army knew perfectly well who I was as I had been out to their headquarters in Lisburn just a week or two earlier for a press briefing. The squad leader stepped aside and spoke into his radio. A minute later, he announced that I could be released. The soldier who had taken such an interest in my photographs apologized and offered to help me pack the boxes again, as their contents were now strewn on the pavement. I refused his help, and both patrols moved on.

I walked the thirty yards to my house feeling humiliated. I told Mrs. Barbour what had happened, but she did not seem too impressed. When I got the gear upstairs and cooled down a bit, I realized I could not expect anyone in this district to be sympathetic. People and houses were searched everyday, and they had been for ten years. How could I think my first thorough, public search was so important?

There were other confrontations with soldiers that year and in later visits, and although I was always a little nervous, I came to take them with the resignation of a native. Once I was pulled aside as a joke. I was on a bicycle, riding up the Springfield Road to Ballymurphy, and I came upon a four-man patrol that had set up a vehicle check point. It was mid-morning, and ordinarily there would have been a fair amount of traffic, but it was riot season—a hunger striker had just died—and people were staying away from west Belfast in droves, fearing their cars would be hijacked and burned. As I approached, a soldier with an impressive moustache stepped into the middle of the road. With exaggerated gestures and a smile on his face, he waved me into a small layby, where the rest of the patrol was waiting.

The other three soldiers thought this was hilarious, as no one ever does a random check of a bicycle. I was very tense in those days, and I laughed easily at odd things, and getting pulled over at a VCP seemed very funny to me as well. The squad leader claimed I had ingeniously disguised an Armalite as a bicycle crossbar and remarked that it was not wise to transport gelignite in a bicycle's handlebars. One soldier began with the usual questions—name, address, date of birth, destination—but on hearing my accent, the others decided there were more interesting things to ask.

"What do you think of this here?" the soldier with the moustache asked, meaning what did I think of the troubles.

I told him that I pitied him, that I suspected that he and his mates didn't want to be there protecting people who for the most part no longer wanted their protection. We talked for about five minutes before I moved on. As I pedaled up the road, I was suddenly uneasy. "What if one of the neighbors saw you back there," I asked myself, "laughing and chatting with the troops?"

Later that week, I saw the same patrol passing the monastery. The soldier with the moustache greeted me with a loud grunt as I rode past. I almost waved, but caught myself, and instead nodded slightly and sped on, hoping no one had noticed.

THREE

THE RULES OF THE GAME

I WAS NOT LONG in Clonard before I began to hear tales of squatting and the impossibility of performing an eviction in west Belfast. I made an appointment to interview Brian Henderson, an amiable press officer for the Housing Executive, and found him a bit defensive. The housing authority was not the only public body with a civil disobedience problem, he said, pointing out that many of the people in west Belfast did not pay their electricity or gas bills either.

"Let's face it," Henderson told me. "In west Belfast there is no law and order."

Henderson didn't know I lived in west Belfast, and I didn't tell him. I also didn't tell him that his analysis of the district was unsound. There was so much normality and order in west Belfast that I knew some rules applied. My trouble was that I didn't know what the rules were or who enforced them. I could see the soldiers were not in charge; if they had been, they wouldn't have been there. I suspected the Provos determined some of the local order, but I couldn't see them or consult their statute book.

Gradually I learned what was expected of ghetto residents. Some of my lessons came from stories told by neighbors or Mrs. Barbour, and some came from accounts of punishment shootings published in the Provisionals' newspaper. Some rules I deduced from warnings painted on walls, others from IRA directives pushed through mail slots in the district.

You were allowed to rob a bank or a post office, for example, but only if you were robbing them for the movement. Stealing from your neighbor was forbidden, but stealing from the government was allowed, and even praised by some as an act of resistance. Teenagers weren't supposed to steal cars or trucks, except during riots when barricades were necessary. During riots, there were still rules: you could steal a bus, but not a black taxi.

Policemen were legitimate targets, anytime, anywhere, of abuse, stones, petrol bombs, or bullets. Firemen, on the other hand, had immunity. There were Catholics on the fire department, and firemen performed their duties as if there was no difference between a Protestant fire and a Catholic one. At the beginning of the troubles, some fire department autos were attacked because they could not be differentiated from police cars. The fire service responded by painting its cars white, and thereafter had little trouble. When things got well out of hand during the hunger strike riots, fire department trucks were also hijacked, but the fire department then threatened to boycott the west side of the city, and their immunity was restored.

Dealing in smuggled goods was permissible, and many grocers sold smuggled butter. Dealing in stolen goods, however, was forbidden. For a short time in 1981, dealing in English newspapers was also on the list of prohibited activities; Joe Early, the newsagent next door, told me he'd been visited and warned. No one cared if you got drunk, but the IRA did not like local establishments to sell liquor to minors, and during my time in Belfast, more than one liquor store was closed for that offense. Heroin was a word heard only on American television programs. Valium was used by almost half the adults in the district.

Looting after a bombing was sometimes allowed. Mrs. Barbour told me that when the Co-op grocery on the Springfield Road was bombed for the third or fourth time, Protestants and Catholics looted together. When Hardin's old hardware store on the Springfield Road was blown up in 1981, however, the Provos sent a notice around the doors of Clonard telling everyone that the missing goods had to be returned or there would be serious consequences. A neighbor told me that people were directed to put the purloined items in the alley one night and that someone collected the material and brought it back to the shop. She claimed that some quite respectable people had ended up with looted material ("You would have been surprised at who was there") and that when they were ordered to give it up, they left their goods not at their own alley door, but at someone else's.

Punishment for these offenses was sometimes swift and usually rough. At other times, however, months would pass between the act and the sentence, and sometimes there was no punishment at all. Sometimes there was mercy, sometimes there were mistakes, and often there were inconsistencies. But, contrary to Mr. Henderson's description, there was indeed law and, as a result, a strange but certain order.

To buttress his argument about the lawlessness of west Belfast, Henderson cited the case of Jimmy Barr, a young man living in Spinner Street, a half mile from Mrs. Barbour's. A week later, another housing official mentioned the Barr case as a sort of landmark, and I thought it might be interesting to meet the legend. After determining that Mr. Barr, like most residents of west Belfast, did not have a telephone, I resolved to approach the man in person. It was not a resolution easily made. I figured that if Barr was such a thorn in the side of authorities, he might well be active in militant circles, and I feared an angry and public confrontation with a man affiliated with one of the Catholic armed groups. I put off the task of knocking on his door for more than a month.

I finally did it in mid-July. A short man with short hair and a moustache answered. His nose looked like it had been broken on more than one occasion, and the tattoo on his arm looked homemade. But for the neighborhood, I might have guessed that he had done military service, perhaps as an alternative to jail.

The man did not admit to being Jimmy Barr. I explained that I was doing a story on housing in west Belfast, that Mr. Barr's name had come up in an interview with a housing official, and that I wanted to interview him. At the mention of the Housing Executive, he was immediately furious. I leapt to my own defense, and explained that I had not been sent by the housing agency, that I had only talked to them, and that I would also like to talk to Mr. Barr. He paused. He left the doorstep and addressed a woman in the front room of the house; it seemed to me that he was asking her for advice. He returned to the door a minute later, and apologetically invited me in.

He was indeed the notorious Jimmy Barr, and the attractive woman he had consulted was his wife, Marie. For the next two hours and on two subsequent visits, Jimmy regaled me with tales of his life. I came to like him, though I also could understand how his nose had come to be so well bent. Jimmy was then in his early thirties and had been unemployed for eleven years. He did not have much to do during daylight hours, and added excitement to his mornings and afternoons by giving passing soldiers a hard time (a fact which would not have seemed notable except that two of Jimmy's sisters were married to British paratroopers). At night, he picked up some small change hustling snooker at the Pound Loney. The Pound Loney is a drinking club with Provisional sympathies; Jimmy described it as "a workingman's club except that nobody in it has any work."

Jimmy told me that in the early days of the troubles, he would pick a fight with just about anybody, that he was interested in women and drink and between the two had no time for the IRA. His cantankerous personality, however, made him suspect. The army picked him up when internment began, and he was in and out of jail for the next few years, sometimes for some minor crime, sometimes awaiting trial, and sometimes as an internee.

A few weeks before I met him, Jimmy had been picked up by soldiers as he entered the city center at Castle Street. He was interrogated, and he thought he came near to being booked on an explosives charge. As a result, he rarely left his own neighborhood, confining his life to a small area bordered by the bookie's, the Pound Loney, and the public baths. Every Monday he signed on the dole. He had told the unemployment office that he would not work outside the district, which is not an unusual statement for a Catholic and is common sense for ex-internees, who fear for their lives in Protestant neighborhoods. Most of the city's jobs, however, are to be found in the industries on the Protestant side of the city.

Jimmy and his wife met in The Nail Bomb, an illegal drinking club, now defunct. Marie, a pleasant woman with large blue eyes and a trim figure, grew up in the Turf Lodge housing project, an ugly development matched only by Divis Flats and Ballymurphy for its misery. After she left high school, she worked as a seamstress at the Ladybird Shirt Factory, but after a short time she abandoned both job and city and moved to London with her mother, seeking a better life. Marie did not feel welcome in England, however, and after nine months, she and her mother came home.

In the first years of their marriage, Jimmy was in and out of jail and he and Marie were together for only short periods of time. While interned, Jimmy built two music boxes for Marie, and today they are prominently displayed in the Barrs' home. Another souvenir from those years is Jimmy's mug shot, which was sent to Marie anonymously while Jimmy was in jail. It was meant to be a threat, a warning that Protestant paramilitaries, who had access to the photo because one of their members had access to police or army files, had their eye on Jimmy and knew where he lived. Though Marie was frightened when she received it, today the picture is in the family album, and it evokes no terror. A chart in the photo lists Jimmy's date of birth and other statistics, including "Religion: RC," which Jimmy says stands for "Rum and Coke."

Although he lost several years of his life in Long Kesh and in Crumlin Road Jail, Jimmy also managed to make more money as a prisoner than he had ever made before, and probably more than he will ever make again. His good fortune resulted from an escape attempt in November 1974, when he jumped into a tunnel dug by other prisoners. He was caught at the tunnel's exit and brutally beaten by the guards. (One of the escapees was shot dead.) The survivors found themselves in a curious legal situation. As internees, they were incarcerated without having been convicted of any crime, but in trying to escape, they broke the law. Jimmy was tried and sentenced to six months.

His wealth came from his claim against the state for the beating he had received. Two years after he filed his suit, he was offered £750 (roughly $1500) to settle out of court. He took it, and the Barrs bought a couch, two chairs, and a dining room set. They also went out for drinks, on which Jimmy spent somewhere between £200 and £250. "At the end of the night," he says, "I was handing out tenners like a saint. I came home with two pounds in my pocket."

Jimmy became a legend, however, not in prison, but in the housing sector, by no means an obscure battlefield in the North. Many observers trace the outbreak of the current troubles to housing problems, specifically to a house in a small village in County Tyrone. In the late 1960s, before the creation of the Northern Ireland Housing Executive, housing was allocated by urban and rural councils, most of which were Unionist controlled. In 1967, as a way of protesting discrimination against Catholics in housing allocation, civil rights organizers urged homeless Catholics to squat in new homes built in Caledon, near Dungannon. In June 1968, the Dungannon Council evicted the Catholic families from the estate and awarded one of the houses to Emily Beattie, a nineteen-year-old unmarried secretary to a local Unionist councillor. Austin Currie, a Catholic representative at Stormont, was infuriated by the blatant discrimination and by Stormont's refusal to do anything about it. He drove to the house in question and, before Ms. Beattie could move in, took it over himself. Currie was evicted by the police, an event that was recorded by television cameras. A march was organized to protest the Dungannon Council's actions, and to the surprise of even the organizers, 4,000 people showed up. A second march was banned by the government, but the demonstrators marched anyway. Policemen responded with clubs, and once again it was filmed by television cameras. The police violence fed more protest, and the movement gathered momentum.

As the troubles escalated in the months and years that followed, people living in mixed neighborhoods came to know the fear of the midnight knock. Houses belonging to those of the wrong religion were torched. Warnings were painted on doors, and mass cards—normally used to express sympathy at someone's death—were sent to some Catholics. Respectable people became refugees overnight, deprived of dignity, scrambling back to any house they could find in the ghettos they had left so proudly years before. A Northern Ireland Community Relations Commission research paper estimated that 80 percent of those fleeing intimidation were Catholic, and that 60,000 people had left their homes.

In west Belfast, 58 percent of the housing is owned by the housing authority, and in the chaos following the great flight, housing officials simply lost control. It became extremely difficult to keep track of who lived where, as people changed addresses overnight and sometimes moved two or three times in as many weeks. In some areas, there were daily gun battles, rent collectors were at some risk, and paramilitaries took over the task of housing allocation, sometimes charging "key money" for their services. Housing officials did not enter some estates for two years. For many Catholics, squatting was not illegal occupation, it was just the way one got a house.

The Barrs set up house in the Lower Falls in 1973. Jimmy was in prison, and Marie was living with her mother-in-law and was anxious to get a place of her own when she heard that a house was soon to go vacant at 22 Plevna Street. In those days, if you heard there was an empty house, you were as eligible as anyone to grab it, and Marie did.

Upon moving into a vacant house, squatters must consider their options. If they pay rent to the Housing Executive at the going rate, they are entitled to wind and weatherproofing repairs, and if they stay in one spot long enough—five years or more—they might be given legal status, which would entitle them to a full range of maintenance and repair work. If they pay no rent, they might save some money for a while, but sooner or later the government would catch on, and it would start making deductions in the family's welfare check. The Barrs decided to pay their rent, which came to about two pounds a month for their two-story brick rowhouse. Many squatters are not so honest, and the Housing Executive admits to being owed millions of pounds in back rent.

As residents of 22 Plevna, the Barrs were just one of thousands of squatting families in Catholic west Belfast (in 1980, when the situation was far more under control, 250 of the 650 homes in the Lower Falls were occupied by squatters). The Barrs rose to fame from that crowd because Plevna Street was marked for urban renewal. The old houses were to be torn down, and new ones were to be constructed. The lucky people who were to become tenants of the new buildings were those with longstanding ties to the neighborhood (some families had been there for generations)—legal residents who had to be temporarily displaced from the Lower Falls so that the new development could be constructed. The Barrs may have been as needy as those slated for the new houses, but so were thousands of other families, and the Barrs were not in the queue. They were, however, in the way.

As the years went by, the families of Plevna Street were gradually moved out. By mid-1979, every home on the block had been leveled but the one occupied by Jimmy and Marie. The Housing Executive offered them other homes, but the Barrs declined the offers. They wanted one of the new houses. The Executive refused to give them one, arguing that there were many others ahead of them on the waiting list, and that the agency would lose all credibility if they gave in to what they saw as blackmail.

Jimmy had the Executive over a barrel. They needed his plot of land. Sewers, electricity, water pipes, and sidewalks for the new buildings had to be laid, and there sat Jimmy in the way of progress. The agency would either have to give in to his demands or alter its plans. The Executive had signed a contract with a builder, promising to turn over an empty tract of land. Once the date for the start of construction arrived, the contractor was within his rights to sue the agency for breach of contract, and he would be entitled to compensation for any expenses he incurred as a result of the obstruction. In a similar case on the other side of the city, a squatter had held up a housing project for seventeen months, and the Executive had been forced to pay the contractor £80,000 in claims resulting from the delay.

The authorities issued an eviction order, but the Barrs paid it no mind. The Housing Executive was not in a position to make good on its threat. They could not evict anyone in the ghetto without an escort of soldiers and policemen, and the last thing the Housing Executive wanted to do was create the impression that it operated in tandem with the army and the police, that it was just another arm of the security forces. Housing officials would then lose all their credibility in an area where they were slowly re-establishing order. People would ignore the agency's waiting list—drawn up without discrimination on the basis of a points system—and would instead go back to seizing whatever accommodation they could get their hands on. The chaos of the early years of the troubles would return, and the people would never escape the squalor that breeds hatred and revolutionaries.

Furthermore, if bailiffs and soldiers were to forcibly remove Jimmy and his family, the authorities would be giving the Provos the opportunity to appear as protector of the downtrodden, and someone might get killed in the process. (The Provos, on the other hand, might be reluctant to be caught in the middle of such a situation: supporting Jimmy would alienate those who were waiting for a new house.)

So there sat Jimmy Barr, prolonging the agony of forty-six families who were living in tenements as they awaited the completion of their new homes. Jimmy, however, was not in the best of positions from which to wage a protracted war. Twenty-two Plevna had no bath, no hot water (just a single cold tap in the kitchen), and no indoor toilet. It was infested with vermin and had a serious case of damp. The situation became more grim when the contractor arrived on the site. He put a timber fence around the entire plot of land, walling the Barrs in with the rest of the acreage. Relatives coming to visit Jimmy and Marie couldn't find their way in, and the binmen had to be shown the round-about path to the Barr residence so they could take away the garbage.

Through it all, I suspect that Jimmy saw himself as a working-class hero, as part of the resistance. In a peculiar way he was. There is no work to be had in west Belfast, so a man cannot achieve any sort of nobility by providing for his family. There is no fulfillment in raising children, as that is considered women's work. So a man who resists, who fights back even though his position might be untenable, has some function, some duty, something to do. Jimmy took his story to the *Irish News* and they published a supportive story, calling the solitary hovel on Plevna "The Little House on the Prairie."

As the months wore on, however, Jimmy found the fight more and more difficult to sustain. The toilet broke, and the sewage flowed into the yard. The smell was horrible, the likelihood of disease immense. The roof fell in, the house was cold, and the family had to move their one dry mattress to the living room. Jimmy and Marie slept on the floor, and their three-year-old son slept between two chairs. Their daughter got sick, and she had to be farmed out to Marie's mother for the duration. Jimmy took to drinking heavily, and he is not a quiet or timid drunk. He and Marie began getting on each other's nerves.

Finally, after holding out for more than nine months, the Barrs could stand it no longer, and Jimmy agreed to surrender. He accepted the Executive's offer of an old house on Spinner Street, just a few blocks away, securing a promise from the authorities to renovate the rowhouse before he moved. The agency even took care of the transfer of Barr's possessions, moving them in a Housing Executive van. To make sure that Jimmy could not change his mind, they had a bulldozer standing by, and, within an hour of the move, the last house on Plevna Street was demolished.

The Barrs' two-bedroom house on Spinner was formerly occupied by a woman with five children. It had no bathtub, so once or twice a week, the Barrs went to the public baths for a swim. Jimmy's four-year-old son quickly adjusted to the new neighborhood and found a derelict house to play in. His mother told me that she had already caught him throwing stones at soldiers.

Tenants began moving into the forty-six new houses in the fall of 1979. To prevent further squatting which could lead to another confrontation like the war with Jimmy Barr, the Housing Executive sanctioned the destruction of its own property: the forty-six families were told that before they vacated their old houses, they had to smash their sinks and toilets, break their windows, rip out their wiring, and pull up their floorboards. As soon as they left, a man from the Housing Executive came by to brick the place shut.

And so an already ugly landscape got uglier. Derelict rowhouses stood as eyesores; they could not be pulled down without damaging a neighbor's home, as each house in the row leaned on the next for support. The roofs of the abandoned houses rotted and caved in. I walked street after street dominated by bricked up doorways, where cement windows seemed to beget cement windows. Shopkeepers also fled, and finally bulldozers would level everything and lay an asphalt top over the entire block. The lot would be covered with scrap in no time.

Every once in a while, a visiting photographer would capture the devastation and attribute it to bomb damage or mobs bearing torches. The people of west Belfast, however, knew it was not that simple.

About a year after hearing about Jimmy Barr for the first time, I met a neighbor I'll call Hugh Curran. Curran, a religious man, had been interned in 1971; upon his release, he discovered that although he had been convicted of no crime, he was considered a security risk by his old employer, a firm which did work for the electricity service. He had to give up his trade, and eventually found work driving a black taxi. In an interview in May 1981, he told me that if the government could rob him of his livelihood, he was perfectly justified in robbing the government in return, and so he regularly claimed unemployment benefits even though he was working.

Hugh's attitude was not uncommon, and it dated back to a civil disobedience campaign organized by responsible Catholic politicians in protest against internment. After the internment policy was implemented in 1971, community groups, civil rights activists, and even moderate politicians lent their support to a rent and rates strike. Catholics who lived in public housing were advised to withhold their rent, and those who owned their own homes were advised not to pay their taxes (called rates). The idea caught on quickly, and some people extended the protest by refusing to pay their road tax and utility bills. In some districts, more than 90 percent of the people withheld funds. "Rent Spent" was added to the slogans of resistance. By September, a month after internment began, the government admitted that 26,000 families were on strike, and the number increased as time went on.

The Northern Ireland government at Stormont responded to the rent and rates strike by passing the Payment for Debt (Emergency Provisions) Act. The legislation was unparalleled in England, Scotland, and Wales. It allowed the government to make deductions from checks a citizen received from the government or from an employer. Enforcement was very expensive (in 1980, it cost a pound to collect a pound), and although the act's purpose was to reduce resistance to the government, it achieved just the opposite. There is no doubt that the legislation helped to break the rent and rates strike, but it also created one more governmental body for Catholics to see as the enemy.

Stormont's new bureaucracy for garnishing unemployment checks, pensions, compensation awards, and paychecks took some time to assert itself, but when it did, many Catholics became desperate. Welfare payments are set at a level that keeps families hovering above the poverty line. When those checks are garnished, families plunge below that line. Rent rebates granted to the poor were denied to families who were found to owe money to the state, and so once people got into debt and were caught, their expenses were greater and their debt multiplied. Eventually some families owed thousands of pounds.

The Payment for Debt Act was passed with the stated intention of operating only as long as the rent and rates strike continued, but after the strike petered out in 1974 and 1975, the act remained in place. It was extended in 1978 so that deductions could also be made for money owed the electricity service and the gas company. The effect on the poor and the unemployed was disastrous. In six years of unemployment, one father of ten in west Belfast ran up a debt of £1,800 to the Northern Ireland Electricity Service. He landed a job as a caretaker for the Housing Executive in 1979, and had been working for five months when the Electricity Service invoked the Payment for Debt Act, arranging to deduct £21 a week from the man's paycheck. That left the man with £38 (roughly $80 a week) to house, feed, clothe, and support his wife and the three children they still had living at home.

In scrambling to rid themselves of their debts, many people resorted to means they would never have considered in normal times. "Doing the double"—working a job while claiming unemployment benefits or a disability check—became common, in part because the fraud section of the Department of Health and Social Services had only six inspectors in Belfast—some of whom were not entirely at ease in Catholic districts. "Given what is happening on the streets," one inspector said to me in 1980, "it is not a wise idea to sit in a car in a Catholic district with a pair of binoculars."

I don't mean to suggest a domino theory here, with internment leading to the rent and rates strike, the strike leading to the Payment for Debt Act, the Act leading to massive numbers of people indulging in fraud. Certainly many people engaged in fraud not because they were pursued by the legislation, but simply because they could get away with it and because they could justify it with their conscience. If the government was going to act extralegally, incarcerating those who had never broken the law, many citizens saw no reason why they should play by the rules. Those with republican sentiments saw their act of fraud as a small contribution to the IRA's economic campaign against the British.

One side effect of the "double" phenomenon was the lowering of wages in some occupations. People who were on the dole were willing to work for less money, and some employers took advantage of this, lowering wages to increase profits. A friend of mine, for example, worked in a laundromat, putting in a forty-hour week, opening and closing the facility, for just £13 per week. Her wages were low because she cheated, and she cheated because her wages were low. Unfortunately, she got caught by the fraud division (she believes a neighborhood busybody turned her in), and now she has no work at all.

There is no way of determining how many of the North's 1.5 million people were doing the double. There are, however, statistics on other forms of fraud and debt. When I arrived in Belfast in 1980, 57,000 people owed the Electricity Service £11.8 million, and the utility was writing off a million pounds a year as uncollectable. The gas industry was owed £3.6 million by 27,000 consumers. Sixty thousand tenants owed the Housing Executive £10.7 million, and 13,000 of those debtors could not be found. And 8,000 people owed £1.9 million in property taxes.

The Electricity Service was the most hated of all the agencies involved. It was also the most desperate. I visited their compound on the

Malone Road in south Belfast in April 1980, and after passing through extensive security arrangements, I sat down in the office of R. J. Thompson, the man who had direct responsibility for "the pursuit and recovery of debt." He was a pipe smoker with greying hair, not at all the ogre I had expected. I felt sorry for him, and as we talked, it was hard to keep in mind the hardships of my neighbors who were in the company's debt.

Thompson told me that a series of crises had hit the utility at roughly the same time in the early to mid-1970s: The intimidation in the housing sector made it hard to keep track of consumers. Income declined further with the rent and rates strike, and the escalating street warfare made debt collection more difficult. The world oil crisis of 1973–74 brought an extreme rise in costs at the same time that unemployment was increasing and consumers had less money to pay their bills. "This forced us to a point where we had to start pressure tactics in order to collect what was owed," Thompson said. "And no matter what you do in debt collection of any kind, you have no friends."

The electricity service is a business, Thompson said, and businesses have to balance their books. "We come into conflict then with those who argue that electricity is a necessity of life and say that we should be precluded from taking the ultimate sanction of cutting off service. And we are not trained to be social judges or means testers. We are trained to provide electricity."

On March 3, 1980, the Electricity Service sent a special crew of volunteers into the Twinbrook estate on the far edge of west Belfast. At 7:30 A.M., the utility's workmen, backed up by eight policemen armed with automatic weapons, cut off service to twenty-two families who owed the Electricity Service money. The Provisionals responded a few hours later by threatening to shoot workmen who did cutoffs in the future.

Thompson explained to me that the raid had "caused an industrial relations situation." While management might think cutoffs were a good idea, the workers were often reluctant to carry them out, even with police and army protection. It was the same problem that Housing Executive workers faced when dealing with squatters: they did not want to be seen as an arm of the law. The electrical workers could foresee the day when the utility's employees would be so hated that even meter readers would be perceived as acceptable targets. Some had already faced guns. A community worker in Divis Flats told me that Electricity Service workers had entered the flats to adjust the coin-operated meters of some delinquent customers so that they would be paying more for the same amount of service; the utility employees were marched out with guns pointed at their heads.

"We have to let the situation cool for awhile," Thompson said in the wake of the Twinbrook raid. And so it did. Four years after the incident, Thompson told me the Electricity Service had not performed another such raid, and that none were contemplated.

Given the tricky morality that prevailed in west Belfast households, it was not surprising that children and teenagers absorbed it. The teenagers I met when I moved into Mrs. Barbour's were five and six years old when the troubles broke out. They grew up seeing their fathers and brothers carried off in dawn raids. Some remember being forced out of their homes in the middle of the night. Others banged bin lids at the sight of an army patrol, cast the first stones at new regiments, and visited older brothers in prison. They were in school when law and order began to crumble, and with it crumbled the established procedure for dealing with truants. Truant officers stopped prosecuting students for nonattendance, in part because they were concerned that they would come to be seen as policemen. It was not until they sat down and worked out an understanding with the Provisionals in the fall of 1980 that the educational welfare officers began using prosecutions again as a means of forcing kids to attend school.

"It's very difficult to try to push education as an end to itself," an educational welfare officer told me in 1981. "They want to know what's in it for them, and the truth is there's not much in it for them. You can't say, 'If you don't go to school you won't get a job. They say, 'What job? There's no job in it for me.' And they're right. You have to say, 'You must go to school or you'll be taken to court.' Before we had the courts to threaten them with, we were just talking in circles."

The threat of prosecution, however, works only on kids from fairly good, stable homes. The others aren't intimidated by the prospect. "Kids used to run away from us," Larry Murtagh, a west Belfast educational welfare officer told me. "But now it's just the same as all other kinds of authority—the police, the army, teachers, the Provos—it doesn't matter. They have no respect, they have no fears."

Adding to the stagnant lives of that ghetto generation is the problem created by the Provisional's decision to streamline operations and use fewer men to conduct their war. While in the early days of the conflict, anyone who wanted to join was accepted, after 1977 only the best of the lot were taken. The result was that teenagers in west Belfast were left with no jobs, no money, no stake in either normal society or in the underground. With nothing to lose, and with an inherited disrespect for the official law and order, a fair number of teenagers took to small-time crime. As they grew older, some took up armed robbery.

Shopkeepers in west Belfast can no longer get insurance against theft, and they cry out in agony as they are burglarized time and again. There is no compensation for burglary except in the most unusual of circumstances. A friend of Mrs. Barbour's who owned a confectionary shop on the Falls Road got so desperate after several burglaries that she began taking her entire stock of cigarettes home with her every night. After her eighth break-in, she sold the shop. A liquor store owner in Andersonstown, after being robbed for the fifty-third time since the start of the troubles, ruefully suggested that he might apply to the Guinness Book of World Records.

A man from Turf Lodge who worked for a well-known bookmaker told me that in his thirteen years on the job, he was robbed twenty-nine times. "The first time I was robbed there was shooting," he told me. "They shot three fellows, one in the toe, one in the chest, one in the arm. After that, as soon as we saw them coming, we just stood back and said, 'Take it.'

"When the hoods did it, they wore masks and showed you guns. Usually they were teenagers. When the Provos did it, they were usually a bit older. They wouldn't wear masks or anything. When the police came we just said, 'We didn't know who they were. They wore hoods.'"

Much of the crime, particularly in west Belfast, is not reported. Some people don't like the police, some think reporting the crime would serve no purpose, and others are afraid of the hoods who robbed them. "The hoods," in local jargon, refers to males from age twelve to thirty who engage in crime for their own ends. Most of them are teenagers. "The biggest policing problem in west Belfast," the superintendent of the Springfield Road RUC station said in 1980, "is not the IRA or terrorism. It's juvenile crime."

The juvenile crime problem was particularly acute at Divis Flats, but then all problems were acute there. The Flats are located at the bottom of the Falls Road, just a few hundred yards from Belfast city center. The housing project—blocks of flats, five stories high, and one twenty-story tower—was only twelve years old in 1980, but it was already a notorious slum. Rats ran on the balconies late at night. Soldiers had put out the lights in passageways between floors to thwart snipers, and drunk men and dogs urinated in the dark corridors. Police appeared only in armored jeeps and bulletproof jackets.

A fair number of the kids from the flats who were dismissed as hoods attended a youth club run by a young man from Derry named Frank Shiels. It was known as Crazy Joe's, named after Shiels's predecessor, a youth worker named Joe Morgan, and it was housed in an old garage. It was drafty, windowless, and damp, and it reminded me of a cave. The club had no organized activities; young people just came and went. They played snooker on two warped tables and watched television on a set that Shiels shook and fiddled to get a fair and steady picture. The club also had a kitchen, where the kids would make tea. Some of those who came to Crazy Joe's had been banned from St. Peter's youth club, which was the local parish's club for well-behaved kids.

Crazy Joe's was Shiels's second posting in the flats. He had also been a community worker there in the early 1970s. "I remember going to the flats on internment night in 1974," he told me. "There were kids, seven and eight years old, drunk on cider stolen from a bottling firm nearby. Kids were puking all over. They were lying on the ground, passed out. Five dozen kids spread over the lot—it looked like the Battle of Somme. There were a lot of parents milling about, they'd go by another parent's kid and they'd say nothing. Parents won't say anything to each other about the kids. It goes back to that concept of touting, the tradition of the informer, and in the flats, nobody touts.

"The sense of morality in the flats has crumbled. For some people, 'Catholic' means it's okay to kill somebody so long as you go to mass. For the kids, stealing has become a habit. Kids steal to finance their drinking and their clothes. I stopped running trips for awhile because the kids were stealing the money to come.

"And invariably they get caught. Virtually every kid I work with, I could name seventy to eighty kids off the top of my head, is up in court. A lot of them face long sentences. But their attitude toward life is, 'Here today, no concept of tomorrow.' My biggest problem with people in the flats is they don't give a damn about tomorrow, and it shows in everything, in attitudes about education, crime, everything.

"The kids do the dumbest things. One tried to steal the lead from the roof of the Queen Street RUC barracks. [Lead can be sold to scrap yards.] It wasn't that he set out to get the barracks in particular as some sort of political act or to show off. Kids had been stealing the lead off the buildings up to it, and the barracks was just the next in line.

"A lot of kids don't feel they are doing anything wrong by stealing. They aren't looking someone in the eye and taking something. They're doing break-ins in the city center. They have no concept that they might be doing anybody any harm. They have no property themselves and so have no understanding of what it's like to have something stolen."

In the fall of 1980, the Provos were paying little attention to public order in the flats as they had a hunger strike on their hands, and the INLA, who were strong in the flats, had neither the will nor the moral backbone to do any law enforcement. A group of vigilantes was organized to "clean up the flats," by which they meant they were going to rid the estate of its hoodlum element. The vigilantes' brief reign was a violent one. Several teenagers who frequented Crazy Joe's were beaten, one ended up on crutches and with stitches in his head. A lad I'll call Tommy Maloney was beaten at the club one night when the vigilantes found him carrying a car key, and he was left with two black eyes.

It was a crime for Tommy to have a car key because he did not own a car. At eighteen, with three years experience behind him, Tommy was one of the best car thieves in the flats. His method involved a key and a pen knife, and he claimed that he had used them, or had been with other teenagers using similar techniques, in the theft of over 300 cars. Tommy and his pals would sometimes steal six or seven cars in a night. They traveled in cavalcades of stolen autos, under the eyes of the soldiers atop Divis Tower. The troops did little about it, taking the attitude that crime was not their responsibility, they were there to fight terrorists.

So Maloney and his mates had field days. They would abandon one car if they saw a parked one that looked faster. If they ran out of petrol, they just lifted another car. They stole cars from the driveways of suburban houses, from parking lots near the city center, and from ghetto streets. They stole cars that belonged to policemen and cars that belonged to Republicans. The object was not profit. Their goal was just to get out of the flats for the night, to break the monotony, to race with their pals, and to challenge the police.

A few of Tommy's friends had been shot in joyriding incidents in the months before I met him, and some had been killed. "I been shot at

twice," he told me, "but it was a good lot of shots. Machine gun fire. You
don't be ascared when you're shot at, but the next day you are. When you
seen them pointin' a gun at you, you be ascared, but see, when you hear
the gun, you don't be scared. I don't be scared. You think you'd be scared,
at the time it happens you're not. It's all over in a fucking five seconds."

Joyriders are fired upon when they drive through army checkpoints.
The second time Tommy Maloney was fired upon, it was because he had
almost run over a policeman: he had forced one cop up against a taxi, and
a second policeman had opened fire. Usually, however, it is the army that
does the shooting and the police that give chase. When pursued, joyriders head for Divis, where their chances of being apprehended are dimin-
ished considerably: policemen fear assassination and so won't leave their
vehicles to chase the driver and his passengers fleeing on foot.

In the first seven months of 1980, fifteen teenagers were shot, three
of them fatally, in joyriding incidents. That first spate of shootings caused
a great outcry from the Catholic community, who argued that summary
execution for auto theft was cruel and unusual punishment. Furthermore, it was a violation of the army's code of behavior, referred to as the
"yellow card instructions." A soldier is not supposed to shoot at a car
simply because it has not stopped at a checkpoint; he should instead note
the direction, make, and license number—and do no more. No soldiers were prosecuted for exceeding those instructions in the joyriding
incidents.

The shooting continued, with less frequency, after the initial hue and
cry. Other joyriders were killed in high speed chases. One kid from Turf
Lodge stole a car and then crashed it, killing his brother, whom he had
taken along for the ride. A few months later, the survivor was out joyriding again. In Lenadoon, a kid was shot by the army and died. The
next night, his pals were out stealing cars. "Death and injury are normal
things to them," Father Matt Wallace, a priest in Lenadoon, told me.
"They are not a significant event in their lives." The Chief Constable's
report for 1980 showed a 20 percent increase in the number of autos
stolen, and it reported that the Springfield Road police district had ac-
counted for 27 percent of all the cars stolen in the entire province.

In the uproar after the first deaths, a proposal was floated in the city
council to establish a stock car racing program to reform joyriders. The
idea had been tried with some success with young car thieves in London.
It proved worthy in Belfast, but dealt with only a small portion of the
offenders. I interviewed a Catholic bureaucrat in the Department of

Health and Social Services at the time of the city council debate, and he thought that while the racetrack might work in London, it would not succeed with west Belfast teenagers because it would not provide enough excitement. "You'll need to have someone shooting at them as well," he said.

The law and order imposed by the Provisionals also involved shooting teenagers, or indeed anyone else who broke certain codes. The difference between the shootings done by the British Army and those done by the Provos was in number and consequence. The army shot teenagers for a single crime and the shootings were often fatal. The Provos shot far more offenders, but at that time they did not shoot to kill, and the punishment was usually imposed for a multitude of sins. The Provisionals clearly saw a distinction between their methods and the army's, and did not hesitate to condemn the soldiers for shooting joyriders, though the IRA was shooting some of the very same lads themselves.

When the IRA decided a kneecapping was in order, they dispatched a punishment squad to do the job. The punishment varied, depending on the seriousness of the crime. A bullet through the fleshy part of the thigh was a light sentence. A heavy sentence could destroy bones and arteries. An offender could be shot in one leg, both legs, or both legs and both arms. (I heard Mr. Meli, the owner of the fish and chip shop on the Springfield Road, once refer to the both legs–both arms option as "getting the silver cross").

Protestants also kneecapped their local offenders, although they did it in lesser numbers. (Punishment shootings were never motivated by sectarian animosity: Protestants shot Protestants; Catholics shot Catholics.) It is commonly believed that loyalist paramilitaries used an electric drill instead of a handgun on some occasions, and the story was repeated by a secretary of state for Northern Ireland in the House of Commons, but police and Belfast knee surgeons I interviewed said the story was apocryphal. RUC spokesmen said the only difference between loyalist and Republican punishment shootings, aside from the difference in numbers, was that Catholics usually filed a claim for compensation as a victim of terrorist crime, while Protestants usually did not.

Between 1973, when punishment shootings started being tallied by the RUC, and the end of 1985, there were 1,110 kneecappings. Dr. James Nixon, an orthopedic surgeon, wrote a dissertation based on a study of 86 kneecapping victims shot between September 1974 and January 1975. Amputation occurred in almost 10 percent of those cases, and Nixon estimated that one in five of those shot would walk with a limp for the rest of their lives.

Kneecap victims received no counseling of any kind, and since they usually had no money, they had no choice but to go back into the neighborhood they came from, where they were intended to be limping examples for those who would stray from the straight and narrow. After a few weeks in west Belfast, I found myself suspicious of every kid I saw on crutches. Although he could have fallen down the stairs or twisted his ankle playing soccer, I always wondered what he'd been kneecapped for.

Sinn Fein spokesman Richard McCauley once explained the Provos' guidelines on punishment shootings. Women were never kneecapped, he said, admitting that this was a sexist policy. Young delinquents—those below age sixteen—were beaten, sometimes severely with hurley sticks, but they too were never shot. McCauley claimed that all offenders received a warning before they had a gun put to their limbs, but I later came to know two teenagers who were shot with no preliminary admonishment. (One, from the Springfield Road, was shot for alleged robberies. The other, from Divis Flats, was shot when falsely accused of rape; the victim later admitted that no rape had taken place.) Sometimes, McCauley said, the IRA concluded that the kid was not to blame. If the parents were deemed lax or irresponsible, the father was beaten up or both parents were banned from the drinking clubs in the district. (Two years after that first conversation with McCauley, the IRA issued a statement threatening to shoot the parents of hoods if they did not keep their kids in line. The first man shot, and perhaps the only one, was a man from Clonard whose sons were notorious in the district.)

Back in the early years of the conflict, when the Provos were ill disciplined, decisions for punishment shootings could be made at a local level; men were shot for disobeying orders, for sleeping with the wife of a man imprisoned for the cause, for having disagreements with Provisionals or members of their families. "People were kneecapped," McCauley admitted, "who should not have been kneecapped."

Dan McGuiness, a Catholic from Andersonstown, was one such example. McGuiness, who later became a Belfast city councilman, was kneecapped in 1972, two days before his eighteenth birthday, because he had let it be known that he supported the police. Local IRA men kidnapped him and subjected him to a fifteen-hour interrogation, during which he was burned on the neck and wrist with cigarettes, beaten with a belt buckle, and sliced with a razor blade. Finally, he was tied to a lamppost and shot twice in the leg. He told me the interrogation was much more painful than being shot.

At that time the IRA also used tar and feathers to punish offenders, though it was not used as often as the gun. (The highest number of tar and featherings was recorded in 1972, when there were twenty-eight.) The Royal Victoria Hospital dealt with many of the cases. The head nurse in the emergency room there told me that some victims had been beaten up before they were tarred and there were fractures underneath the coating they had received. In those cases, removing the tar had to be done with great care. Thick diesel oil was used as often as tar, she said, and she had found that eucalyptus was the best solvent for its removal. At one time the Royal Victoria Hospital was using more eucalyptus than any hospital in the UK.

The tar and feathers punishment was sometimes abbreviated, and offenders were simply doused with paint. "We had to call the painting foreman in," the nurse told me. "He told us how to remove it. We used acetone."

The IRA has largely given up paint, tar, and diesel oil, in part because the procedure is too conspicuous and takes too much time. A punishment squad in the early years of the troubles, back in the days of no-go areas for the police and army, could afford the exposure that a tar and feathering involved. Today, with random police and army patrols and a greater respect for the exposure of volunteers, the IRA resorts to the punishment only on rare occasions.

So the Provisionals of 1980 relied primarily upon kneecapping to keep the community in line. Whether the technique succeeded in that goal, however, was open to question. "This is not a normal society," Andy Tyrie, the leader of the loyalist UDA told me. "You have to instill fear in those sort of people, but it never works if it occurs over a long period of time. People get used to being threatened. I know someone who has been kneecapped three times and is still doing the same things he was kneecapped for."

"You ask them how's the knee?" a priest in Lenadoon told me, "and they're not emotional or embarrassed about it. They'll tell you, 'Oh, it's fine,' or 'I'm going back tomorrow for a checkup.' They joke and talk about it freely, and everyone knows they were kneecapped. I went to see one lad in the hospital and the first thing he says to me is, 'Father, is it true I get 3,000 pounds for each knee?'"

In 1980, compensation ranged from about £800 for a flesh wound to £4,000 for bone or artery damage, and someone severely crippled could expect far more. Belfast knee surgeons, however, are among the best in the world in treating high- and low-velocity bullet wounds, particularly to the leg, and so many young men have come to see a clean, no-complications kneecapping not as a deterrent, but as money in the bank. "The way these hoods see it," Richard McCauley told me in 1980, "if you were kneecapped, that's something to be proud of, and if it's been done twice, that's better, they're looked up to by other hoods. It's not a very happy state of affairs because we are not dealing effectively with the problem. We are only scratching the surface. But you've got to do something. Our people demand that we do something.

"I have talked to people who demand that if the IRA wants to seriously deal with the problem of hoods, they'll have to shoot them dead, and there has been considerable pressure on the IRA to do just that. But they won't do that hopefully. They'd just be playing into the hands of the Brits."

The IRA took no particular delight in the shootings. They continued to do them largely because the ghetto needed policing, and if they didn't do it, people would eventually turn to the police. Acceptance of the police would ultimately result in rejection of the IRA, as people who talked to the RUC about delinquents would eventually talk to them about where the weapons were stored and who was likely to use them. So the Provos were forced to act. They disliked the obligation in part because it exposed IRA volunteers for something other than the war effort. In 1982, for example, a Sinn Fein spokesman told me that it had taken nine volunteers to carry out the kneecapping of a hood in the Beechmount district, about a half mile from Mrs. Barbour's.

"You've got to have weapons brought to the men, safe houses for them to go to afterward, and a dump for the weapons," he said. "You keep the men and the weapons separate as much as possible. You need masks, a change of clothes, and scouts to check the area to make sure that it's clear of patrols and civilians who might get involved. It's not just a matter of giving a volunteer a gun and telling him to go out and shoot somebody."

During my time in Belfast, I met nine men who had been kneecapped. One of them was a friend of mine, a man I'll call Peter Murphy. Peter was kneecapped in 1974 by the IRA; in his version of the story, it started when his child got into a fight in Divis Flats with another child. Peter's wife went out to break the two up, and she ended up fighting the mother of the other child. Peter then went out to break up that fight, and he ended up swinging at the other child's father, who was a member of the Provos. Shortly thereafter, Peter was kneecapped. About two years later, Peter's brother robbed a pub that was controlled by the INLA. Peter was accused of the crime and punched his accuser. Shortly thereafter, the Irps shot him in the arm.

For the first offense, Peter was taken to a cemetery at gunpoint, shot, and abandoned. He almost bled to death. The second shooting occurred in an alley, and the nerve and muscle damage in his arm was so severe that today his hand is limp.

"If you're kneecapped," he said to me one night, "it always stays in your mind. You're afraid because you never know who's coming, who's knocking at your door, or when it's going to happen again. And the police are always after you to find out who did it. The first time, they started to question me before I even got in the operating room."

Peter is particularly bitter because he comes from a Republican family and was a member of the IRA himself in the early years, even serving time in jail for a hijacking. During his days in the movement, he was one of the chief persecutors of the delinquents in his neighborhood, and after he was maimed, some of the local hoods sought revenge. Just before I met him, he had been drinking heavily, and late one night, coming home from a pub, he was beaten up and relieved of his money and his shoes.

"I had them tortured at one time," Peter told me. ("Tortured" is a word used loosely in Belfast; it can mean anything from "inconvenienced" to "beaten bloody.") "The way the hoods go about now, they never did that when I was in the IRA. Years ago, we had them brush balconies or we tarred and feathered them. We never lamed anybody. I kneecapped a guy with a .45 once. I told him I would just graze him, burn him with the discharge. He got two burns, one on each leg. That was it. He thanked me for it."

Peter believed that kneecappings and beatings were not the way to deal with hoods. "I'd shoot one dead," he said to me, "and there'd be no hoods afterward."

He submitted the idea in May 1981, a few days after IRA volunteer Bobby Sands had died on hunger strike. The neighborhood was barricaded with burned out vehicles. We were talking in Peter's living room, and his wife Marie was watching "Mork and Mindy" on the television set, listening sometimes to us, sometimes to the program. Marie's cousin came by with some beer, and so I met Frankie Moore, once a great racketeer, now, at twenty-six, trying to get his money together to leave the North and move to the Republic. (Frankie Moore is not his real name.) The thrills were gone, he drank too much, and his wife had run off, taking his child with her. He sat down, bummed a Valium, sipped his beer, and picking up on our conversation, told his own story.

In years past he had access to a shipping warehouse, where he stole appliances and boxloads of merchandise meant for department stores. He sometimes stole to order, procuring a washing machine for someone who needed one, and at other times he just took what he could get and sold it in the flats. He'd once made off with a great quantity of brassieres, all of them an off shade of brown, and they had sold extremely well. He took some delight in the fact that for a time he could predict with some accuracy what many of the women in Divis Flats were wearing underneath their street clothes.

For the Provisionals, however, there is also an acceptable level of violence. When a man becomes too flagrant a criminal, he risks attracting the attention of the police. Once caught, the police may offer a deal in exchange for information, and then IRA volunteers are jeopardized. Frankie exceeded the Provisionals' acceptable limits, and although his customers included some Republican families, he was placed on the list of those to be kneecapped. His brother, an active IRA man, warned him, but he figured that there was nothing he could do.

One night, two gunmen confronted him in a drinking club in Andersonstown. "I said to them, 'Wait a minute,'" Frankie told us. "I took off my coat, told my friend to hold it." The coat was worth ninety pounds, and Frankie didn't want it ruined. It survived unscathed, but Frankie told the authorities that it had been destroyed in order to increase his claim for compensation.

"One shot went through my trousers," he said. "I thought I'd been hit, but actually the bullet had just cut through the cloth. I thought, 'Jesus, this is easy.' Then came the second shot, and I knew I was done. I didn't shout for help, though, until he got out.

"I was hit in the knee. They took arteries from one leg and moved them to the other. My toe bothers me, and I don't get pulse into my feet. See I was shot with a .45 automatic from far away, and the further away it is, the worse it spins, the more damage it does."

There was one major difference between Frankie's kneecapping and the two suffered by my friend Peter. Under the government's rules for personal injury claims, no one who has been a member of a proscribed organization is eligible for compensation as a victim of terrorist crime. As a convicted IRA man, my friend Peter could collect nothing. Frankie, on the other hand, was what the security forces refer to as an ODC, an ordinary decent criminal. His wound was severe, and he was awarded £4,000.

Unfortunately for Frankie, the Payment for Debt Act was invoked after he was awarded his claim, and by the time his back rent, electricity, and gas bills had been paid, he was left with only 2,000 pounds. He told me that he drank a thousand of it in a week, and the other thousand over the next five. He admits that he will probably never have that much money again, but he doesn't regret for a second the way that he spent it. If he got that much money again, he told me, he would probably wind up dead, as he would drink it all himself the next time around instead of buying so many drinks for his mates.

Before he was kneecapped, Frankie was offered the option of sweeping the footpaths in his neighborhood as his punishment. He chose to be shot. Sweeping sidewalks, he said, would be embarrassing. Like Peter Murphy, he was against the policy of kneecapping, in part because he thought it was cruel punishment, in part because he didn't think it achieved what it was meant to. He understood, however, why the IRA resorted to it. "They aren't exactly in a position to put you away for six months," he said.

Frankie agreed with Peter that the only solution for the problem of hoods was more drastic punishment. He cocked his hand as if it were a gun and pointed it at his head. "I think the only thing left for them to do now," he said, "is to clean your ears out."

The people of west Belfast were full of good will for the Provos then, as Bobby Sands had just died. Had I met Frankie at another time, I'm not sure he would have been so forgiving of the IRA. Looking back, he said, he had no animosity toward the movement for shooting him. "Put it this way," he said, "they must have thought I needed it to keep me in line, and when you get a guy who starves himself to death, my kneecapping is nothing compared to that."

While punishment shootings seem barbaric to outsiders, to ghetto residents they were acceptable, and there was little sympathy for those punished. The Provos even expressed concern at the community's preference for kneecapping over attempts to work out softer sentences. My barber, an affable man who worked in the shop just up the Springfield Road, told me that hoods should not be shot in the leg, but in the ankle, because he believed ankle shooting would cause more permanent injury. Even a woman from the district who had contributed to the Peace People, exasperated by one of the local hooligans whom she had just caught breaking into a shop, asked me if I couldn't talk to someone to have the lad "taken care of."

When I arrived, I was fascinated and horrified by the custom, but over time I too became calloused. At this point, I can look at the notes of my conversations with McCauley, see his statement that the shootings are "now being done on a much more rational basis," and understand exactly what he means.

One of the reasons why good Catholics can accept the shooting of their delinquents, and one of the reasons why I can understand McCauley's seemingly contradictory statement, is because the state also attempts to control working-class Catholics with rules that violate normal standards of justice. The government relies heavily on two laws, the Emergency Provisions Act (EPA) and the Prevention of Terrorism Act (PTA).

The PTA was presented to the House of Commons in 1974 by Home Secretary Roy Jenkins. "These powers are draconian," he said. "In combination they are unprecedented in peacetime. I believe they are fully justified to meet the clear and present danger." The law allows the state to imprison suspects for seven days without charge. It also provides for the use of an extraordinary device called an exclusion order. An exclusion order can be served against any Northern Ireland citizen in order to prevent him from entering England, Scotland, or Wales. In effect, it means the Northerner can be arrested, interrogated, held for seven days, and deported back to his province *and he has no right to learn the charges against him and no right of appeal.* (Imagine a young black man leaving Detroit, hoping to find work in Miami. Upon entry into Florida, he could, if the United States were to adopt a similar law, be sent back to his ghetto in Detroit without explanation, and told never to leave Michigan again.) In application and in its mere existence, the law maroons many Catholic men who might want to leave the ghetto and start anew elsewhere in their country. An ex-internee is particularly vulnerable, as his time in Long Kesh would show up on the computer and would certainly color the judgment of the arresting officer—even though his incarceration may have resulted from no crime at all.

The Emergency Provisions Act allows for detention without trial and searches without warrant. It outlaws membership in proscribed organizations, professing membership in such an organization, and giving or inviting financial support to such a group. Under the EPA's provisions, it is illegal to dress or behave in a public place in such a way as to arouse reasonable apprehension that one is a member of a proscribed organization. The EPA also established special courts to deal solely with terrorist offenses. (The courts were named after Lord Diplock, who chaired the commission that recommended that terrorist crimes deserved special treatment.) In Diplock courts there are no juries (the government feared that jurors were biased and likely to be intimidated), and in certain cases, a man or woman is presumed guilty unless he or she can prove his innocence.

One might expect there would be a certain amount of embarrassment in Britain for having "draconian" legislation on the books, and that that shame would generate rigorous examination and continuous monitoring of the effect of the legislation. Such has not been the case. Parliament has renewed the emergency powers legislation repeatedly with little debate, little dissension, and little research, ignoring the arguments of British civil liberties advocates. The London-based National Council for Civil Liberties argues that the laws violate international standards on human rights, that there is no evidence that the PTA has reduced terrorism, and that the emergency legislation has in fact increased violence in Northern Ireland. Others argue that the laws do not discourage membership in organizations like the IRA; on the contrary, the legislation is used as a justification for violence and actually encourages membership in proscribed organizations.

The Cobden Trust, a civil liberties foundation, has funded several academic studies of justice in the North under the emergency legislation. The most recent, *The Use and Abuse of Emergency Legislation in Northern Ireland* (Cobden Trust, 1983), was written by Dermot Walsh, a former researcher in Queen's University's law department now on the law faculty at University College in Cork. Walsh found that 90 percent of those arrested under the emergency legislation in the first ten months of 1980 were released without charge. He interviewed a sample of sixty people, Catholic and Protestant, who had been arrested and released without charge in the first three months of 1981. Almost three-quarters of them said they had not been questioned about any specific terrorist incidents, but that they had been asked details about their families, their neighbors, their political views, and the political views of people they knew. Walsh found that those arrested were often so relieved to find they were only being screened, not interrogated about some illegal act, that they were quite willing to chat away when asked seemingly innocuous questions.

It is not easy for the police or the army to install undercover operatives in ghettos like west Belfast, where everyone knows everyone else, and so low-level intelligence information can be quite useful. The seemingly unimportant information extracted in a screening arrest can be collated with material from informers, telephone taps, and the army's already large data bank, and a larger picture may emerge. A teenager, for example, picked up for a screening, may mention that he went to a Provisional drinking club in Andersonstown on Sunday night, as it is one of the few places in west Belfast where a man can get a drink on the Sabbath (all the pubs are closed). The police may ask their prisoner who he saw in the club. The kid may mention that he saw his neighbor there, a man we'll call Mickey Flynn, and, that Mickey was singing away with the rest of the crowd when the band played "The Belfast Brigade." The police consult the computer on this fellow Flynn, and they find he grew up in the Lower Falls in a house with no bath. Furthermore, the computer shows that three days ago Flynn was stopped near the university at a vehicle checkpoint in a car driven by an ex-internee; that he was questioned by a foot patrol in Lenadoon the following day; and that his brother is doing two years for membership and six for possession of a firearm. Mickey begins to look like a man to keep an eye on: he's mobile, he hangs about in Republican quarters, he grew up in poverty, and he's probably been fired up by tales of beatings by prison guards when he visits his brother in the Maze. Actually, Mickey may have no political views at all.

But as the police repeatedly arrest him, trying either to figure him out or to keep him off the street, he may well acquire some.

Continuing in this fictional case, let's say that the Provisionals ambush a government minister as he enters the university to give a commencement address, and that, as usually happens, the gunmen make good their escape. The police recall that they have spotted Flynn near the university, and lacking suspects of more significance, they arrest Mickey and take him to Castlereagh for interrogation. If this is Flynn's first visit, he'll be scared before he gets there, a lingering effect of the torture that went on there in the 1970s. When he arrives, his personal effects are taken from him—rings, watches, scapular, wallet, etc. He is taken to a small cell with bare walls, a chair, and a bed chained to the floor. The room may be overheated. The light may shine constantly. There will be no reading material of any kind, and Flynn will see no other prisoners, no member of his family, no one but policemen for the next forty-eight hours. After forty-eight hours, regulations require the police to allow him to see a solicitor. (In his survey, however, Dermot Walsh found that access to an attorney was often denied.)

Flynn will be interrogated in another small room with bare walls. His questioners may include several two-man teams, each with a different technique. Sometimes there is a policeman who wants to beat the suspect bloody; that cop is kept from doing so by his partner, who can barely restrain the mad detective. (One man I know was interrogated first by a good guy/bad guy team, then by an older man—a father figure—who compared the prisoner to his own child, and finally by a man who quoted the Bible.) The sessions vary in length, from fifteen minutes to more than two hours, and there may be more than ten interrogation sessions per day, with many of the questions repeated over and over again, seemingly for no purpose. Exasperation, loneliness, and fear all work in the interrogator's favor.

Flynn may also be intimidated by the fact that his interrogators seem to know everything about him. They can tell him where he drank last week, what his brother does for a living, and who his friends are. Dermot Walsh told me that some men were surprised when detectives called them by their nicknames; that others were taken aback when they heard jokes that they had told their friends in a pub repeated to them by interrogators in Castlereagh; and that others were amazed when the police produced surveillance photographs showing the person with friends or at public gatherings. One man interviewed on the BBC's Spotlight program said he had cracked and agreed to work for the police as an informer after his interrogators were able to tell him that he was two-timing his girlfriend. Tom McGurk, writing in Dublin's *Sunday Tribune* on April 18, 1982, attributed the police's extensive data to screening arrests, examination of tax returns, phone-tapping, other intelligence-gathering techniques, and the use of informers.

In Walsh's survey for the Cobden Trust, one-third of those he interviewed said that the police had tried to enlist them as informers. Some said that they had been threatened, others that they were offered money. One teenager Walsh interviewed was told that soldiers would approach him as he stood in his local pub with his friends, and that the troops would say, "Are these the lads you were telling us about?"

Walsh was also impressed by the response of the people he asked for interviews. Often they told him that they would be happy to comply but they predicted that he would probably be disappointed. "Nothing happened," they explained, by which they meant they had not been beaten up or mistreated physically. That they had been threatened, incarcerated for up to seven days for no reason, denied access to a solicitor, and asked questions that had nothing to do with any crime did not seem to them remarkable.

Walsh concluded that the police were using the emergency laws to compile dossiers on individuals in ghetto areas; to force people to pass on information; and to harass activists whose politics the government did not appreciate. All were purposes for which the emergency laws were never intended.

After the survey on arrest and interrogation, Walsh went on to study the operation of the Diplock Courts, analyzing the 170 cases heard in the first three months of 1981. He found that in 88.8 percent of the cases in the special courts, the accused was alleged to have made a confession, although 20 percent of those charged had not been suspected of any particular crime when they were arrested. "The very distinct impression I get from these cases is that the accused is not giving the confession voluntarily," Walsh wrote. Furthermore, Walsh said, due to the pressures applied by interrogators, it is "highly unlikely" that the confessions would stand up in a court of common law. Under the emergency legislation, however, all confessions were admissible except those in which the prosecution failed to prove beyond a reasonable doubt that the confession was not obtained by torture or inhuman or degrading treatment, or in cases where the judge decided to exercise his personal discretion and reject the confession.

An earlier Cobden Trust survey found that in almost all cases, the confession was written by the detectives, rather than by the subject himself. A confession need not be written at all, however, for it to be accepted by the court. If, for example, during the twentieth interrogation session in two days at Castlereagh, a suspect is told for the fifteenth time that he is a member of the IRA, and he replies in an exaggerated, sarcastic manner, "Sure, I'm a member of the IRA," that statement can be treated as a confession.

Of the cases Walsh examined, the most shocking example of an admissible confession involved a man who was being interrogated for the thirty-third time after almost three days in custody. One of the detectives left the room, and the one who remained—a man who has a reputation among Catholics for employing dubious interrogation methods— later emerged from the session with the news that the man had confessed. The judge handed down an unusually severe sentence: six years for membership in a proscribed organization.

Dermot Walsh and the Cobden Trust are not alone in their concern. Amnesty International has also questioned the Diplock process and some of the convictions that have resulted. In its 1982 annual report the organization highlighted the case of Michael Culbert, a Belfast social worker, who was arrested in May 1978. After four days in custody, Culbert was charged with the murder of a policeman. "At Castlereagh he was interrogated for long periods," Amnesty International's report stated, "but he was not physically ill treated. He was alleged to have made a verbal confession, which formed the only evidence against him. Michael Culbert denied having made such a confession. He maintained that at the time of the alleged confession he was completely disorientated as a result of continuous interrogation, lack of sleep, and being made to stand for long periods during interrogation. (The police denied that he had been forced to stand.) He was tried by a special court some 18 months later in October 1979. The only issue in the trial was the admissibility of his alleged verbal confession. The court held that the confession was admissible, convicted him of murder and membership of the Irish Republican Army, and sentenced him to *life imprisonment*" (italics mine).

The result of years of life under the Diplock rules is entirely predictable: no one in the Catholic ghettos believes that a fair trial is possible in the special courts. When a policeman at Castlereagh threatens to charge a young man with a crime he did not commit, the prisoner knows he can be convicted whether he committed the crime or not. This may well lead him to plead guilty to a lesser charge.

Furthermore, it is obvious to all that justice in the North is not blind. *Ten Years On in Northern Ireland,* the 1980 Cobden Trust study of 300 trials, found that charges of membership in proscribed organizations were more frequently brought against Republican than loyalist defendants. The professors who conducted the study also pointed out that a higher standard of proof was required for the conviction of a member of the security forces. A committee headed by English Crown Court Judge Harry Bennett found that up to the end of 1978, there had been no final conviction of a policeman arising out of the hundreds of complaints of ill treatment during interrogation, although that ill treatment was well documented.

Perhaps the most extraordinary conclusion of Walsh's study of the Diplock courts was that although they were created to deal only with terrorist crimes, the special courts are now dealing with ordinary crime as well. More than 40 percent of the cases in his sample did not qualify as terrorist crimes, but were "ordinary criminal actions carried out for ordinary criminal motives. Most concerned armed robberies," Walsh said in his report, "although there were some truly bizarre cases, such as attempted rape and indecent assault."

It is easy to understand why the police use the special courts in these ordinary cases. The procedures allowed under the emergency legislation free them from common law requirements for a valid arrest, and the rules of the Diplock courts make for easier convictions. And so the abnormal, once again, is accepted as the norm.

One might expect that in an area so firmly identified with Catholicism, the Church would be a great help to its members in sorting out the rules imposed on them. The clergy, however, is as divided as the flock. Bishop Cahal Daly, the man who rules the Belfast diocese, seems pro-British, while Cardinal O'Fiaich (pronounced O'Fee), the head of the Church in Ireland, has not kept secret his opinion that the British should leave. On the whole, the Catholic hierarchy is very thorough in denouncing the violence of the IRA, but it celebrates men who used the same methods of terrorism and guerrilla warfare in securing independence for the Republic sixty years ago.

The priests of west Belfast are a mixed lot. Some speak only of the kingdom of heaven, while others are deeply involved in the problems of the communities they serve. I came to know Father Patrick Buckley, one of the activists, because I spent a lot of time in his neighborhood. I liked him; many others didn't, some because they didn't like his opinions, some because they didn't like his readiness to express those opinions to reporters.

"The Church is like an ostrich with its head buried in the sand," he told me one day in 1982. "Somebody gets killed. A bishop here or a priest there stands up and condemns the killing. It's gotten to the stage now where it's a cliche and it's a laugh, as if priests and bishops were only for condemning atrocities. It's almost like the keeners we used to have in Ireland; we used to hire women to cry at funerals. We in the North have become just criers over atrocities.

"I think it is remarkable that there has been such a huge argument about the North, but there has never been a seminar or a gathering of the clergy to ask the question, 'What moral position should the Church take on the North of Ireland? Who does the North belong to, and what are the implications of that?'

"If, for instance, you asked that question, and from a moral point of view you came up with the answer that the North is rightfully Ireland's, well, then the Church would be quite justified in saying, 'Yes, it's a sin to kill, but it's also a sin to steal, so give these people back their country.' That hasn't been faced up to."

Buckley believes many priests fail in their responsibilities as moral leaders, preaching sermons about the next world when burning issues are "just inches from the pulpit." "If priests were being shot for their preaching," he told me, "I think that would be a very healthy sign for the Church, although I must say I wouldn't like to be the first one shot."

Buckley, the oldest of seventeen children, spent most of his youth in Dublin. He had never been to Belfast when, at age twenty-six, he was transferred from a small parish in Wales to St. Peter's parish in the Lower Falls, perhaps the roughest, most brutal community in either Ireland or Britain. He told me that in his four years on the job he had come

to understand the legal and institutional injustices in the North, the forces
that make an IRA man do what he does, but at the same time he could
not sanction the IRA's activity. That attitude put him squarely in the no
man's land between the guerrillas and the security forces, a position occupied by a few other priests as well. Those clergymen have become
negotiators between the government and the guerrillas, and sometimes
between delinquents and the IRA.

When I met Buckley, he had mustered a group of thirty tenants who
lived in Divis Flats and formed an organization called the Residents Association; one newspaper, realizing the priest was trying to develop an
alternative to the police and the Republican guerrillas, referred to the
group as the Third Force. The Association hoped to make the flats more
livable by maintaining pressure on the Housing Executive to perform repairs, by cleaning up the flats themselves, and by trying to control the
rioters who were responsible for much of the neighborhood's misery.
Buckley's fellow priests in the parish berated him, and took to referring
to him as the Lone Ranger.

Buckley believed that 40 to 100 kids were causing most of the trouble.
His parishioners, he told me, were powerless to stop them: they were
reluctant to go to the RUC because the police had such a bad name in the
flats (a name Buckley said was well deserved); they were also reluctant
to go to the Provos or the Irps to ask that the offenders be punished.
(While many west Belfast residents have little sympathy for those who
have been kneecapped, no one wants to be the direct cause of a shooting.) The only alternative, Buckley thought, was community pressure,
but his parishioners were afraid to take a stand because they feared the
hoods would break their windows or beat up their children. Many also
had the feeling that in some mysterious way, the IRA or the Irps were
behind the rioting, so if a man or woman took a stand against the rioters,
he or she would be opposing the Republican movement. As a result of all
these fears, nothing was being done.

Buckley hoped his Residents Association would change that. The Association was composed almost entirely of women, in part, he said, because women have more courage in confrontations with the local powers. A man confronting another man can be threatened with a beating or
with being shot. There is still a taboo, however, about beating or shooting a woman who is not your wife. Also, although women often do not
have the final say in family and home affairs, those matters are still con-

sidered their responsibility, and so meetings that involve those issues draw mostly mothers and wives.

The Residents Association's efforts against delinquency began with informal night patrols. They destroyed caches of petrol bombs and took down the names of any youths they spotted committing an offense. They visited the homes of the kids who were causing the problems, hoping that the parents, once informed, would do something.

Buckley admitted that the group had not made much progress with its appeal to the delinquents' parents. "Either they're out drinking, or the father has left the home, or they won't listen to you," he said. "They'll tell you lies. You've seen a kid out making trouble and his parents will swear blind that he was in bed, or that he was watching TV with them. Parents seem unable to accept that their kids are doing wrong."

Writing down the names of the offenders didn't promise to be particularly effective in the long run either. Buckley was hoping that the kids would find it intimidating to see a priest or an adult recording their names when they were doing something they knew was wrong. Buckley, however, had no idea what to do with the list. He certainly wasn't about to give it to the RUC or the IRA. Similarly, he went out with a camera on several occasions, hoping the kids would be intimidated by having their photos taken. There was, however, no film in the camera, as Buckley had no one to give the pictures to.

With so many rules and so many conflicting authorities in west Belfast, it is easy to get caught in a squeeze between the great powers. Sometimes those squeezes can have fatal results.

"Fellows who are doing vandalism or petty crime, when they see the Provos or the INLA coming, they know they'll be shot," Father Denis Faul told me in the spring of 1982. "So they run to the only people they know, the RUC, to ask for protection. I had a case no later than yesterday. The INLA was after two boys from south Belfast. The police stopped the boys, took them to Castlereagh, and said, 'If you don't cooperate with us, we'll keep on arresting you and we'll put out the word that you're acting as touts. We'll arrest a number of the prominent men and tell them that we arrested them on your information.' Then once they start to work for the RUC, they can't stop, or the police will let it be known that they are informers, and they will be shot dead."

The Church, in the person of Father Faul, provides people caught in that position with a sort of sanctuary. Once he has exposed a case of intimidation, the victim is often left alone.

The Church is not so kind to certain young women, however, who are abandoned because of an unwritten treaty between Church and state. In 1978, I dropped in on a school for girls caught between those two powers. The school had been started by Frank Shiels and Rowan Davison (another social worker who labored in Divis Flats), and it met in the ill-heated rooms of Shiels's youth club; on the days when I visited, the students never took their coats off. The class consisted of six girls, aged twelve to sixteen. The school's proper name was the Divis Education Project, but if you asked the kids where they went to school, they'd tell you they went to Crazy Joe's.

The six girls lived in the flats and came from families afflicted by all of the social diseases of west Belfast: wifebeating; child abuse; alcoholism; one-parent families; unemployment; paramilitary involvement; imprisonment; beatings by the security forces, the IRA, or the Irps; enormous debts to the utilities, the coal man, and the Housing Executive (one mother owed £3,000); and welfare checks reduced by the Payment for Debt Act. They had brothers up for petty theft, brothers shot, brothers on the run, brothers in jail, and brothers dead. Some of the girls were themselves involved in petty theft, and one was on probation for shoplifting.

Those six girls, however, were the liveliest I met in all Belfast, generous, and full of funny stories. In school, they wore no uniforms, they used whatever language they pleased, and they smoked whenever any of them had enough cigarettes to go around.

I was in their class shortly before Christmas, and Eleanor McClorey, a young woman with long black hair who was the school's teacher, began reading a story to her students about a Polish family imprisoned in a concentration camp during World War II. She stopped when she came to the name Hitler.

"Who can tell me who Hitler was?" she asked.

Colette, one of the older students (I have changed all of their names here), spoke out. "He was the leader of the Nazis," she said.

Bridget, twelve years old, a small child with a raspy voice, asked for clarification. "Was he a Catholic or an Orangie?" she said.

Ms. McClorey hardly flushed. She explained that Hitler was German, not one of those who fell into the category of Fenian or Orangie. Colette, the older student, added that Hitler had hated Jews.

"What's a Jew?" Bridget asked.

McClorey explained that Jews are people who came from Palestine, and that in fact Jesus himself was a Jew.

"Then Hitler was an Orangie," Bridget concluded.

Bridget and her fellow students are not unintelligent, but their view of the world outside the flats is hazy. The haziness is due in part to the fact that they have rarely been outside Belfast, and in part to the fact that their formal schooling was terminated by Catholic authorities who told all six girls that they were no longer welcome in Catholic schools. The six had attended St. Louise's, a local Catholic girls secondary school with a national reputation for its fine programs. They had been dismissed for committing a variety of offenses including cutting classes, smoking in the washrooms, hopping on the back of lorries while wearing the school uniform, and being disruptive in class. One of the girls was sent home after only three weeks in the school, and she spent the next four years getting no education at all.

There is no doubt that the six were difficult kids. What is considered normal behavior in Divis Flats is considered wildly aberrant by some of the nuns and middle-class students at St. Louise's. On the face of it, the expulsion of some of the girls seems routine. The principal told me that she had done all that she could for them, that they are now the state's responsibility.

It would seem logical that after being expelled from St. Louise's, Colette or Bridget or any of their four schoolmates would simply enroll in another Catholic school or would attend a state-run institution. The other Catholic schools, however, are afraid of becoming dumping grounds for St. Louise's more difficult students. There have been exceptions, but the general rule is that once you have been expelled from one Catholic school, you are not wanted in another. And attending state schools located in Protestant areas is out of the question for most Catholics.

"If a Catholic parent sent his kid to our school," one educational welfare officer at a Protestant school told me, "he would be murdered." The welfare officer went on to relate the story of a boy called Sean who was beaten by his classmates on his first day at school. The boys had simply assumed that with a name like Sean, the child must be Catholic. In fact, he was Protestant.

Someone unfamiliar with the dynamics of Northern Irish society might think that the state could provide schooling for children like Colette or Bridget simply by building a special school in Catholic territory. That option, however, was not acceptable to the Church for two reasons: such a school would provide no religious instruction, and it would be seen as an indictment of the Catholic schools for abandoning difficult children. One might assume that the state would easily dismiss those objections and begin plans for construction, or that it would force the Church to provide the schooling, using as leverage the state funding of all Catholic schools. The state, however, feared the Church too much to insult it or order it to do anything.

"The Department of Education will never allow the Catholic monopoly on the education of Catholics to be destroyed," Tony Spencer, a Catholic member of the Belfast school board told me. Spencer, a professor of sociology at Queen's University, claimed that the Department of Education's worst fear was that the Catholic bishops will hurl spiritual bombs at them. "They know that the last people you must antagonize are the Catholic bishops. All it takes is something like the Cardinal visiting the Maze or commenting on the treatment of suspects in police custody. He could comment on any issue in the exercise of his pastoral function, and he could present it to the world as pastoral concern. The political implications are explosive. If the bishops want to create mayhem, they can do more than the IRA can. They could make the province ungovernable."

So the state did not provide for the likes of Colette and Bridget, and neither did the Church. The children went back to their ghettoes and were easily forgotten; the Belfast Law Centre documented fifty cases of children in that educational limbo in 1982, but no one knew how many other kids were in the same position. Although the archdiocese's guidelines for expulsions cited "extreme misconduct" as justification for suspension, the Law Centre's sample found pupils expelled and suspended from several Catholic schools for not wearing their school uniform, for having their hair too short, for poor attendance, fighting, smoking in school, glue sniffing outside of school, and poor performance in the classroom. In half the cases in the sample, there was no contact between the school and the parent; the child was expelled or suspended, and was simply told not to come back. In only 20 percent of the cases was an educational welfare officer contacted. Some of the parents were not sure if their children were expelled or suspended, and the Law Centre cited two cases in which the school seemed to change its story when social service authorities or a community organization inquired about the expelled child's status (in one case the child was taken back, having missed several months of school). Although the law requires schools to notify the education authorities when a child is expelled, that statute also seemed to be ignored by the Catholic school principals.

When I sat in at Crazy Joe's school, there were no boys in attendance, though several had asked to be admitted. The boys' schools in west Belfast posed a different problem. Most headmasters expelled no one, but many boys were consistently truant. If Eleanor McClorey had taken a truant into the Divis Education Project, she could have been brought to court for keeping a child from attending school, as the classroom in Crazy Joe's was not recognized as an educational institution by the state authorities. The result was that many of the boys in the flats went nowhere.

The Church and state policies left McClorey and her students in a curious position. The state would provide no funds, but since some members of the school board were sympathetic, the school was permitted to occupy a state-funded youth club; if the board really wanted to close down the school, it could have evicted it. The Board members may also have given the project a wink and a nod because they feared that evicting the class might provoke a lawsuit. The state is required by law to provide for the education of every child, and the authorities were clearly not fulfilling their legal obligation. (Social workers who thought that a legal battle might result in policy changes or in something more concrete than a makeshift school, had found that it was difficult to muster a test case. None of the Catholic parents they contacted wanted to fight the Church.)

The Church authorities were not fond of Crazy Joe's. They would not support it because they had no control over the school and because religious instruction was not part of the curriculum. But while McClorey could count on no aid from that quarter, she could also count on no attack: the Church had plainly washed its hands of the girls and had chosen to ignore the morality of that washing. To have that pointed out in public would indeed be embarrassing. And so Crazy Joe's existed because the two giants pretended it wasn't there.

The girls studied math, history, grammar, and literature, all with donated textbooks. On Monday afternoons, McClorey took her pupils to the kitchen in the Community Center for a cooking class, and on Wednesdays, a folksinger, a friend of McClorey's, came in to teach music. Occasionally the girls wrote stories in class. One of the older ones, a teenager who had been out of school for three years until Crazy Joe's started, penned her own version of "The Twelve Dancing Princesses," a fairy tale she had read in one of the books donated to the school.

In the original version, a king was very worried about his twelve daughters. Every night they went to bed with new slippers, and every morning the slippers were worn out. The expense didn't bother the king because he was very wealthy, but he wanted to know how the slippers deteriorated so quickly. Many nobles came forward to help solve the riddle, but none succeeded. Finally a common soldier volunteered his services. He was tipped off by a beggar that he should not drink the wine the girls offered at bedtime, and as a result, he discovered that the girls danced all night at a magic castle. The king allowed him to marry one of the princesses as a reward. Eventually, the soldier inherited the kingdom, and everyone lived happily ever after.

The Crazy Joe's version went like this: Once upon a time, there was a poor king. He had twelve daughters who were very good dancers, and every day he had them dance down in Castle Street [the street where the black taxis congregate just outside the city center]. Many people liked the girls' performances, and they threw them coins, but the dancing princesses remained hungry and poor. They did not understand where the money went. One day, one of the princesses followed her father and discovered that he spent all of the money in the bookie's and the pub. So the princesses decided to withhold some of the daily proceeds. The poor king, however, discovered their plot. And so he killed them.

THE WALL AND THE PEOPLE BEYOND IT

ENSHRINED in the Ulster Folk Museum, on the outskirts of east Belfast, are several spades. One of the tools comes from the northeast part of the island of Ireland, where Protestants are the majority population. The Protestant spade has a short shaft topped by a T-shaped handle. Other spades on display come from different parts of the island, where Catholics are the majority, and they have straight, long shafts, with no special handles; the digger is meant to hold those shovels by the shaft. Because of the difference in design, a man with a Protestant spade usually used his left foot for his labors, while a man with a long-shafted tool used his right. Today, an Irishman who has never lifted a spade, when unsure of a new acquaintance's religion, may ask "What foot does he dig with?" Often, the reply will be that the person "digs with the other foot."

Any Northerner can tell you it takes no great talent to tell a Catholic from a Protestant. In Belfast, for example, the most segregated city in the North, one can quickly determine a man's religion just by asking him where he lives or what school he went to. Often one can tell from a person's name what church he or she holds dear: anyone named Sean, Seamus, Kieran, Patrick, Damien, Eamonn, Malachy, Theresa, Bernadette, Deirdre, Finnoula, or Colette is Catholic. William, Sammy, Ian, Hope, Joy, and Grace are all Protestant. A former resident of the Ardoyne, writing in the *Irish Times* in 1981, said that Orangemen parading past his old neighborhood sang an altered version of "If You're Irish, Come into the Parlor" to irritate the local Catholics. The original song includes the words, "If your name is Timothy or Pat, As long as you're from Ireland there's a welcome on the mat." In the Orangemen's version, if your name is Timothy or Pat, "you'll never get into the shipyard with a Fenian name like that."

One can sometimes tell a man's faith by his vocabulary. A Protestant will often call the city of Londonderry by its full name, while Catholics will call it Derry. (Television reporters, in an attempt to be objective, often call it Londonderry in the first reference and Derry in the second.) Anyone who refers to a "Roman Catholic" is a Protestant; the other sort will just say Catholic. A Protestant may call the North "Ulster," a word Catholics rarely use. Catholics call the province by a variety of names, including the "Six Counties" (referring by omission to the other twenty-six counties that make up the rest of the island), or the "North of Ireland" or just "the North."

If a man says the "queen," you can't really tell, but if he says "the British queen," you can assume the speaker is Catholic. Similarly, if he says the "pope of Rome," he's Protestant. If he calls a cop "a peeler," he's probably Catholic, and he'll almost certainly call a prison guard "a screw." Often, one can tell by the way a man or a woman pronounces the letter H, which comes up in discussions of the prison, where the prisoners are housed in H-blocks (rows of cell blocks in the shape of the letter H). A Protestant will say "aitch," while many, but not all, Catholics will say "haitch."

You can tell a man's religion from the cemetery he buries his people in, from the newspaper he reads, from the bus he rides, from the football team he roots for. In some neighborhoods, you can guess a man's faith quite accurately by noting which side of the street he walks on. If a kid plays cricket, he's not Catholic. If he carries a hurley stick, he's not Protestant. If he wears a scarf of green and white or red and white, he's certainly Catholic, as those are the colors of Catholic-backed soccer teams.

Many Protestants and Catholics in the North say that they can often tell a person's religion by his or her physical appearance. This seems a preposterous claim, but after spending some time in Northern Ireland, I can't help but wonder if there is something to it. Frank Burton, a British sociologist who studied the Catholic Ardoyne in the early years of the troubles and was at first skeptical of those who made the claim, found that he was making the same sort of judgments, albeit subconsciously. In his book, *The Politics of Legitimacy* (Routledge and Kegan Paul, 1978), he tells of running for a bus in the city center one day and suddenly deciding that he should be in no hurry. The bus stop he was heading for was served by two different bus routes. One went to a Protestant district, the other to the Ardoyne. Burton realized that he had stopped running because he had determined that the people getting on the bus looked Protestant. He ran ahead to check his perception against the vehicle's destination sign, and found he'd been right.

I feel uncomfortable, however, talking about the differences between the two communities. The troubles have had an erosive effect on those differences and today the two communities have far more in common than they did when the troubles began. Unemployment was largely a Catholic experience in 1969; today, with 14 percent of Protestants unemployed and 28 percent of Catholics, both communities feel the pain of joblessness. Protestant superiority in government has declined as well. Some of today's city and town councils may have as big a Protestant bloc as they had before the troubles, but those blocs have been stripped of most of their power under direct rule from London.

The sense of alienation from the police force, the courts, and the government, common to Catholic communities, is now also shared by many loyalists; in 1984 and 1985, Protestants, upset by government policy, attacked the constabulary with bricks, bottles, stones, petrol bombs, and in one incident, bags of urine. That dismay with British rule is so heartfelt that Andy Tyrie's UDA, the largest Protestant paramilitary group, now advocates breaking the tie with Britain—long the goal of the IRA. (The difference between the two groups' stated goals is that the IRA wants a united Ireland, while the UDA wants to establish a Northern state independent of both Dublin and London, a proposal unpopular with Catholics who fear their rights would be denied just as they were under the Stormont government.)

The encroaching similarity of the two communities is a great challenge to those who wish to preserve the differences, and they must work hard at their task. They are aided by physical barriers constructed between the two communities, the most prominent of which is at Cupar Street, at the back end of Clonard, about two hundred yards from my house.

When I moved into Mrs. Barbour's, Cupar Street was a no-man's land. An administrator in the Department of the Environment referred to it as "the frontier," as if it were a stretch of wilderness between two nations across which there were daring escapes. Other bureaucrats I interviewed called it "an interface." To the unknowing eye, it was just a street. The neighborhood to the south was Clonard—densely packed, working class, and Catholic. The neighborhood to the north was Shankill—working class, not so dense, and Protestant. Between the two was a wall commonly known as the peace line, an entirely inaccurate but commonly accepted term adopted by the government years ago.

In 1980, the peace line at Cupar Street was a few hundred yards long and made up of bricked up rowhouses and sections of corrugated iron. The iron portions were twenty feet high, topped with barbed wire, and they stretched across two intersections and a section of Cupar where the buildings had been leveled after a bombing. At the far end of the structure, where Cupar Street doglegged into Catholic territory, the army had installed an iron gate to prevent automobile traffic. The gate reminded me of drop arm barriers I had seen at border crossings between eastern and western Europe, but for two details: first, the Cupar street gate was designed to swing horizontally, not vertically; and second, it never swung in any direction, as it was always locked shut.

The gate at Cupar Street was not designed to prevent pedestrian traffic, and every morning and every night, Protestants who worked at Mackie's crossed the peace line there. No one paid them much attention. A few Catholic women from Clonard crossed to the Shankill to do their shopping, but they were considered bold, if not foolhardy, by most of their neighbors. Protestant and Catholic adolescents gathered at the unmanned gate in the evenings and passed the time pelting each other with stones and bottles, and so the street and sidewalks around the dogleg were always covered with glass and debris.

Before the troubles began, all of the houses on Cupar were occupied, and the street was mixed—Protestants and Catholics lived side by side. There were no physical barriers between the two communities. Protestant men patronized the bookie on the Kashmir and their wives used the laundromat on Clonard Gardens. Many Catholic women shopped on the Shankill. Pubs, usually owned by Catholics, catered to both sides. Peace and calm prevailed.

In Belfast, however, peace and calm never lasts. The Cupar Street area figured in the riots and uprisings of 1886, 1898, 1920–22, 1935, 1964, and 1969. Today's peace line was installed by the army not long after August 15, 1969, the date known in Clonard as "the night they burned Bombay Street." The wall was merely a formalization of what was already there, as both communities had thrown up barricades. Troops installed iron curtains at several other Belfast flashpoints, and over time the walls became accepted urban design, facts of life no one thought about from one day to the next.

In 1972, when the Unionist government at Stormont finally collapsed and direct rule of the North from London began, one of the priorities of the new government was a drastic reformation of housing policy. Unionist ministers over the previous five decades had dragged their feet when it came to providing social services, and they were particularly poor providers of public housing. The 1961 census, for example, reported that 19.3 percent of the homes in the North had no piped water supply and 22 percent did not have a flush toilet. A government report published the following year said that the house-building rate of 6,000 a year was entirely inadequate, that 10,000 homes a year would have to be built for the North just to stand still in the housing sector.

The homes on the Shankill were as miserable as any on the Catholic side. Some of the houses standing in the 1970s had been condemned as unfit in 1890. In the early 1970s, the newly created Northern Ireland Housing Executive turned its attention to the Shankill, and eventually began a £3 million redevelopment project on the Protestant side of Cupar. When I arrived in 1980, the ground was well broken, and just by chance, at a dinner party in a Belfast suburb, I met Richmond Stokes, the architect assigned to the Shankill project.

Stokes, thirty-five, a straight talker, a patient man, and an atheist of Protestant descent, had come to the North from Wales when he was twenty-two, and he made it clear to me straightaway that he was a Welshman, a different breed. He told me that when he arrived on the

Shankill site, he found a neighborhood in an advanced state of decline. After the troubles broke out in 1969, many of the families on the Shankill had abandoned it for neighborhoods where the battles were not so constant. Protestants had more places to flee to than Catholics, and so while the houses in Clonard right up to the peace line remained occupied and were even sought after, the houses on the Protestant side of the wall, once deserted, stayed that way. The structures began falling apart, in some cases almost overnight. Once a house was vacant, the drains would jam and damp would take over; soon the house next door would suffer similar problems, and its inhabitants would move out. The deterioration crept down the rows of houses, and by 1980, it had advanced through whole streets.

The residents who were the most resourceful—the best educated, and the ones with the most money—were the first to leave, and by the time the redevelopment project broke ground, there were few community leaders left. Vandals and hooligans were a major problem. The houses near the peace line that remained occupied were constantly getting their windows broken; the Department of the Environment would provide metal screens for windows after they had been broken three times. Looking out from the inside of one of those homes was like looking out from a prison cell.

When a family gave up and moved away, local delinquents broke into the empty house and tore it to pieces, making sure to remove the lead, which they sold to scrap yards. The district was so blighted that Stokes welcomed these acts of destruction, as they prevented the odd squatter from moving in and wrecking the rehabilitation schedule, as Jimmy Barr had done on the other side of the wall.

The police, meanwhile, weren't particularly active, seemingly more concerned about the revolutionaries in Clonard than about delinquents on the Shankill. The UDA and other loyalist paramilitary groups were active, but they rarely acted to keep order (though in one notable incident in the fall of 1980, the UDA kneecapped three youths who had raped a nurse). Two men who had done work on the redevelopment scheme told me that the local paramilitaries demanded protection money from the builders who came into the district to do the rehabilitation, that the practice was so common that contractors wrote the cost of the protection into their bids for Housing Executive contracts, hiding the outlay under innocuous titles. In effect, the Executive was subsidizing the paramilitaries. Officials in the Executive denied it, and could cite instances when they had stood up to paramilitaries who had tried to shake them down, but in truth, the Executive had no control over the situation as long as contractors cooperated with the extortionists. (According to Dr. Alistair McDonnell, a city councilman from the Social Democratic and Labour Party, there were shakedown schemes of a different sort in Catholic districts. McDonnell claimed that a contractor would sometimes start work on a job without any trouble, but that one day he would arrive and find the site occupied by a dozen men. The group's leader might then tell the builder that he wanted the men hired, and, according to McDonnell, they often were. Sometimes the men were qualified, and sometimes they were not, and so the quality of the construction varied considerably.)

On the Shankill, the grimmest sight of all was the peace line at Cupar Street. In one stretch of rowhouses, every roof had caved in, so as you stared at the row from a distance, it looked comical: each house had a chimney rising into the sky, but nothing next to it, no roof at all, and every window and door was made of cement.

Yet those peculiar structures were of the utmost significance to Belfast, to Northern Ireland, to the United Kingdom, and above all, to the people of Clonard and the Shankill. Those deformities were the brick portion of the peace line, all that stood between gunmen of one side and gunmen of the other, perhaps the only thing that prevented the area from becoming engulfed in a full-scale civil war.

Stokes was deeply troubled by those derelict buildings. He thought the Cupar Street shells were a great weight that dragged down the whole community. He could have restored them to some livable condition, but that would have served no purpose. No Protestants would move into them, and while an extremely desperate Catholic might make the move, the act could be perceived by Protestants as a government-sponsored invasion. The boundaries have been clear for more than a century, and one family stepping over might ignite a new holocaust. Stokes decided to propose that the houses be torn down, as they were of no use to anyone anyway, and that the strip be left open as a landscaped green, a small park which would act as a buffer between the two communities.

The people of both sides of the peace line rejected Stokes' idea. They argued that a green would simply give the two sides a clear shot at each other, and when there was no shooting, the park would amount to nothing more than an arena for the stone throwing hooligans of both religions. Stokes realized that removing the Cupar Street shells would probably only change the location of his dilemma. The new frontier would be a row of houses a few yards into the Shankill side of Cupar: as the last homes on the battlefield, they would soon be deserted, the deterioration would begin again, and he would end up with a whole new community millstone. When I met Stokes he had just spent £90,000 rehabilitating houses on a street that ran parallel to Cupar. If he tore down the peace line buildings, he would have to write off that investment. No one would move into the rehabilitated homes, as they would become the new peace line.

A group of Shankill residents proposed to Stokes that instead of tearing down the shells and replacing them with a green, he should bulldoze the houses and replace them with a brick wall. Stokes was uneasy with the idea, but went back to the drawing board and came up with a design for a six-foot structure. The community told him that it wasn't enough, and police at the Springfield Road station, hoping to thwart the local stone throwers, asked for a barrier of at least twenty feet.

The architect then came up with a plan for a twenty-foot wall with a four-foot fence on the top. The structure was to be sixteen inches wide at the bottom to withstand the burrowing efforts of the local hoods. It was to be made of Tyrone brick, which would blend in with the other buildings in the district. Next to the wall would be a landscaped area with trees and thorny shrubs (thorns would make unauthorized removal of the shrubs difficult). The Catholic side of the peace line would remain relatively unchanged, as there was no space on that side to do anything fancy. The homes ran flush against the boundary, and all were inhabited.

The design met with approval on the Shankill, and it was then shown to a group from Clonard. They too were well pleased. Months passed, however, and no brick wall appeared. "It is a serious plan," Stokes told me, "but everyone is holding off because no one wants to build it. The cost of construction of a brick wall, coupled with the feeling that you'd be dividing the city off with a Berlin-type wall, is just too much for people outside the two communities to take."

Stokes told me that Belfast politicians could accept the row of corrugated iron and crumbling brick. It was formidable and so served its purpose, and at the same time it looked so terrible that it seemed a temporary measure. A brick wall, on the other hand, would be permanent, a national monument to the failure of the Northern Irish state.

The people of the Shankill and Clonard were less troubled by those lofty ideals. Hooligans broke through the derelict homes that formed the wall and regularly invaded the other side's turf, breaking windows and painting slogans on walls. After the hooligans broke through the brick sections, the crumbling houses became dumping grounds for rubbish, and rats threatened to become a serious problem. The people on both sides of the line argued that a brick wall would be far more sanitary, far more effective in eliminating hooligan raids, and far less unsightly than the wall of ruins.

Stokes did not want to build the wall, but he saw no alternative. "You get divided communities all over the world," he said to me, "but it is not often that they live literally within a stone's throw of each other. People here live much closer to each other than the two sides of the Berlin wall. There is not enough distance for an open field, there's just seventy feet, and a road runs through that, so there really is no distance at all. If you assume that you have to separate the two, and you can't separate them with distance, you have to separate with height."

I came to know people who lived on both sides of the wall. Teresa Quigley, a Catholic in her mid-fifties who lived in Bombay Street, had been burned out of her house on that hot August night in 1969, and had later come to inhabit one of the new homes built to replace those that were torched. She argued that a wall was necessary, that both sides needed to be protected from the other's hoods, and that Catholics needed protection from Protestant paramilitaries. She made her argument not long after loyalists had shot dead a young man in Leoville Street, the avenue just behind my house, and she cited two other fatal sorties into the district by loyalists that had occurred in the previous two years. Those shootings, however, had taken place in spite of the presence of the wall, and whether more would take place if the wall was removed was not possible to say.

William Johnson, who lived in Sugarville Street on the Shankill side (and whose name I have changed here at his request), agreed with his neighbors that the primary problems were hooligans and stone throwers, but he argued that a wall was not the solution, that it was instead a provocation. He said that he had seen teenagers throwing stones over the wall blindly, not knowing who or what they were hitting on the other side, and he thought they wouldn't do that if there was a green along Cupar instead of a wall. At the gate where Cupar bends toward the Springfield Road, he had watched kids from both sides throw missiles at each other, and he claimed it was not as bad as many people thought, that in all the years of stonings across the divide, nobody had been seriously hurt.

Rich Stokes, the architect, told me a similar story. "I swear this is true," he said as we walked around the district one cold day in March 1980. "I was out there one day and there were two kids throwing stones at each other. One of them shouts, 'Sean, I've got to go home now for my tea. I'll be back about six.' 'Okay, Billy,' says the other one, 'Cheerio.'"

The more interviews I did, the more confused I became. I found it hard to determine the function of the wall. If it weren't there, would there be more stone throwing? Or were there only a finite number of stone throwers on each side? If there were no wall, would there be more hooligan raids, more vandalism, and more bitter graffiti? Or would the pattern of targets simply shift, as the lads from one side dared each other to strike deeper and deeper into enemy territory?

Would the shootings, then rare, increase if the wall was torn down? Loyalists shoot a small number of Catholics at random every year. Would they shoot more if they had more targets, or would only the location, and not the total, of the corpses change? Would the IRA and INLA increase their attacks on the security forces if the wall were removed? Perhaps not, as the number of potential targets would not be increased significantly by the wall's elimination. Again, the locations might change, but not the body count.

If there were no wall, of course, there would be the threat of a re-enactment of the battles that raged on that night in August 1969. It might be argued then that the wall was the solution to that problem. It might also be argued, however, that the wall was the problem, that as long as there are walls between the two communities, they will never become reconciled to each other.

The whole issue seemed moot, however, when I considered how the wall could be dismantled. If it were taken down by government fiat, it seemed entirely likely that both sides would go back to the barricades that preceded the peace line. The invasion of 1969 is a long way from forgotten in Clonard, and the siege mentality of the Ulster Protestant is as robust on the Shankill as it is anywhere.

The different bureaucracies dealing with the question favored different solutions. The Housing Executive would not agree to Stokes's original plan for a green. By 1980, they had spent £3 million rehabilitating the homes on the Protestant side, and they wanted to protect that investment from any potential riot. They also wanted those new homes to be lived in; if Protestants would not move into some of the homes near Cupar if there was no wall, then a wall was necessary.

Stokes told me that the Northern Ireland Office, which would have to clear the final plan for Cupar Street, favored a wall, but preferred the one that was already in place, decrepit and ugly though it was. As long as there were houses there, the NIO argued, even though they were derelict, there would be the recognition of the fact that people had once lived there and that they might do so again.

Lawson McDonald, a Department of the Environment official who worked in an office on the peace line, was slightly irritated by my interest. He warned against "getting too hung up over a bit of fence. . . . We're talking about a few hundred yards of street in Belfast. I think that when a decision is finally made about what to do there, it will not be made at a very high level." (About eighteen months later, the *Guardian* and the magazine *Scope* uncovered the fact that the British Army was making major decisions for the Department of the Environment, that the army was planning Belfast, altering its geography, and that decisions like the one that had to be made at Cupar Street were made not at low level, but at the highest level of authority.)

McDonald argued that if the shells went, the residents would demand a very tall structure—"a monster of a wall"—to replace the old one in order to thwart snipers and stone throwers. Since no one had asked the department to increase the height of the derelict buildings, McDonald figured he could prevent further fortification of the borderline by simply doing nothing at all. He suggested that a contractor might be called in to shore up the shells which were in danger of collapsing.

"One argument against putting up a permanent wall," McDonald said, "is that it is far easier to put them up than it is to take them down. By and large, it looks like we have built a psychological barrier, and it's the psychological barrier which is hard to take away."

━━━━━

Putting up psychological barriers is one thing, but maintaining them is quite another. It takes hard work to maintain the difference between yourself and your enemy when your enemy has the same color skin and worships the same God.

The most impressive maintenance work is done during "marching season," the summer months when the members of the Orange Order take to the streets. The Order's marching bands start practicing in late May and early June, and they don't hang up their costumes and banners until mid-August. The season peaks on the Twelfth of July, the day Protestants celebrate the victory of King William over the Catholic King James at the Battle of the Boyne in 1690.

As July approached in my first summer in the North, I heard Catholics speak of "the Twelfth" not as a day in the month but as a mean and bitter season. Those who worked alongside Protestants in shops and factories told me that their coworkers grew cold and distant as the holiday approached. I knew from my reading that the British government was wary, preferring to shelve all legislation having to do with Northern Ireland until after the season was over. History told me that times of great marches are times of great violence. Yet as the Twelfth approached, all I could feel was a sense of anticipation for a holiday.

In late June, the people of the Shankill began painting their curbs red, white, and blue (the colors of the British flag) and hanging plastic pennants of the same colors over side streets. They installed Union Jacks and Ulster flags over doorways and taped photographs of the queen to windows. Elsewhere, huge murals of King William of Orange on his white horse, were restored to blazing color. While I could understand Catholic resentment of those symbols, I did not initially understand their fear and anger. I was reminded of Fourth of July celebrations of my childhood, and I actually looked forward to the great parade. It was the 290th anniversary of the Battle of Boyne, and 80,000 men were scheduled to march at seventeen sites, with the biggest parade—an estimated 30,000 participants—scheduled for Belfast.

My neighbors share a superstition about the Twelfth, believing that it is always blessed by fine weather; since fine weather is rare in Belfast, it seems to the people of Clonard that God digs with the other foot that day. On my first Twelfth of July, however, it rained. Undaunted, I left west Belfast with great expectation.

I was disappointed, as I think anyone would be who has grown up with American spectacles. There were no clowns, no floats, no beauty queens, no celebrities waving from convertibles, no tubas, no trombones. The parade was largely made up of row after row of men wearing dark suits, orange sashes, and bowler hats. They ranged in age from teenagers to pensioners; a few of the former wore mirror sunglasses. The only females I saw were the Shankill Rangers Girls Band and four overweight, middle-aged women clad in dresses made of Union Jack material, carrying Union Jack umbrellas, prancing gaily but embarrassing to behold.

The monotony of lodge after lodge of men dressed all the same was relieved by the marching bands, whose uniforms were dashing, occasionally even rakish. The selection of musical instruments, however, was limited almost entirely to tin whistles and bass drums. Aside from the traditional loyalists songs like "The Sash My Father Wore," the bands of 1980 played "We Shall Not be Moved," "When the Saints Go Marching In," "The Halls of Montezuma," and "The Ballad of the Green Berets."

There was also some relief in the curious and magnificent banners, perhaps six feet high and five feet wide, held aloft by standard bearers from each Orange Lodge. The banners were embroidered with the name of the lodge, a motto, and two pictures (one front and one rear) of Protestant icons. The Sydenham Loyal Orange Lodge No. 1361, for example, carried a banner with King William on one side and the Harland and Wolf shipyard crane on the other. Another banner depicted a woman, afloat in a stormy sea, clinging to the True Cross; under the picture was the question, "If God be for us, who can be against us?" The Northcoate Temperance Lodge's banner carried the slogan, "Total Abstinence, the Source of England's Greatness." Christ in Gethsemane, David and Goliath, Lord Mountbatten, and Queen Victoria also appeared. Depictions of King William (known in the North as King Billy) were common, as were scenes of "The Relief of Derry" and the Mountjoy, one of the ships that broke the seige of Derry in 1689. (In April of that year, 30,000 Protestants, surrounded by the forces of King James, locked themselves inside Derry's walls. King Billy's ships, loaded with supplies and reinforcements, sailed to the city, but when they arrived in the River Foyle, they found their way blocked by a wooden boom. The Protestants starved—many ate their dogs and cats—but they would not surrender. At the end of July, the British ships finally tried to break the boom; they were successful, and so the loyalists' ordeal came to an end. In that siege was born the famous Protestant motto, "No Surrender," and also the suspicion that although England was an ally, she could not be counted on, and that Ulstermen would, from time to time, have to take matters into their own hands.)

The six-mile parade route ended in Edenderry Field on the outskirts of the city, where concession stands sold soup, soda pop, "No Surrender" cassette tapes, and Ian Paisley tea towels. I felt sorry for the marchers, as they were only half done; after speeches from their leaders, the Orangemen had to march all the way back to where they had come from.

The speeches were mean spirited. Imperial Grand Master Martin Smyth blamed the civil rights movement for twelve years of violence and called for "equality for all and special rights for none." By "equality for all," Smyth meant that he was opposed to any form of government in which Catholics and Protestants would share equally; such a government would be undemocratic and unequal in Protestant eyes because the Catholic minority would have a greater voice in government than their votes would dictate. The fact that Northern Ireland owes its very existence to an undemocratic decision (the majority of the people of Ireland did not want the nation split in two) holds no sway in this line of thought.

The Reverend Ian Paisley addressed his own group of Orangemen on a field at Ballycastle, and concerned himself with the threat of Catholicism. The Labour Party in Britain had recently attempted to amend the Act of Settlement, passed in 1701, which forbids anyone who is Catholic or married to a Catholic from becoming king or queen. Paisley and other Northern Unionists were enraged by the attempted amendment, assuming (incorrectly) that the proposal was triggered by rumors linking Prince Charles, then a bachelor, with the Catholic Princess Marie Astrid of Luxembourg. The Parliamentary debate had come to a head just three days before the Twelfth. In an unusual step designed to make certain that no fuel would be added to the Protestants' heated celebrations, Buckingham Palace issued a statement denying that any romance existed between Charles and Marie, adding that the Queen had no intention of asking Parliament to amend the 1701 legislation.

Paisley took his text from the Princess Marie threat. He spoke of the "darkness and drudgery of Romanism and paganism" which the unwary would be plunged into, and he warned that the queen's advisors were "using every Jesuitical trick to subvert and overthrow the Protestant throne."

"We will never be loyal to a Papist monarch," Paisley said. "Let us spell it out loud and clear. If the monarch ever becomes a Romanist, my MP's Oath of Allegiance immediately falls." Paisley is the member of Parliament representing North Antrim and consistently draws more votes than any other politician in the North. His popularity in the Protestant community results from the perception that Britain wants to abandon Ulster, and that Paisley, extreme though he is, is their final champion, their last bulwark. The Ulster Protestant sees his world in collapse: the ship-yard is doomed; the queen has met the pope; scores of good Protestant men are in jail, serving time for their loyalty to Britain; polls on the main-land indicate that a majority of the British would like to tow Ulster into the middle of the ocean and sink it. In the midst of all this uncertainty, Paisley stands firm for the old values. He has all the answers and deliv-ers them with the confidence of a man who knows God personally, who had lunch with Him last week.

That night, as is the custom, the BBC broadcast a tape of the parade, covering it as a sort of quaint folk festival. At that point it was very clear to me that the Twelfth was a festival for some folks and not for others; police had installed canvas screens, twenty feet high, around two Catho-lic districts that day in order to shield the residents from the marchers and the marchers from the residents. The Twelfth is also a celebration full of contradiction and inconsistency. The holiday is held on July 12, though the battle it commemorates took place on July 1. Protestants use the occasion to celebrate the subjugation of Catholics, but at the actual Battle of the Boyne, the pope was allied with Protestant William, not with Catholic James. The Orangeman's uniform calls for a derby, but the hat has no political significance whatsoever. It was invested with its mythical importance in 1911, when Protestants threatened violence if Britain instituted "home rule" (i.e., rule from Dublin), and the men who took to the streets wore bowlers; they wore them not as any sign of pro-test, but to keep their heads warm, and, as they were the fashion of the day, Catholics were wearing them as well.

The Reverend Paisley epitomizes the Twelfth; both the holiday and the minister serve the same end—that of keeping the two camps apart—and to understand the holiday, one really needs to know something of the man. A large, bellowing preacher with a huge head and white hair, he is durable, complex, inconsistent, malevolent, kind, stern, and amusing. When I first came to Belfast, I could not understand why he was still alive, given his blatantly bigoted remarks, and I heard two theories. The first, advanced by an American diplomat, was that Paisley was the safest man in Ireland, as his murder would precipitate incredible revenge and the Provisionals would not be able to protect their people. The second theory was put to me by a British reporter: "When I hear some of the things he says," she told me, "even I want to join the IRA."

Ian Paisley was born in 1926, the son of a Baptist minister, and was preaching in a mission near the Harland and Wolf shipyard when he was

only nineteen years old. At age twenty-five, he founded the Free Presbyterians, a sect that now has more than forty churches in Ireland, Canada, and the United States.

His educational credentials are dubious. He has a bachelor's degree,
received by correspondence course, from a theological seminary in
Rockford, Illinois; an M.A., received through the mails after a six-week
course, from a seminary in Colorado; and an honorary doctorate of di-
vinity from Bob Jones University of Greenville, South Carolina, a school
which achieved some notoriety in 1982 when the Reagan administration
announced it would extend tax benefits to the school which are normally
denied institutions that practice racial discrimination.

Paisley's dubious credentials, however, should not be taken as an indication of his intelligence. He is a nimble-minded man with a keen grasp
of scripture, a formidable opponent in a debate, a master politician, and a
hard-working man who understands the needs of the poor. Paisley, who
won his seat in the House of Commons in 1971, is also one of three elected
representatives from Northern Ireland in the European Parliament. He
heads his own branch of the Orange Order, his own political party (the
Democratic Unionist Party), and his own army (formed in 1982, pledged
to defend Ulster from its enemies, and known as the Third Force, Paisley once claimed it had 50,000 members).

Like the Twelfth, Paisley is full of inconsistencies. He once said he
"would welcome a referendum in England, Scotland, and Wales. If we are
in the United Kingdom without the wishes of the United Kingdom, then
we ought not to be there." Yet when a London *Sunday Times* poll showed
that a majority of the people on the mainland would vote the North out of
the UK if they had the chance (by a margin of almost 2 to 1), the Reverend paid the poll no heed.

Paisley claims he hates Catholicism but not Catholics, and he does indeed go out of his way to help a Catholic constituent who comes to him.
(It is not rare in Belfast for a Protestant to seek out a Catholic politician
or for a Catholic to go to a Protestant, as both sides believe that politicians of the other sort will occasionally work harder for them in an
effort to score points against the opposition and to prove that they are
not bigots.) Paisley's distinction between Catholicism and Catholics, however, is not well understood by some of the people he inflames. He points
to the pope as the enemy (referring to him as "the Scarlet Whore," "the
anti-Christ," and "the slanderous bachelor who lives on the banks of the

Tiber"); he says the Catholic Church supports the IRA; and he calls for Britain to invade the Republic of Ireland to root out terrorists there. Then when some Protestant takes up arms and shoots a Catholic, Paisley washes his hands of him.

Paisley is a man who condemns murder but calls for war, a law-and-order politician who has served time for provoking riots, a clergyman with an army. He stands in favor of the right to free speech, but he urges the police to arrest peaceful demonstrators with Republican views. Paisley preaches liberty, but when his party is in power, as they are in Ballymena, they are notoriously intolerant.

There is also a benign view of Paisley, however. In 1980, some officials in the Northern Ireland Office toyed with the idea of abandoning direct rule from London and creating a new government for the six counties with Paisley as its head. The idea, wrote two *Irish Times* reporters at the end of that year, was that "Paisley's intolerance and his rabble-rousing are functions of his insecurity and of the insecurity of the people he represents. Change the context, the argument goes, and you might well find yourself dealing with a practical, sensible, responsible politician."

The insecurity of the Ulster Protestant came to mind as I watched my fourth Twelfth of July parade in 1984. Loyal Orange Lodge No. 1018 marched past with a banner featuring Oliver Cromwell and the motto "Trust in God and Keep Your Powder Dry." At Edenderry Field, small boys ran around in Union Jack caps and "Proud to be a Prod" tee shirts. A procession of Orange Order officials at the speakers platform denounced the pope, the Dublin government, Tip O'Neill, and the Kennedys (John Kennedy was denounced, not only as a Catholic, but also as a womanizer). It occurred to me that the Orangemen assembled were proclaiming their Britishness in terms no one on the British mainland considered a twentieth-century sentiment, in outfits no one else in Britain would consider wearing, all the while claiming a history that hadn't happened. (If a resurrected King Billy had led the parade that day, he might have told the speakers to lighten up a bit, particularly about that bachelor on the banks of the Tiber.)

When I thought about it later, however, I realized that the costumes, banners, and speeches were not simply displays of Britishness meant to remind Britain of a tie that was 370 years old. The most important audience was not on the mainland but in the North. The festivities reminded Catholics that they were a defeated people and reassured Protestants that although they lived in the same sort of houses, ate the same food, and collected the same dole as Catholics, they were indeed a superior race.

In addition to being a statement of superiority and a turn toward Britain, the Twelfth is also a turn away from the Republic of Ireland. Ulster Protestants have very good reason to be angry with those who suggest that they should look on those south of the border as their brothers. When a Northern Protestant looks south, he sees a state that until recently refused to extradite IRA men, a state that, in the eyes of a hardline Orangeman, shielded the murderers of Ulster policemen and national guardsmen. The Northern Protestant also sees the Republic as a sectarian nation with laws dictated by Catholic beliefs. Divorce is illegal in the south, contraception is largely unavailable, and it is a criminal offense to entice a man or woman away from his or her spouse. The Irish government bans books it judges indecent or obscene; current titles on the Register of Prohibited Publications included *Looking for Mr. Goodbar, Portnoy's Complaint, A Clockwork Orange, The Ginger Man, The Painted Bird*, and *The Joy of Sex*. Also banned are books which advocate birth control or abortion, including such works as *What to Tell Your Children About Sex, Roman Catholic Methods of Birth Control, Sex and Disease, Everyday Sex Problems, Having a Baby: A Guide for Expectant Parents, Modern Russia, Planned Parenthood*, and *Is Birth Control a Sin?*

The 6 percent of the population of the south that is not Catholic has done well economically, but many Northern loyalists look beyond that wealth and are alarmed by the drastic decline in the Republic's Protestant population since independence. Protestants numbered 250,000 in 1921 in the twenty-six counties; fifty years later there were only 98,000. Some of the decline is attributable to the Catholic Church's insistence that in a mixed marriage, the children must be raised Catholic (an insistence that has softened in recent years). Paisley and his followers fear that their "Protestant way of life" (something they have some trouble defining) would vanish in a united Ireland. Protestants in the south experience no outright discrimination, but many feel a sense of irrelevance.

The Republic has done little to quell the fears of Northern Protestants. While most of the residents of the south claim they would like to see peace in the North, and most also say they would like to see a united Ireland, until 1983 the issue was not high on the list of the government's priorities. It was trotted out during every election, but went back on the shelf soon thereafter. There is great ambivalence in the south about the war. While the Provisionals claim a direct line of descent from the heroes of 1916, the state those heroes created denounces the IRA, jails its members regularly, and cooperates with the intelligence services of the IRA's professed enemies.

Northern Protestants also find themselves in a tricky position. They seem to object not to the interference of church with state in the south, but to the fact that it is not the Protestant church that is doing the interfering. In Northern towns and cities where Paisley's party is strong or where the Lord's Day Observance Society is active, Protestants have been more than happy to let their beliefs dictate the behavior of nonbelievers. There have been campaigns against Gaelic football pitches because they were in sight of a Protestant community; the mere sight of Catholics playing that game on a Sunday was said to be offensive to those who observed the sabbath more rigorously. As for censorship, Paisley and his crowd like the idea. They have demonstrated against the showing of certain movies and plays (among them Brendan Behan's "The Hostage," Monty Python's "The Life of Brian," and Bertolluci's "Last Tango in Paris"), have campaigned against the teaching of Darwinism, and have assembled a list of books they would like to see taken off the shelves in secondary schools (among the offensive works was *Of Mice and Men*, which earned such disfavor because the characters in it curse). Nor are Paisley and his followers great advocates of divorce, and on the issues of integrated schools, abortion, and liberalization of laws against homosexuality, Protestant and Catholic clergymen have stood firmly together in opposition.

Many observers have said that the Catholics and Protestants of Northern Ireland have far more in common with each other than they have with the British. What psychological barrier keeps them apart? What freezes them in their separate trenches, preventing the two from working out a destiny both could accept?

In Catholic districts, and lately in some loyalist areas as well, it is the British who are held to be at fault. At the end of World War II, Britain gave the Unionists a guarantee, saying that the North would remain a part of the United Kingdom as long as a majority of its citizens wanted to belong. That sounds like the British sense of fair play only if you forget that the British ignored the wishes of the majority in order to create the state.

That guarantee gives Ulster Unionists great license. They have no reason to negotiate with Catholics and no need to share power with them. The Unionists have what they want—membership in the United Kingdom—no matter how they behave.

Removing the guarantee, however, would not be enough to set Unionists on the straight and narrow. The troops would have to go also. If the British set a date by which the troops would be withdrawn, then Unionists and Republicans would be forced to work out their destiny in talks which would probably also include representatives from Britain and the Republic. What would emerge? Perhaps a state with ties to both nations. Perhaps a state within the Republic of Ireland. Perhaps an independent nation, though that seems least likely, as in an independent Ulster, Catholics would have no protection, and no reason to trust the government, which would probably resemble a resurrected Stormont.

The British argue that a troop withdrawal would be followed by a bloodbath. Furthermore, they say, it would be Catholic blood that would flow in the streets and gutters, as Protestants have the superior numbers and weaponry. Most Catholics, however, are willing to take the chance. "Certainly if the Protestant hard men do adopt a scorched earth policy," writes Tim Pat Coogan in his book *The IRA* (Fontana Books, 1980), "it's going to be one of the few occasions in history in which the haves turn guerrilla against the have-nots, for it is, after all, the Protestants who have the jobs and the houses which would be set at risk by warfare. This circumstance should make for pressure to compromise in the ultimate, however unwelcome this might be, rather than to destroy."

Coogan's reasoning makes great sense to me when I sit at my typewriter in Chicago. But when I am at Edenderry Field on the Twelfth, or at the Cupar Street peace line during a time of high tension, I fear for the day the troops pull out.

━━━━━

Two days after the Twelfth is the annual Sham Fight, the reenactment, in costume, of the Battle of the Boyne performed at the village of Scarva in County Down. As the outcome of the battle never changes, it is hard to imagine that the production would have much suspense, but it draws thousands of spectators anyway. The tradition goes back more than a century, and in 1980, the same two men from Scarva had played King William and King James for thirty-five years. "We've been doing it so long," King William told a reporter that year, "that we don't need any practice."

The Twelfth parade and the Sham Fight have the effect of maintaining the barriers between Catholic and Protestant, but they lack a vicious, killing spirit. The celebration that precedes them, however, the night of bonfires on the eve of the Twelfth, is quite different. The Eleventh night is a night of tangible hatred, a night when bitterness is passed on to children. It is one thing to build a wall, another to maintain it, but it is most damaging, I think, to keep building walls from generation to generation.

The ritual starts in May, when children in districts like the Shankill and Sandy Row begin to collect tires, cardboard, old furniture, mattresses, doors, scrap wood, and anything else they think will burn. The great heaps take on a mythical quality: what would be called a trash pile anywhere else is called an "unlit bonfire" in Belfast newspapers. Children collecting the wood take great pride in the size of their accumulations. Vigils are kept to prevent rivals from other Protestant neighborhoods from raiding the stack or setting it aflame.

I spent my first Eleventh night on the Shankill, and it started mildly enough. On Cambrai Street, a small fire was lit early in the evening, two hours before the night's major conflagrations would begin, and it burned innocently, with no one standing around it. I had the impression that it had been lit at such an early hour for the benefit of the five and six year olds who played nearby, who were too young to stay up until midnight for the major fires. Three women, their hair in curlers, stood on the sidewalk behind two tables full of sweets. A cheap stereo played records at high volume, but the songs were traditional Irish, songs without politics. There were children all over the street, and in other doorways, old women stood watching, eyeing the fire from a distance, chatting to each other.

A policeman and a policewoman patrolling on foot without riot gear or plastic bullet guns stopped and gratefully accepted a sweet and a soda pop. I was on a bicycle, and after I stopped to watch the activity, the women with the magnificent table offered me sweets and soda. I had a cookie. No one asked who I was or what I was doing. The women broke into little jigs every few minutes, and I had the feeling then the fire was as much fun for them as it was for the kids.

I stood around for a few more minutes, thanked the women, and then moved on. At the end of Keswick Street, in front of a small factory, I came on another modest tower of wood, perhaps twelve feet high. A friendly woman of forty-five, wearing red lipstick and a new pair of slacks, was keeping her eye on the kids who were climbing the woodpile and on a dog she called Sparky, a mongrel that looked as if he had received his name as a mean joke. When I stopped my bicycle, she warned me of the days to come. The nails in the woodpiles would survive the fire, she said, and would litter the pavement. "There'll be nothin' but punctures around here for weeks," she said.

She was in a grand mood, and she told me that the only problem with the Eleventh night was that it was so hard to get up the morning after to go see the parade. As we talked, children ran back and forth to the pile, adding bits and pieces. One boy, perhaps nine years old, climbed up the stack and tied a pair of stuffed red sweatpants to the top of the pile.

"What's that?" I asked.

"The pope," he said.

The figure had no head, arms, chest, or feet. The woman I'd been chatting with, perhaps sensing I was not amused, assured me that the stuffed figure didn't represent John Paul, that it actually stood for Charlie Haughey, then the prime minister of the Republic.

Burning effigies of the pope is not a custom born of the troubles. Effigies of the pope were burned in the United Kingdom back in the seventeenth century, and then not so casually—sometimes a cat was put inside so that its screams would heighten the dramatic effect. I saw another stuffed pontiff just a few blocks from the Keswick Street effigy, this one on a woodpile at the corner of Riga and Snugville streets. A kid I took to be about nine or ten was tying a babushka to the head of a full-bodied figure. "Hey mister," the kid called to me. "This is the pope." Why the pope would wear a babushka is anybody's guess. Beneath the pope was the duke of York, a wooden cutout figure, about five feet tall, in redcoat and leggings and wig. I had seen it just the week before advertising traditional music outside the Duke of York pub in the city center. I suspected that the duke's keepers didn't know he was soon to be immolated, but I was not moved to attempt a rescue.

Instead I went to a cafe on the Shankill to pass the time, waiting for the hour when the major fires would be lit. By the time I returned to Riga Street, both the pope and the duke had been consumed. Dozens of people stood around the fire. Orange songs blared from a record player up Riga, and a half dozen children, none taller than four feet, carried boards from a stockpile to the bonfire. It did not take much imagination to picture them dragging boards to a barricade by the time they were teenagers.

The flames were intense. A door stood upright in the middle of them, and I could see the ridges and the keyhole even as it burned. Finally it fell flat, charred with little black canals. A large spool burned alongside, and a chair was thrown in. Springs from a mattress that had already expired sat hot at the edge of the flames. A car turned into the street, and the beams of its headlights rippled in the waves of heat.

A drunken middle-aged man wearing a suit left his wife, who appeared to be sober and supporting him, and came straight at me. He grabbed my collar. "Take pictures of them," he commanded, pointing at a group of young men in Riga Street. "Take pictures of the teenagers. They will protect us. They do all the protecting around here." He let go of me and staggered back to his wife. A nineteen-year-old blonde in tight white jeans came up the street and stood close to the flames, drinking beer from a brown bottle. She watched for just a few sips, then threw the bottle down at the pavement, where it smashed loudly, and then she too staggered off.

At Ainsworth Avenue, the site of the biggest fire I had yet seen, a Benson and Hedges billboard caught fire. On Canmore Street, just across from Rich Stokes's redevelopment office, I watched a dozen parents and children cheer when two effigies caught fire. One was labelled "IRA," the other "BURN-adette Devlin."

Catholics also raise some enormous fires on their chosen holiday in August, and it might be argued that they too are passing hatred on from one generation to the next. Having observed both sides' fires for several years, however, I would argue that there is a distinct difference between the two. The Catholic fires are a show of defiance and solidarity and remembrance of abuses past, but I never saw anyone burn an effigy of the archbishop of Canterbury or Ian Paisley or even Mrs. Thatcher. The season's graffiti may be as crude and brutal as "Fuck the Queen," but I saw no equivalent to the "All Taigs are Targets" I saw in a Protestant district in East Belfast in 1981, or the "Kill All Taigs" I saw off the Ormeau Road in 1982 (Taig is a slang term for Catholic). No priest thumps his pulpit about the evils of Protestantism. No bishop calls Paisley a heretic or a whore. Catholics do curse loyalist politicians for their past misdeeds or for their put-downs of Catholicism, but I never heard anyone in west Belfast curse an Orangeman for his religious beliefs. It seems to me that every July, loyalists begin to think the future boils down to "squash

Catholics before they squash you." Catholics, on the other hand, perceive the conflict as political. Their graffiti is "Brits Out," not "Prods Out."

After the double effigy fire at Canmore Street, I decided I had seen enough, and I started for the peace line crossing. I was uneasy as I dismounted my bicycle at the Cupar Street gate, as I was open to attack at that moment from both sides—from Protestants who would have realized that someone from the other side had been in their midst, and from Catholics who might be alarmed to see an invader from the Shankill, particularly on this night. Once I got past the barrier and the carpet of broken glass, I got on my bike again and rode quickly down to the Springfield Road. Instead of turning toward home, I decided to visit one more fire, the conflagration at Woodvale Avenue, which proved to be the most vicious of them all.

Woodvale was once a mixed district. Today it is Protestant. Every year on the Eleventh night, the neighborhood's bonfire is lit at the intersection guaranteed to give the best view and the greatest offense to the Catholics who live on the other side of Springfield Road. The fire is always a big one. When I had stopped to size up the enormous woodpile a few days before, a passing policeman told me that in 1978, the flames could not be contained and that a house had caught fire and burned to the ground.

As I rode up to the fire, I passed a group of soldiers and two Saracens, parked in a dark empty lot next to the Co-op grocery, ready to spring from their position if Protestants invaded Catholic turf from Ainsworth Avenue or Mayo Street. A few hundred yards up the road, a dozen policemen in flak jackets, some with plastic bullet guns, stood on the Catholic side of the Springfield, opposite the Woodvale fire, keeping their distance and their eyes on the celebrants.

I rode over to the fire from the Catholic side of the road, and I stood on the side nearest the police. On the other side of the flames, firemen were hosing down the roofs of two abandoned houses which had been ignited by sparks that leapt up from the street. Even as they sprayed the roofs, teenagers were throwing more wood on the fire. The firemen made no move to turn their hoses on the cause of their troubles; if they had, they would have been overwhelmed by the mob. The fire service departed not long after I arrived, and just a few minutes later, sparks from the fire flew back to the sprayed houses, and one roof's underside spurted flame all over again.

I took out my camera and began taking pictures. A girl, about sixteen years old, turned and screamed.

"He's a Taig!" she shouted.

I lowered my camera immediately. Given that night, that place, and those passions, it was a killing accusation. I had no idea how the girl reached her conclusion, unless perhaps she assumed I was Catholic because I had come over from that side of the road. She was drunk, bold, and very loud. A small group turned away from the fire to examine me, and others turned when they saw the beginnings of a new commotion. My accuser stepped forward, clutching a can of beer.

"Are you a Taig?" she asked.

"I'm an American," I said. The answer had always worked in the past.

"American Catholic or American Protestant?"

"Just American."

"American what?" she demanded. "Catholic or Protestant?"

I was raised a Catholic, but by 1980 I hadn't practiced for many years. I disagreed with many of the Church's teachings. I had no great fondness for the pope. In short, I didn't think I qualified as Catholic. I was being offered an opportunity many believers would have envied, a chance to stand up for the faith in the face of persecution. I was not enthusiastic. I was scared by the crowd and by the mean spirit I had seen on the Shankill, embarrassed by my uncertainty, and angry that a mob of drunken arsonists, led by a teenage girl, threatened to get the best of me.

I have since decided that I should have claimed Catholicism and solidarity in one breath, admitting that I had been raised a Catholic, but hastily adding that I worked for a living just as the people stoking the fire did, that I ate the same food, that I lived in the same sort of house, that in fact the only difference between us was that I didn't go to a different church than the one that they didn't go to. Belfast Protestants and Catholics would do well to receive strong doses of reality to dispel their myths about each other, and my claims of practicing non-Catholicism would have been a small contribution.

Instead, I lied. I claimed I was a Jew. It was probably one of the few times in the recent history of Europe that someone has claimed to be a Jew in order to avoid religious persecution.

My accuser made a rhyme with the word Jew, but I didn't catch it. In a conciliatory gesture, she offered me a sip of her beer. I declined. Another girl, no more than twelve years old, who had been standing behind my interrogator, stepped up and offered me a large green soda bottle. "Vodka and Seven-Up?" she asked. I declined again, but politely.

I stayed where I was, watching the fire, taking no pictures, knowing that a hasty exit would arouse suspicion. The group that had gathered turned back to the flames but for a middle-aged man who came from the curb and stood beside me. He said nothing. I watched him out of the corner of my eye.

Finally, he pointed to the burning roof nearby, and shook his head, indicating he disapproved. It was just a small gesture, but I sensed that he wanted to say something more. I told him that I had heard from a policeman that another home had burned down at this site a few years earlier. He said that was true. People were leaving the neighborhood, he said, not because of religion, but because of vandalism. After the Catholics took flight, he told me, a low class of people moved in, and the teenagers attacked anyone, even an old woman who lived nearby.

A few minutes later he told me that he was the last Catholic in Woodvale. A brick had been thrown through his window and his car had been stolen and burned in 1973, but that other than that, he said, he had had no trouble. He had lived in the district for twenty-five years, and, particularly in the early years of the troubles, had thought about leaving, but he had no desire to live in the Catholic ghetto, as he was afraid his son would "get involved" (in Belfast jargon, someone who is "involved" is a member of some armed force). If he were to put his house on the market, he said, he could get only about two-thirds of its value, so he had no financial incentive to do anything but stay put. The Catholics who had moved out, he claimed, had done so mostly because the women of the family got scared. "The wife gets scared, what you gonna do? You got to move," he said. "Lucky my wife doesn't get scared. She's more afraid of a mouse than of the neighborhood."

Half of Belfast goes on vacation after the Twelfth; some factories close down for the whole fortnight. The Catholic told me he was leaving for Donegal in the morning. "Every year I come back," he said, "and I come up the Springfield Road here, and I look at this place, and I get sick. It looks so horrible. I think, 'This place is a curse.' But then you get back into it and after a couple of days or a week, it doesn't bother you."

After talking with that Catholic stranger, I was ashamed that I hadn't claimed the faith earlier, and the denial still haunts me. In the days that followed, I considered going back to church, not out of belief, but because in Belfast it seemed that you had to dig with one foot or the other. That seemed a twisted reason to take up Catholicism, however, and in the boring peace that overtakes the city in the two weeks after the Twelfth, the urge passed completely. The closest I got to a Catholic service was the sudden prospect of a funeral, when four weeks later, the young Provisional put a gun to my head to check my identification.

THE NEIGHBORHOOD IN FLAMES

THE HISTORY of Northern Ireland often seems to follow a script, with scenes repeated in each generation. The climax is some explosive act which diminishes all the ordinary violence and renews the troubles for the next generation. The leading man is often dead, or soon to be.

I was not long in Belfast before I heard stories of Tom Williams, one such leading man, born and raised in Clonard, who died almost forty years before my arrival. I heard his name first from a middle-aged woman in Bombay Street, then ran across a ballad about him in the IRA song-book, and then met an old woman, the mother of two IRA volunteers, who still had the memorial card printed after Williams's death stuck in her daily missal. I later pulled the newspapers from 1942, interviewed the dead hero's brother, and eventually came to understand something about the role of dead rebels, an understanding that would be useful in understanding the IRA hunger strike in 1981.

Tom Williams was raised in Bombay Street, and in 1942, at age nineteen, he was a lieutenant in C Company of the Belfast Brigade of the IRA. On Easter Sunday that year, the IRA command was scheduled to gather in the Lower Falls for its annual Easter commemoration, and Williams and five other volunteers were assigned the task of creating a diversion in Clonard to draw the attention of the police away from the day's real business. In the North, Easter is a combination of the Fourth of July and Memorial Day. It's a day when Catholics celebrate the 1916 Easter Rising, which eventually led to British withdrawal and freedom for the south; it is also a day that Catholics honor the men who have died in the struggle against Britain since the Rising.

In 1942, the Easter celebration was to be a relatively quiet and brief affair, and the planned distraction was simple enough. Williams and his comrades were to fire over a police patrol in the Kashmir Road, flee down an alley, drop their guns into a woman's handbag, and disperse into the warren of streets off the Kashmir. The police were expected to retreat to the Springfield Road RUC station and return with reinforcements, by which time Williams and his men would have vanished.

All went according to plan except that the police did not retreat. The conspirators ran into the entry behind Cawnpore Street (an alley is called an entry in the North); they dropped off their weapons and moved on at speed, but the two women who were supposed to take the guns away panicked. Instead of setting off in the opposite direction, they followed the gunmen down the alley.

The men found an entry door open at 53 Cawnpore Street, the home of Mary and Francis O'Brien, and they ran inside, past the terrified Mrs. O'Brien, who was eating her dinner in the kitchen. The gunmen and the women were about to run out the front when they heard policemen knocking at the rowhouse next door. Someone then spotted a policeman in the entry, and Tom Williams took his gun from the handbag and snuck into the scullery behind the kitchen.

The policeman in the entry was Patrick Murphy, a Catholic and a father of nine, and he entered the O'Brien's yard with his gun drawn. He and Williams stood a few feet from each other, and one of them opened fire. Williams staggered back into the kitchen and fell to the floor, wounded twice in the thigh and once in the left forearm. Constable Murphy, himself perhaps wounded at this point, walked into the kitchen, stood over Williams, aimed his gun, and pulled the trigger. The gun misfired.

One of Williams's comrades, seeing the policeman about to finish off his comrade, started shooting. One bullet went through the constable's heart, and he died instantly. The identity of the man who fired the fatal shot has never been established.

The dead constable's colleagues entered the house a few minutes later. In the first bedroom upstairs, they found Mr. O'Brien, who had been in bed since breakfast, and the two women conspirators. In the second bedroom, the police found the six IRA men, with Williams in bed and the others standing, unarmed, around him. They surrendered without firing another shot. Williams was taken to the hospital, and one of his comrades was given a good beating.

On Easter Tuesday, the six conspirators were charged with Murphy's murder. Williams, convinced that he was going to die, confessed from his hospital bed that he had killed the constable and that no one else had fired a shot.

Williams, however, did not die, and the six rebels went on trial at the end of July. The prosecution argued that the confession was a lie, that Constable Murphy had been hit by bullets from two different weapons, and that all six men should be held responsible. The jury agreed, and on July 31, the judge sentenced them all to death. The sentence made legal history in the United Kingdom, as it was the first time that six men were to be hung for the death of one.

Catholics organized a petition drive, asking for a reprieve for the condemned men, and 200,000 signatures were collected, including those of the cardinal, three bishops, 464 priests, 70 doctors, 50 lawyers, and 10 Protestant clergymen. A wide range of organizations expressed support, including the Association of Irish Protestants, the Turf Accountants Association, the Irish National League of the Blind, and the Irish Amateur Swimming Association. Telegrams were sent to Winston Churchill at 10 Downing Street. A representative of the Dublin Reprieve Committee visited the United States to ask President Franklin Roosevelt to intercede.

Three days before the execution, the Governor of Northern Ireland reprieved five of the six condemned men. He refused, however, to show mercy to Williams. Williams's supporters argued that Britain was going to hang the one man of the six whom everyone—including the Crown prosecutors—knew had not killed Murphy. The reprieve committees re doubled their efforts, sending telegrams to the Archbishop of Canterbury, the British Home Secretary, the King, and Churchill, pleading in public meetings that the nineteen-year-old from Bombay Street be spared.

At eight o'clock in the morning on September 2, 1942, Tom Williams received the last rites and was hanged on the gallows at Crumlin Road jail. At noon, he was buried in an unmarked grave in the prison grounds. The press was barred from the proceedings.

Catholics in Belfast took to the streets. Women who had been holding a vigil outside the jail knelt on the pavement and sang hymns. People hung black flags from telephone poles. Shopkeepers and publicans shuttered their businesses. A large group of mourners marched to the city center, where they engaged the police in minor combat. In Dublin, shops, offices, and factories closed so workers could attend eleven o'clock memorial services.

At dawn the next day, police threw a dragnet around west Belfast and, in raids lasting into the evening, ransacked homes and detained hundreds of Catholic men. The police and the IRA exchanged fire, both in Belfast and along the border. Four days after Williams was hanged, two policemen were shot dead.

Williams's co-conspirators were pardoned in the late 1940s. The authorities, however, have repeatedly refused to release the corpse of Tom Williams, and he remains today in an unmarked grave in the jailyard at Crumlin Road. The government knows well that in Ireland, dead men are dangerous, and cemeteries are not just repositories of the dead, but museums of political history, tourist attractions, and forums for outlaws.

When I first pinned down the details of the Williams story, I could see each step that led to the Clonard teenager's demise, but even with those facts, it was hard to understand how it could have occurred. It happened in the middle of World War II, when many Northern Irish Catholics were fighting voluntarily in the British armed forces. The Luftwaffe had already bombed Belfast, killing 949 people in three separate raids; in the crypts of Clonard monastery, Catholics and Protestants had huddled together for protection, and the Dublin fire department was cheered by

Northern Protestants when it came North to give aid. Yet a year later, a nineteen-year-old construction worker, making no speeches and dying all alone, rekindled all the old passions: Clonard Catholics wept for him, Shankill Protestants drew hangman's nooses on gable walls, and the British displayed a complete lack of understanding of the situation.

I was no longer mystified about the Williams legend after the 1981 hunger strike, an explosion that once again rekindled the troubles. Until Bobby Sands and his comrades started leaving prison in coffins, the conflict was defined in terms of 1968 and 1969; the hunger strike began the troubles again at year zero.

Before I relate the events of those months as I saw them at street level, it is necessary that I fill in some background about the creation and abolition of "special category" status for prisoners; the protest of imprisoned IRA men and the response of their keepers; the attempts of the Catholic clergy to mediate the dispute; and the aborted hunger strike of 1980.

The hunger strike of 1981 had its roots in a hunger strike in 1972. At the end of the 1972 fast, Secretary of State for Northern Ireland William Whitelaw decreed that men and women in the North who were sentenced for crimes related to the political upheaval would be entitled to "special category" status. In establishing special status, the state was merely recognizing that something extraordinary was happening on the streets, that many of the Northern Irish being sent to jail were not ordinary criminals.

The special category prisoners were allowed to wear their own clothes. They were allowed more visits and food parcels than other convicts, and they were not required to work, although everyone did. The men were housed in Nissen huts, not in cells, and each compound of huts was the domain of one paramilitary group; a member of the Provisional IRA, for example, would be housed only with his own comrades. The recreation and education in each compound was often determined by the prisoners.

In 1975, Secretary of State Merlyn Rees announced that special category status would be phased out, that anyone convicted of terrorist crime after March 1, 1976, would be treated as an ordinary criminal. Under the new rules, all prisoners in the Maze would wear prison garb and do the bidding of the warden, not the commander of their paramilitary group. Political convicts would not be housed in prisoner of war fashion in Long Kesh; they would instead be incarcerated in the Maze, a new prison on the same site made up of eight sets of cell blocks, each set built in the shape of the letter H. The prison came to be referred to as the H-blocks.

Rees's decision was part of a much larger strategy, a campaign of normalization, criminalization, and Ulsterization. The plan was to make the province look as normal as possible: men who committed arson and political assassination would no longer be POWs; they would be arsonists and murderers. Their leaders, who had once been flown to London at state expense for talks with the government, would now be "godfathers" not recognized by the state. As much as possible, the security of the province would be turned over to the police force, with the ultimate goal of getting the army off the streets entirely.

The change in prison regime had been recommended by a commission, chaired by Lord Gardiner, which had concluded that the state had lost control of the prison. The prisoners in Long Kesh maintained their quarters on the order of their elected leaders, not on the order of their keepers. They stood in military formation every morning, recognized a military chain of command, and punished their own. There were gun lectures, lessons in Irish history, and Gaelic language classes. Those might seem powerful arguments for eliminating the special category, but in fact the recidivism rate for those who served time in those compounds was far lower than the rate for those who were later denied that political status.

The government's abolition of special category was greeted by rioting and bus burning, primarily by Protestants. Both Republican and loyalist paramilitaries believed they were not ordinary criminals: the government had set up special courts for them, courts in which there were no juries, and normal rules of evidence did not apply. No one who went through the system believed it was ordinary, fair, or impartial, and so men convicted in those extraordinary courts felt they deserved extraordinary treatment in prison.

The first Republican denied special category status was a young man named Kieran Nugent. He took his sentence without protest, but when he arrived at his cell in the Maze, he refused to wear the prison uniform. The only alternative was the blanket on his bed. Within a year, several hundred other men had joined him "on the blanket," including a small group of loyalists. Nugent and his comrades had adopted an old tool of prison protest. At different points in Irish history going back 100 years, Republican prisoners had gone naked, worn newspaper, and covered themselves with blankets to claim recognition as political prisoners.

For this relatively minor gesture, the men were severely punished. They were not allowed to sit or lie on their beds during the day. Visits and exercise were prohibited unless the men would don the uniform. Letter writing privileges and parcels from their families were denied, as was access to radio and television, hobby materials, and occupational training. For a time, the Bible and various religious pamphlets were the protestors' only reading material. They were allowed out of their cells only to go to the toilet once a day (there was a chamber pot in each cell) and to go to Sunday Mass. They were subjected to regular body searches, including an anal passage search, initially done by hand, and later done by having the prisoner squat over a mirror. The government also decided that the protestors would forfeit all remission of sentence (in the North, prisoners who conform serve only 50 percent of their sentence; by taking away all remission, the government was in effect doubling the blanketmen's sentences).

A spiral of malevolence began. The prisoners adopted attitudes of complete resistance, refusing to cooperate with even simple requests of their jailers. They refused to move to other cells; those refusals were met by physical force from the prison staff. Denied educational facilities, the men shouted lectures in Irish history and Gaelic. Denied letter writing privileges, they smuggled notes out, some to be used as propaganda, many of them written on toilet paper and passed on the tongue to a visiting wife (some of the prisoners took visits, though it meant wearing the uniform for part of a day). Denied tobacco, they smuggled it in up their anal passage encased in hollow ballpoint pens.

"It's well up so nothing will show when the screws search us," one blanketman told *Irish Press* editor Tim Pat Coogan. "It's amazing what fits up there. One fellow brought three pencils that way and another hid a pen, a comb, and a lighter. You don't feel it unless the casing is too long, but you do bleed all the time and sometimes pieces of flesh come off."

The men refused to cooperate with the anal searches, which provoked their keepers, who retaliated by forcing the prisoner's legs apart. The men complained that they were hit in the testicles and that sometimes the same finger used to search their rectum was then used to search their mouth.

The prison guards were almost entirely Protestant, and included men who had served in the national guard, the army, and the police; from the start, they were not likely to hold much sympathy for their Catholic prisoners. As the conflict in the Maze escalated, the Provos added prison guards to their list of legitimate targets, and twenty officers were shot dead (a few were shot by loyalists). The life of a prison warder became increasingly difficult; he faced abuse on the job and possible assassination at home. The salary and benefits, however, were considerable, and were supplemented by overtime, the Northern Ireland "emergency allowance," and a daily bonus for those who worked in the blanketmen's blocks. Those wages attracted some men whose professionalism was open to question.

In 1978, the blanketmen extended their campaign of noncooperation by refusing to empty their chamberpots. Prison orderlies assigned to the job were allegedly slow to perform it, and so the pots overflowed. (Occasionally, a member of the prison staff may have purposely spilled a pot in a prisoner's cell or on his mattress.) The blanketmen responded by breaking the windows of their cells and throwing the contents of the pots outside, an action which also made their cells drafty and cold. (They claimed that guards assigned to cleaning duty outside picked the excrement up in enormous gloves and threw it back into the cells.) The prison authorities then installed metal grilles on the windows to prevent the men from emptying their pots outside. The men responded by tearing pieces of foam from their mattresses and using the foam to spread the excrement on the walls of their cells. Maggots appeared, and diarrhea became common.

The warders moved the prisoners to clean cells every two weeks and steam cleaned the fouled walls, but the process left the cells damp, and the moves to the clean cells became the usual combination of prisoners' resistance and warders' force, with prisoners sometimes dragged by the hair. The clean cells would then be fouled until the next move, which would be accompanied by more force and beatings, and so on. At the same time, the men were refusing to wash, shave, or have their hair cut, and so their campaign of resistance came to be known as the dirty protest.

By February 1980, 360 Republican prisoners were on the blanket. They festered. There was no movement on their demand for political status after three and a half years of protest. They had nothing to give meaning to their lives but their determined resistance, their hostility to their keepers, and, for some, their religion. The government was quick to point out that the blanketmen's hardships were self-imposed. The prisoners argued that they had no other choice, that their cause was just, and that they were protesting with the only tools at hand.

On four occasions, the men wanted to start a hunger strike, but IRA leaders outside the prison, who had only a tenuous hold on their incarcerated comrades, prevailed upon them not to. The prison protest became a millstone around the Provisionals' collective neck, draining their resources and distracting their attention from building a political organization in ghetto communities.

When I arrived in west Belfast in 1980, the periodic marches in support of the prisoners were miserably attended, but tension in the Maze was mounting daily. Cardinal Thomas O'Fiaich and Bishop Edward Daly of Derry were drawn in to negotiate with the government on behalf of the prisoners. The basis for their negotiations were five demands put forward by the men in the Maze, demands which later were referred to in shorthand as "political status." The men wanted to wear their own clothes; to have some say in what work they would do in the prison; to have the right of free association with other prisoners; to have one letter, one parcel, and one visit per week; and to have their lost remission restored.

The two clergymen and the government met over the course of five months in 1980 and seemed to be making some progress, but the discussions finally came to naught. Cardinal O'Fiaich and Bishop Daly left the final meeting in London with the feeling that the British had not been negotiating in good faith, that they did not understand the gravity of the situation, and that their policy was one of confrontation.

If indeed the British wanted a confrontation, they were not disappointed. On October 28, five days after the breakdown of negotiations, six IRA men and one member of the Irish National Liberation Army refused breakfast, and the first hunger strike began. The seven were hard men: four were doing time for murder, and charges against the other three included attempted murder, robbery, and kidnapping.

The hunger strike gathered support in the Catholic community in a way that the dirty protest did not. A coalition of groups, some vehemently opposed to the Provisionals' military campaign, mustered support for the prisoners' five demands. Bernadette Devlin came out of the wings and played a leading role as organizer and spokesperson. (She had been off stage for years, raising three children with her husband Michael McAliskey.) She spoke forcefully of the spectre of coffins coming out of the Maze and of the bloody forces that would then be unleashed. Attendance at prisoner support rallies soared to ten and fifteen thousand. The

participants were of all ages, of many neighborhoods, and almost all working class. Teenage girls wearing school uniforms marched beside grey-
haired grandmothers. Mothers of blanketmen wore blankets themselves.

The parade organizers went to considerable lengths to keep the
marches peaceful. The IRA brought its military campaign to a near stand-
still so as not to jeopardize the growing support for the prisoners. Inside
the jails, the Provos escalated the campaign: not long after the strike
started in the Maze, three women prisoners in Armagh also began refusing food, and in December, thirty more men in the Maze joined the
strike. The government's position was hard to grasp; officials seemed
anxious to settle the matter one day, unwilling to bend the next.

As time passed, Clonard and other ghetto districts grew more and
more tense. We were bombarded with bulletins almost daily about the
deterioration of the "Magnificent Seven." In the seventh week, teenagers in Derry rioted for three days. Ian Paisley began to threaten his
own violence, upset not only by the growing support for the men on the
fast but also by the talks that Margaret Thatcher was then having with
Charles Haughey, prime minister of the Republic—talks that Paisley saw
as the first step on the road to a united Ireland.

On the fifty-third day of the strike, prison doctors said that Sean
McKenna, the hunger striker with the slightest build, would probably die
within twenty-four hours, and the young Provisional was given the last
rites. That night, between 6:45 and 7:15, McKenna's comrades called off
the fast, much to the surprise of the IRA command outside the prison.

The end of the fast was shrouded in confusion, with both the government and the prisoners claiming victory. The prisoners thought there
were signs that the government would grant concessions if it was allowed
to save some face. Mrs. Thatcher, for example, had said there would be
no concessions to hunger strikers, but she had not said there would be no
concessions to the seven if they were no longer on the fast. Furthermore, Secretary of State Atkins, who had a far better record than his
predecessor in introducing reforms, seemed to concede that the government had been inflexible in the past. On the day McKenna received the
last rites, Atkins gave the prisoners two documents that set out in great

detail the privileges available to those who conformed. The documents were conciliatory; they promised, for example, that the prison work requirement would not be interpreted narrowly, that education would count as work.

It appears that the hunger strikers became certain that they, and they alone, held the key to McKenna's life. They decided to trust in the government's willingness to end the confrontation, and called off the fast. McKenna was fed, and survives today.

All of the North breathed a sigh of relief when the men came off the strike. Tension abated even in the prison, and there were demonstrations of good faith by both sides. The government allowed Bobby Sands, the Provos' commanding officer in the Maze, to meet with his junior officers to explain the ending of the strike. The mirror searches were suspended. Twenty test prisoners, men who had been on the dirty protest, took baths, shaved, and submitted willingly to haircuts. Seventy-six other blanketmen stopped fouling their cells.

In the month that followed, however, the prisoners began to doubt the government's good faith. According to a study published by the Peace People in mid-February 1981, the prison authorities refused to accept some articles of clothing brought by the prisoners' families; according to the documents provided to the hunger strikers, prisoners were to be allowed to wear their own clothes at certain times of day, and civilian-style clothes issued by the prison would be worn the rest of the time. "The chief disagreement appeared to be over—of all things—underwear," wrote Tom Foley, the Yale law student who was the author of the Peace People report. The prison authorities insisted that civilian underwear was not proper attire even during the time the men were allowed to wear their own clothes.

That action helped seal the prisoners' opinion that the government was as intransigent as ever. The government, meanwhile, was bothered by the test prisoners' attitudes toward prison work: the men were willing to labor in the laundry, the canteen, and the sections of the prison in which they resided, but they would not make their warders tea or do any other work that was for the sole benefit of their keepers. The government insisted that it would grant "the full range of privileges" only to prisoners who conformed to 100 percent of the rules.

On January 25, 1981, Bobby Sands said that "the spirit of cooperation" had broken down, and two days later, the test cases smashed their cell furniture after what they felt was an unreasonable delay in being allowed to wear their own clothes. On January 29, all ninety-six test cases went back on the dirty protest, and on February 5, the Republicans inside the Maze announced that a new hunger strike would start on March 1.

The Provos outside the prison were opposed to the new strike, and the H-block coalition also advised against it, but the men inside the jail, feeling that they had been cheated, plunged ahead. They decided to stagger the fast in order to prevent both a failure of nerve, which some prisoners felt had ended the first hunger strike, and a doublecross by the authorities. Control of the strike was placed in the hands of a nonfasting prisoner appointed by the IRA leadership outside the Maze. As the first strike had been timed to peak at Christmas, the second was timed to come to a head at Easter.

In the meantime, tension was building outside the prison. The Provisionals had resumed their military operations, and planted bombs in London and Belfast. On January 16, 1981, three members of the Ulster Defense Association tried to assassinate Bernadette Devlin McAliskey in her home in rural County Tyrone. The loyalists shot the former MP in the chest and both legs, and shot her husband in the head, stomach, and right arm. The two might have bled to death had an army patrol in the area not responded quickly after hearing the shots.

Bernadette McAliskey was the fifth Republican activist shot by loyalists in less than a year, and the only one to survive. The IRA retaliated on January 21, executing Sir Norman Stronge, 86, and his son James, 48, in their castle in south Armagh. The elder Stronge had been a leader of the Orange Order and a member of Stormont for thirty-one years. The younger Stronge had succeeded his father when he retired. The two qualified for execution primarily because they were vulnerable; they were not significant in the pantheon of hardline loyalist leadership, and they certainly had no connection to the assassinations of the Republican activists or the attempt on the McAliskeys.

On February 5, Ian Paisley unveiled a new paramilitary group called the Third Force. In the middle of the night, four journalists were blindfolded and taken to a remote field, where 500 men stood in military formation and, at Paisley's command, waved firearms certificates. Paisley went on to denounce the summit meetings between Mrs. Thatcher and Charles Haughey as "the most nefarious conspiracy that has ever been hatched against a free people." The clergyman said his men would "resist to the death. . . . We will stop at nothing."

And so on March 1, in a season of assassination and escalating unrest, the prisoner Bobby Sands refused breakfast, an event that would have enormous ramifications.

Few outside the prison had ever heard of the twenty-six-year-old from the Twinbrook housing project. Unlike Brendan Hughes, the leader of the first strike, Sands had had no brilliant military career. He had killed no one, had escaped from no prison, had taken part in no legendary Provo operation. He had been in jail for a third of his life, and had spent every Christmas since he was eighteen behind bars or barbed wire. The London *Sunday Times* dismissed him as "an obscure Republican with a long history of imprisonment, but little else to his name."

Bobby Sands had grown up in Rathcoole, a largely Protestant district in north Belfast, and was fifteen years old when the troubles broke out. As sectarian tension mounted in the years that followed, he was harassed by his former playmates, attacked with a knife, and finally forced at gunpoint to abandon the only job he ever had. In June 1972, with marching season underway, the police and the army made no effort to protect the Catholic minority in Rathcoole. Intimidation became commonplace. Shots were fired at the Sands's house and a garbage can was hurled through the front window. The family fled soon after.

They were among fifty Catholic families who left Rathcoole in a hurry that month and moved to the newly constructed Twinbrook estate. Some families fled on such short notice that they arrived with no furniture. Others moved into homes that had no electricity. Others had no plumbing. Sands's sister Bernadette later recalled that one family of ten set up house in a one-bedroom flat.

After a short time in the new neighborhood, eighteen-year-old Bobby Sands joined the IRA. He was involved only a few months before he was arrested, charged with possession of four handguns, and sentenced to five years in Long Kesh as a special category prisoner. He served three years, and while imprisoned studied Irish history, Gaelic, and revolutionary theory, as well as the guitar. After his release in April 1976, he returned to Twinbrook, where he helped organize a tenants' association, worked on a newsletter, and organized social nights in the church hall, during which he sometimes sang himself. He also re-enlisted in the

Provos. He was on the street for six months before he was arrested on charges connected with the bombing of a furniture store.

He was interrogated over the course of six days and later wrote that he had been denied sleep, that he was punched in the head and neck, and that he had been kicked in the testicles. In September 1977, he was found not guilty on the explosives charges, but guilty of possession of a gun. When arrested, he had been traveling in a car that contained a single handgun; the driver of the car and his three passengers were each sentenced to fourteen years for possession.

Sands was transferred to the Maze after his conviction, and he immediately joined the blanket protest. He wrote articles for the Provisionals' newspaper on sheets of toilet paper, using the pen name "Marcella" (the name of his favorite sister), telling of the monotony, the maggots, the cold, the mutual hatred between screws and Republicans, and the bitterness growing inside him, "a hatred so intensive it frightens me."

For the first seventeen days of his hunger strike, Sands kept a diary, and in it he comes across as a modest, self-effacing man, well aware that he is going to die, capable of joking about his impending demise (he notes that his contraband cigarettes are bad for his health), and yet near tears when he thinks of the birds he can hear from his cell (he had once dreamed of being an ornithologist). He wrote of being taunted by guards, who shoved food in his face, and by the governor of the Maze, who, upon seeing that Sands was reading a short book, commented that the text was a wise choice, because if Sands had chosen a longer work, he would not ever find out how it ended. Sands also wrote of his comrades' attempts to bolster his spirits: his fellow prisoners said the rosary in Gaelic twice a day, and on Sands's twenty-seventh birthday, nine days into the fast, they held a sing-song and called for a speech, which Sands gave, noting later that he doubted its worth. On the whole, however, the prisoner portrayed in the journal is lonely, cold, and often bored.

The diary is extraordinary not so much for what it says as for what it doesn't say. Through it all, Sands makes no mention of the five demands or political status, and more to the point, he does not spend a word on the election held in County Fermanagh that many thought would save his life. The election was unexpected and a fluke. It was called because Frank Maguire, a fifty-one-year old publican, died suddenly four days after the hunger strike began. Maguire, who had been active in the IRA in the 1950s, was the member of Parliament for County Fermanagh and the southern portion of County Tyrone.

Fermanagh–South Tyrone is a curious district, an underpopulated land of small farms, no great wealth and no great poverty, full of lakes and known for its fishing. The border there runs a very crooked line. In some sections of Fermanagh it is possible to travel two miles south, east, or west and be in another country—the Republic.

After the creation of the Northern Irish state, Fermanagh became a case study in discrimination against Catholics. Catholics were a majority in Fermanagh, but they were denied housing, representation in county councils, and employment. (In March 1969, for example, the Fermanagh council employed 338 Protestants and 32 Catholics.)

Yet it was not a bitter land. Catholics showed their spunk peacefully, using their majority in Parliamentary elections to vote in maverick MPs. The district consistently had the highest voter turnouts in the UK (almost 90 percent), but citizens' participation was more a pledge of allegiance (Catholics to the Republic, Protestants to the Union) than a belief that the outcome of the election would make a great difference in their lives.

Even after the troubles started, the district was largely tranquil. When I went to Northern Ireland in 1977, I met a tourist board spokesman who told me that the board had made considerable progress in selling German and Swiss anglers "the peace and quiet of County Fermanagh."

Two years later, however, that peace was undermined by an IRA campaign. The Provos had been killing members of the national guard and the police in the area since 1971, but the campaign escalated in 1979, and for one nine-month period, an area near the border in Fermanagh had a higher murder rate than anywhere else in Northern Ireland. And the killings had been gruesome. One man was shot in the head so many times that police at first thought his skull had been smashed by an automobile.

The assassins operated from inside the Republic. While Fermanagh Protestants believed that no one in the local Catholic community was pulling the trigger, many felt they were being set up for assassination by their Catholic neighbors, as the killers seemed to know their victim's habits. Almost every Protestant family had someone in the security forces, and as widows multiplied, Protestants girded for battle and talked of taking matters into their own hands. "If there's going to be a civil war," one resident said in late 1980, "it's going to start in Fermanagh."

When Frank Maguire died, several contenders in both communities prepared to run for the seat, but both sides realized the importance of not splitting their constituency's loyalties. The dust did not settle until the last minute, and it revealed a classic confrontation. Harry West, a Unionist of considerable renown, stood for the Protestants, and would run under the label "Official Unionist." Bobby Sands stood for the Catholics, and would be listed on the ballot as "H-Block/Armagh Political Prisoner."

The Sands candidacy was a great quirk. Convicted felons have historically not been eligible to run for office in the UK, but in 1967, when the Representation of the People Act was revised, the prohibition against felons was inexplicably omitted. Felons could thereafter stand in elections in which they were not allowed to vote.

Although Sands was the first Provisional IRA man to stand for election anywhere, his candidacy was not really a test of the IRA's popularity. The central theme of the campaign was that a vote for Sands was a vote to save his life; that surely Mrs. Thatcher could not refuse a democratically elected member of Parliament the right to wear his own clothes; that surely the election of a man to Parliament whose campaign proposals were merely the "five just demands" would secure those rights for the prisoners. Once those demands were secured, Sands intended to resign, and so the end result would be a new election, probably based on broader issues. (The five demands were not a burning issue in Fermanagh; the county had only nine men in the H-blocks.)

Sands was denied access to television, so he could win no support through broadcast interviews or speeches. Owen Carron, an unemployed schoolteacher, was named Sands's election agent, and he became a stand-in for the candidate. In the meantime, Harry West campaigned hard, and the national guard helped his effort by harassing Sands's workers.

The most significant event to occur during the campaign was the assassination of Mrs. Joanna Mathers, a twenty-nine-year-old mother, who was killed by a masked gunman while she was collecting census forms in a Catholic enclave in Derry. The Provisionals had been encouraging Catholics to boycott the census as a way of striking a blow against the government, but no one expected they would take the campaign that far, and it did not seem a typical IRA operation. The Provisionals denied responsibility for the act, claiming it had been carried out by loyalists to discredit Sands's candidacy, but the police issued a statement claiming that the gun used in the incident had been previously used in IRA punishment shootings.

The killing became a major issue in the election campaign, with many clergymen blaming the Provos. In the House of Commons, Don Concannon, Labour Party spokesman on the North, joined in the chorus, saying that a vote for Sands was a vote of approval for the perpetrators of the La Mon massacre, the Warrenpoint explosions, the murder of Lord Mountbatten, the killing of the census worker, "and all the other senseless murders that have taken place in Northern Ireland over the years."

For a Catholic, however, the alternative to Sands was unthinkable. Harry West, who was favored to win, stood for Unionism, the set of beliefs and mores that had oppressed Catholics for generations. Worse than the historical record, however, was the fact that West did not recognize it. The grievances of the civil rights movement, he had said, were "nearly all imaginary." Asking Catholics to vote for West was asking them to vote for a party that would not share power with Catholics, for union with Britain, and for Mrs. Thatcher's stand on the hunger strike. The *Observer*, the London Sunday paper, advised Catholics not to vote at all.

On election day, 62,818 people—86.8 percent of the electorate—went to the polls. They elected Sands by a margin of 1,446 votes. Sands supporters were quick to point out that their man had received about 10,000 more votes than Mrs. Thatcher had drawn in her last election. (In the British electoral system, citizens vote only for their local member of Parliament; the leader of the party that wins the most seats becomes prime minister.)

Sands detractors were outraged. Loyalist politicians denounced the Catholics in Fermanagh as "30,000 potential accomplices" of murder and as people who would stand at the graveside of the census enumerator and give "three cheers for her murder." The *Times* of London called on the House of Commons to unseat Sands immediately and to change the rules to make sure his ilk could not be elected again. Some Labour MPs objected to the move to unseat the prisoner, as did John Hume, the leader of the Social Democratic and Labour Party, claiming the move was tantamount to telling Northern Catholics, "Send us someone more to our liking"; Hume said the government was trying to reverse the democratic choice of a public representative, telling 30,000 voters who had peacefully expressed their opposition that the government would not tolerate dissent. An *Irish Times* cartoon depicted the House of Commons with a sign outside saying "No Irish need apply."

The victor heard the results on the radio in his cell on the forty-first day of his fast. He was having trouble walking. His eyes hurt, and he was plagued by cold and headaches. There were reports that the MP's body had begun to smell as his vital organs were consumed, and he believed he had two weeks to live.

Four days later, on Tuesday of Holy Week, Humphrey Atkins, Secretary of State for the North, told the nation to expect Sands's death. On Holy Saturday, April 11, the young man from Twinbrook was given the last rites.

Easter dawned sunny and bright, and I went down to the Falls to photograph the IRA's parade. The crowds were thick and decked out in bright colors, and many wore badges that said, "We support the hunger strikers" or "Smash H-Block." People seemed both jovial and defiant, and the gathering felt more like a parade than a demonstration. Teenagers flirted, women walked baby buggies, men perched small boys on their shoulders.

IRA men wearing black ski jackets, black berets, dark sunglasses, and gloves assembled in a side street in Beechmount, and then, accompanied by the Clonard Martyrs marching band, began the half mile walk to Milltown cemetery. None of them seemed to mind as I wove in and out snapping pictures. The police were nowhere to be seen, and the only sign of the army was a helicopter overhead.

At the cemetery gates, two vendors sold ice cream cones. Inside, a few speakers came and went, and then a group of armed IRA men emerged from nowhere and fired a volley of shots into the air. The crowd cheered, and the men disappeared.

The Provos held a similar commemoration and parade in Derry that afternoon. After the ceremonies were over, a group of about fifty teenage spectators wound up on Infirmary Road and began stoning policemen and soldiers. The game took place on the usual spot, with the usual weapons and the usual abandon. The kids joked with each other, filled with the sweet anxiety that precedes a good chase.

As the pelting continued, two army Land Rovers came over the top of Rosemount Hill, above the action, behind the stone throwers. According to a BBC reporter on the scene, the jeeps were moving at 50 miles per hour and the drivers made no attempt to slow down. The vehicles smashed into the crowd. Jimmy Brown, an eighteen-year-old baker, was hurled into the air and landed near a lamppost, dead. Gary English, nineteen, an unemployed barman, heard or saw the jeeps and ran a few steps, but the soldiers drove right up his back. The driver stopped the jeep, threw it into reverse, and backed over the body.

In the hours that followed, Catholics screamed murder and demanded that the soldiers be prosecuted. On Monday, David Mitchell, a minister in the Northern Ireland Office, responded for the government. He asked citizens to remember that 250 people were killed on Northern Ireland's roads each year and that during riots the risks were much greater. The *Sunday Times* account on April 26 carried Mitchell's response with that of a police spokesman who said, "The incident will be treated as a road accident, until or unless the Director of Public Prosecutions says otherwise."

The Catholic community hardened fast after that, though some still thought the confrontation could be resolved before Sands died. The SDLP, the Catholic moderates, called for the government to grant concessions to the men on the fast, and Cardinal O'Fiaich suggested that the strike could be ended if the government simply made prison work and the wearing of the prison uniform optional. The Provisionals' military wing maintained a low profile so any negotiations that might take place would not be jeopardized, and issued an appeal to the youth of Belfast and Derry, asking them to refrain from rioting.

Thatcher and Atkins, however, would not be moved, and the kids rioted anyway. In Derry, thirty-one cars and buses were stolen and burned on Easter Monday and Tuesday, and acid bombs, made with chemicals stolen from local schools, were lobbed at the police.

On Easter Monday, three members of the Irish parliament were permitted to visit Sands. The government hoped that the emissaries from Dublin would talk him off his fast. Sands told them that the prisoners had offered a compromise back in December, when they had called off the first hunger strike and the dirty protest; it was now the government's turn, he said, to give a little. As the politicians rose to leave, Sands pointed out that he had not once mentioned the words "political status." They left believing that Sands was willing to call off the fast in exchange for modifications in the prison regime, that he was not holding out for political recognition.

After leaving the Maze, the three emissaries asked for a meeting with Mrs. Thatcher as soon as possible. "It is not my custom to meet MPs from a foreign country," she replied, "about a citizen of the UK." Referring to the Irish as foreigners seemed a strange view for someone who had referred to "the totality of these islands" (Britain and Ireland) after meeting Charles Haughey just a few months earlier.

At that point, Citybus cancelled service to west Belfast and the *Andersonstown News* advised readers to stock up on groceries. My neighbors began sewing black flags, and young men hung tricolors from telephone poles and plastered posters of Sands and the three men who had joined him on the fast on every block. A graffiti artist with gymnastic ability painted "Blessed are those who hunger for justice" high on a gable wall at the bottom of Bombay Street, and in other districts, elaborate murals began to appear, some depicting bearded hunger strikers in Christ-like images.

The Protestant community was also busy. On Thursday, April 23, leaders of five loyalist paramilitary groups set aside their sometimes murderous feuds and formed an Ulster Army Council to coordinate their activity. Andy Tyrie, the UDA commander, emerged as leader, and five days later, he assembled a large force on the Shankill side of the peace line, a stone's throw from Clonard. Press reports quoted UDA spokesmen claiming that they had mustered 2,500 men; that it was purely an exercise so that the men would know their posts if they were attacked; and that the UDA did not intend to attack anyone themselves. Few of my neighbors, however, bought that line, and a few days later, Tyrie offered no comment to a reporter when he was asked if members of the Ulster Army Council might be planning to assassinate prominent H-block activists.

At that point, the Protestant community was full of contradictions. "Let Bobby Sands Die," "Let Bobby Sands Rot in Hell," and "Don't be Vague, Starve a Taig," were written on walls in loyalist districts, and the Reverend Robert Bradford, Unionist MP from south Belfast, was demanding a "ring of steel" around the "republican ghettoes." Yet loyalist prisoners had endorsed the five demands and just five months earlier had briefly staged a hunger strike themselves when it appeared that the starving republicans would get what they wanted.

Similarly, while many Protestants were upset over the publicity Sands was beginning to gather (not one of the policemen murdered in all the years of the troubles had received such attention), there were still people even in the hard-line loyalist districts who expressed pity for Sands, believing that his death would achieve nothing or that he was afraid to come off the fast for fear of what the IRA would do to him if he did. Others expressed sympathy for Sands's parents.

On Sunday, April 26, eight days after the MP had received the last rites, 15,000 people marched in Belfast in support of his demands. The parade took two hours to reach the Busy Bee shopping center in Andersonstown. I went down to hear the speeches and saw teenagers lining the rooftops. Bernadette Devlin McAliskey, back on a Belfast platform for the first time since the assassination attempt two months earlier, said that if Sands died in the next few days, H-block campaigners could expect to be arrested en masse.

Her vision was only slightly inaccurate: the police did not wait for Sands to die, but began the arrests the next morning. By Wednesday, sixty activists were in jail, booked under Section 12 of the Prevention of Terrorism Act, which allowed the police to detain them for seven days without charging them with any crime. The arrests were illegal: the PTA requires that police must have reasonable suspicion that those arrested are engaged in terrorism. Those arrested were peaceful protestors.

By this time, my neighbors were hoarding food and local shops had run out of dried milk, bread, coffee, and tea. On Tuesday, I ran into a woman I'll call Mrs. Murphy, a most dangerous gossip, as she was on her way to the grocery store. She denied that she was going in for emergency provisions. Her parents had been put out of their house before she was born, she said, and she had been taught a lesson about worldly goods from an early age. "My father always told us," she said, "it's easier to move a bank book than a piano."

That night, a hastily formed defense committee held a meeting in our local bingo hall. Three priests were present, but they walked out when the Provisional IRA walked in. The Provos asked for the names of those present who had cars, saying they would be needed to transport food if lorries refused to come up the Falls to make deliveries or if loyalists threw up Reverend Bradford's ring of steel to blockade west Belfast. The

Provos also said that arrangements had been made in Andersonstown to take refugees from Clonard. Clonard was expected to be the front line, Andytown the rear.

"That's great," one woman said in response to the suggestion. "We're gonna leave here and let the hoods raid our houses?"

The Provos told the woman not to worry, that the hoods would be taken care of, but the remark was greeted with some skepticism. Two days later, the IRA circulated a leaflet in west Belfast that offered a "final warning" to the hoods: "The Republican movement will not tolerate any acts of vandalism or destruction against our people. Anyone caught hijacking essential services such as milk floats, bread vans, etc., stoning private cars, looting, or using the situation for personal gain will be dealt with most severely."

On Wednesday afternoon, the day after the meeting in the bingo hall, a bulletin came through Mrs. Barbour's mail slot announcing that the Clonard Welfare Committee, our local defense organization, was setting up headquarters at 10 Kashmir Road, a derelict building just around the corner. I decided I should introduce myself, as I wanted no replay of the gun-to-my-head incident of the previous August. I walked in on a meeting of about eight men, most in their late teens or early twenties, and it turned out that I needed to produce no credentials, as the August gunman was among them. The committee was sponsoring a first aid session in the bingo hall that night that I was interested in observing, and their leader said my attendance would cause no problem.

I was one of twenty people who showed up, seventeen of them women. The instructor, a paramedic from St. John's Ambulance Corps, opened the meeting with the announcement that he usually offered a four-month course, but, given the circumstances, he was going to cover the material in a single session. In the next three hours he touched on gunshot wounds, burns, compound fractures, punctured lungs, the loss of an eye, and injuries caused by plastic bullets. He told us that the bingo hall might become a field hospital, but he was skeptical that the Provos could provide the bandages and medicine necessary.

After the class had ended and most of the group had dispersed, the paramedic's supervisor arrived. He was disturbed and confused. He was mad because he had not been told of the meeting (it had been organized only that afternoon). He was upset because the Provisionals had accosted some workers at the Royal a few nights before, demanding medicine and bandages, and the senior ambulance man wanted nothing to do with supplies received in that manner. And finally, he was angry because he did not know what to do. He first said that the first aid training should have been started three weeks earlier, and then he muttered that it should probably not be done at all. "Listen, I know from experience," he said. "As soon as it all starts, these people aren't gonna stick around. They'll be away. I know it. That's what happened in 1969. It will happen that way again."

Wild stories made the rounds in the days that followed. A Clonard widow told me that Sands was already dead: she had heard it from a Protestant who had heard it from a prison warder. Another neighbor told me over tea that a corner grocer was letting his shelves go bare, refusing to add to his stock because he had heard that the IRA was going to take over local shops if food got short. Even Secretary of State Atkins got into the act, claiming that the Provos had plans to burn the Short Strand, a Catholic district, that they would afterward blame the fire on Protestants, and that householders had already been ordered to cooperate with the scheme. When asked for comment, the chairman of the local tenants association, a well-respected Quaker, pointed out that not only was no one moving out, but there were many people anxious to move in if any house went vacant.

By Friday, May 1, we were all sore from waiting, and still Sands hung on, three weeks after receiving the last rites. "I don't think the devil wants him," one Protestant woman told a *Sunday Times* reporter, "he's taking so long to die." By that point the world press had accumulated in Belfast in great number, and photographers and television crews were everywhere. The *Irish Times* reported that ABC and CBS had four crews each and that one of the networks estimated it was spending about $10,000 per day. The rioting, however, had almost ceased, as Easter vacation was over, the kids were back in school, and the Provos had issued their anti-riot proclamation, which may actually have had some effect. So while tension in west Belfast was as thick as I had ever seen it, the foreign camera crews were having a hard time, as tension without combat is hard to capture on film. One Canadian morning news program even described the city's mood as calm.

On Saturday, a barman came across a stash of gelignite in a storeroom in the Blackstaff, a pub sixty yards from Mrs. Barbour's front door. The gelignite was "weeping," an indication that it was in unstable condition. The army bomb squad was called in, and the police knocked on doors up and down the Springfield telling residents to evacuate. Mrs. Barbour scoffed at the cop who carried the warning. "I've got a house to clean and washing to do," she told him. "And besides, if it's the Blackstaff, it's been blown up twice before, and both times I was in the house and it didn't matter."

And so Mrs. Barbour and I did not evacuate, and she did indeed finish her washing. I did not sit easy, however. I was working in the sitting room for the six or seven hours that the bomb squad labored, and as the room faced the street, I was afraid that I might be hit by flying glass at any moment. I closed the blinds and pulled the curtains, but Mrs. Barbour came in a few minutes later and yanked the curtains back.

"Ach, John, you needn't worry about the glass," she said. "The blinds will stop that. That's the beauty of blinds."

The army set off a controlled explosion in the afternoon, and at several points during the night, the disposal experts signaled to the police and soldiers to take cover. I waited for another blast, but it never came.

———

So ended a week of mass arrests, mobilized Protestants, food hoarding, emergency medicine, and wild rumor. It had also been a week of dashed hopes. Father John Magee, an aide to Pope John Paul and a native of the North, had been dispatched from the Vatican to urge Sands to abandon the fast. Sands, however, would not be moved.

John Hume, leader of the moderate Catholic Social Democratic and Labour Party, had suggested that the government should send someone to talk to Sands, an idea stunning in its simplicity. No one in the government had bothered to talk to a man whose death might cause civil war. Mrs. Thatcher refused to dispatch an emissary lest he be seen as a negotiator; for the prime minister, there was nothing to negotiate. There was almost universal agreement, she said, that "criminals" and "men of violence" had no right to political status. She repeated that her stand had the backing of the European Commission on Human Rights, which had ruled the previous summer that it could find no basis in law for political status for the prisoners. Mrs. Thatcher seemed to have forgotten that the Commission had also criticized the government's "inflexible approach," an approach which, according to the Commission, seemed more concerned with punishing those who broke prison rules than with "exploring ways of resolving such a serious deadlock."

Mrs. Thatcher's man in Belfast gave her full support. "What the prisoners are asking for," Humphrey Atkins said, "is the right to control prisons. . . . The government will not yield to this emotive form of blackmail. . . . The five demands amount to political status. . . . The lives of the hunger strikers remain, as they have since they began their protest, in their own hands."

By the time Sands started his fast, the prison authorities had largely satisfied three of the prisoners' demands, acting, in the government's view, not in response to the pressure of the prisoners, but in response to the European Commissioners' belief that there was room for humanitarian reform. Two crunch issues remained: the demands that the men be allowed to wear their own clothes and that they be able to determine their own work, which would mean refusing to do certain kinds of prison labor.

The government had tried to resolve the prison uniform issue just before the 1980 hunger strike began, abandoning the old denim uniform in favor of "civilian-type" clothing (slacks, shirts, and sweaters) and allowing prisoners who conformed to the rules to wear their own clothes in evenings, on weekends, and during visits. For the protestors, the issue was not the style of the prison uniform, but its very existence, as it marked them as criminals, which they did not believe they were.

If the government had allowed the prisoners to wear their own clothes at all times, would that necessarily mean that they had granted them political status? Cardinal O'Fiaich pointed out that the women in Armagh prison had been wearing their own clothes for a decade and that no one claimed that they therefore had political status. Other moderates pointed to Spain and Scandinavia, where inmates wear their own clothes, and no one argued that they were therefore political prisoners.

Was the work issue unresolvable? It did not seem so. The Provos were willing to do prison work, they just weren't willing to clean their warder's quarters or do other jobs which to them seemed to support the prison or the state without making the lives of the inmates any easier, and they wanted some say in the way jobs were allocated. It seemed obvious that a cleaning service could be hired to do the disputed jobs, or that the tasks could be assigned to "ordinary criminals," perhaps with a bonus of extra remission of sentence or commissary privileges for taking them on. (Rewarding those who would do the work would in effect be punishing those who would not, a maneuver which would seem to fit well in the government's usual line of thinking.)

Would granting these demands give the Provos control of the prison? IRA men serving time in the Republic's Portloaise prison were already enjoying the five demands the Northerners were asking for and no one believed that the IRA controlled Portloaise. The Irish government had solved a similar crisis, also brought to the fore with a hunger strike, by winks and nods and flexibility. The British also argued that granting any kind of special status would be granting a license to kill, yet there was no evidence that the Republic's solution had encouraged terrorism.

Furthermore, if the British were to grant the privileges to all prisoners, the authorities could then well argue that only humanitarian reforms had been instituted, that no one had special privileges or status. The Provos might have claimed victory, but it would have been made to look like a very minor one if child molesters and common thieves were awarded the same status. Later in the hunger strike, the Republican prisoners made it clear that they had no objection to the extension of those reforms to everyone in the North's prisons. Whether they had that view when Sands was in his sixtieth day without food is unclear. No one from the government went in to ask.

Those who supported Mrs. Thatcher's stand argued that it would be wrong to talk with Sands or with the Provos' commanding officer in the Maze because that would amount to recognition of the Provisionals' command structure, and would amount to giving political recognition to terrorists. Yet the government had recognized the IRA's command just four months before when they had allowed Sands access to his junior officers to explain the settlement of the first hunger strike. And as for recognizing terrorists, Lord Carrington, Thatcher's Foreign Secretary, had only recently engineered the transition of Rhodesia into Zimbabwe through talks with Robert Mugabe and Joshua Nkomo, two men whom Mrs. Thatcher had denounced as terrorists in 1979.

Others who supported the government's position thought that negotiating with Sands and working out a settlement would result in a loyalist backlash. However, as the loyalist prisoners endorsed the five demands, it seemed possible that the backlash might have come only from the verbal terrorists, not from the gunmen.

There were also ways out of the crisis that would have spared the government's vanity. After Sands reminded the three Irish parliamentarians that he had not mentioned political status, Atkins or Thatcher might have seized the day, saying that for the first time it was clear that Sands only

wanted minor reforms, that the government was on the road to introducing those adjustments at the behest of the European Commission,
and that the Minister of Prisons would be happy to speed up the time-
table so that all "common criminals" could enjoy the new regime. The
government might have sent in John Hume, the moderate Catholic leader,
as negotiator, and then when concessions were granted, credit would
have gone to the moderates, not to the Provos.

Perhaps the greatest factor working against a settlement, however,
was Mrs. Thatcher's personality. In Britain she is known as the Iron
Lady, and she does not mind the nickname. She is ill disposed toward
Irish Republicans; in 1979, the INLA assassinated her right-hand man,
the war hero Airey Neave, who had escaped Colditz, served as a prosecutor at Nuremberg, and was the Conservative Party's spokesman on
Northern Ireland at the time of his death. While some observers had
viewed Sands's election to Parliament as a point in his favor, proof that a
large constituency wanted the prison reforms he was asking for, other
commentators believed Sands's election only served to get Mrs. Thatcher's back up, that the victory in Fermanagh–South Tyrone might prove
to be the kiss of death.

"The British are thought to be a people much given to the idea of
compromise and honest brokering," said an editorial in the *Irish Times*.
". . . But not a move on Sands; not a sign that Carrington or Whitelaw,
well known negotiators, have a thought beyond 'No Surrender.'. . . There
is a certain amount of old English hypocrisy in all this. . . . A BBC program recently reminded listeners how often British MPs have launched
themselves on foreign countries pleading for jailed politicians. There is a
sudden and strange lack of chivalry in that most famous of all clubs at
Westminster. . . . Will there not be one in the British establishment to
regret that, when so little effort was needed, none at all was made?"

That sentiment in Dublin, however, was a far cry from the prevailing
mood in London. On May 3, the sixty-fourth day of Sands's fast, the
Observer wrote that there was no doubt that the strike was for political
status, that the three members of the Irish parliament who had visited
Sands and had asked the world to note that the MP had said nothing
about political status were "willing dupes" claiming that "the British Government was letting Sands die over a quibble about clothing."

And so the sides were very clearly drawn. In England, Bobby Sands
was a terrorist, a gunman asking for political status. His fast was black-

mail, his death would be suicide. In west Belfast and Catholic communities throughout the North, Sands was the long-haired smiling lad in the campaign poster, a hero, the kid from Twinbrook elected to Parliament. To the people of Clonard, Ballymurphy, and Divis Flats, Sands was asking for simple prison reforms, and he was dying at Margaret Thatcher's hands.

So the two sides marched inexorably forward, each with a firm grip on its own reality. And the prisoner rotted away, relieved of boredom by his great pain.

On Monday, May 4, I turned on the radio as soon as I woke up, expecting to hear that Sands had died during the night. He was still alive after sixty-five days without food.

It was a bank holiday, and if I had given it any thought I could have predicted there would be riots, as the schools were closed. I was passing Divis Flats that morning and came upon a burning lorry surrounded by sixty boys stoking the fire with material from a nearby building site. Most wore stocking caps over their faces with eyeholes cut in the material, or scarves over their noses like bandits in the cowboy pictures. I met two of the girls from Crazy Joe's among the few spectators. They told me the riot had started at 6:30 that morning in response to a police and army raid. It was then almost noon.

Two camera crews and five photographers recorded the scene. The police could be seen off in the distance. A helicopter hovered overhead, and the soldiers on top of Divis Tower were probably also involved in the surveillance. No one, however, was doing anything to stop the activity, or to remove the barricades that now sealed off the flats. The army had confessed its strategy in one of the Sunday papers. "We plan to contain any violence in the Catholic areas," a senior officer said. "We do not seek a robust role of confrontation, so we will only intervene if violence overflows into the other community or threatens the commercial heart of Belfast or Londonderry."

The oldest rioter on the scene, his face hidden by a blue hat and a wool scarf, gave an interview to the two camera crews, who jostled each other for position, setting the flames and the flats in the background of the shot. The leader claimed that the action behind him was just a taste of what would happen if Sands died, trying to put a political veneer on what was really just a street game.

When the interview ended, the masked man came over to where I was standing with my two friends from Crazy Joe's. "Did you recognize me?" he asked, raising his hat slightly. I had to admit that I hadn't. The master of ceremonies was a man who had once been an activist in the campaign to demolish Divis Flats. While the driver of a passing truck made as if he would happily run over the kids who threatened to hijack his vehicle, I asked the mob's spokesman how a petrol bomb was made. "You take a bottle and fill it about three inches full of petrol," he said. "You put in a little soap powder or sugar to make it stick. Then the rag goes in, soaked in gasoline, and you light that." A companion of the former activist explained that it was best to hold the bottle from its base, not its neck, when you threw it. I asked why the lads never seemed to set their arms on fire, since they would have been handling gasoline just minutes before they lit the fuse. The young comrade explained that petrol dries very quickly and is really no problem.

My masked acquaintance lost interest in the conversation and left to join his mob. I said good-bye to my friends and moved off toward home. The riot had nothing to do with Sands, and I felt dirty watching it.

When I got back to Mrs. Barbour's, an Indian swami, swaddled in orange cloth, was walking up the Springfield Road, trailed by eight followers. I stopped one of them, a young man with a beard, and he gave me a flier that identified the orange man as Swami Vishnu Devananda. The swami was a Canadian citizen, the paper said, best known for dropping peace leaflets over the Suez Canal in 1971, the same year that he and Peter Sellers demonstrated for peace in Belfast. The bearded follower told me that the group planned to walk through both Catholic and Protestant neighborhoods that day, and he invited me to come to City Hall at 3:00, where the swami and his disciples were going to stand on their heads for an hour for peace.

Clonard was aswarm with strange faces. It was also disorganized. Other districts had made arrangements for medical supplies, food stores, and even communication systems, but Clonard, for all the talk of evacuation, field hospitals, and first aid, lagged far behind. There was no consensus in the district. Some thought Sands's death would bring holocaust. Others thought it would all blow over in a day or two. Some alternated between those two views and prayed that even at this late date, something would happen and Sands would not die.

Emmanuel Davey, the father of five children, an ex-internee, and one of the leaders of the Clonard defense committee, blamed the clergy for the district's lack of preparedness. "In other areas, people have clubs, and the clubs lend their rooms for meetings and storage," he told me on May 3. "In this area we don't have anything that doesn't belong to the Catholic Church. We have to convince them that we are not connected to the Provos or any other organization, and it's like getting into the confession box. I mean it. I felt like I was in Castlereagh. They accuse us, they say we're scaremongering, we're raising the temperature. But any time they need anything, they come over and ask, and they don't have to ask a second time. They just say, 'We need you,' and I go. Yet when you go to them, that's the way you're treated."

Many Republicans were critical of the clergy at that point. The *Andersonstown News* had reported that Belfast's bishop did not want Sands to be given a public funeral mass. Cardinal Basil Hume, the Catholic archbishop of Westminster, had condemned the hunger strike as "a form of violence" and stated that in his view, the MP's death would be suicide. Hume's statement was not supported by many in the Irish hierarchy, and in west Belfast, it was dismissed as English thought, not Irish. The *Andersonstown News* answered Hume's "form of violence" charge, saying that Northern Catholics knew quite a bit about forms of violence— "illegal and undemocratic partition; disenfranchisement; discrimination in every field; being suspect before the law because of religion; being the subject of continual legal violence by both police and judiciary; being the subject of loyalist assassination and pogroms with the connivance of the police; internment . . . ." The paper noted that Cardinal Hume had never raised his voice about those forms of violence.

The evening news carried footage of the swami, standing on his head. I went to bed at about 1:45, only to be roused twenty minutes later by the clatter of bin lids and whistles, coming from somewhere near Bombay Street. I assumed that the government had turned to some form of internment and mass arrests had begun. I ran out of the house and up the Kashmir. Just past Meeghan's pub, I asked a man standing in a doorway what had happened. He thought that Sands might be dead. He was right.

At the corner of Clonard Gardens and the Kashmir Road, a few yards from the laundromat, twenty women had gathered. Some banged lids on the pavement, others blew whistles. A sixty-year-old man held an African drum under his arm, and he thumped it with a large spoon. Over the clatter, the drumbeats, and the shrieks of the whistles, a friend told me that she had heard the news on Irish radio at 2:00 A.M. Sands had died at 1:17.

I had expected that as soon as Sands died, Clonard and other key districts would be flooded with soldiers. I was wrong; there was not a soldier in sight. People flowed into the street. One man who stood near me wore pajamas, slippers, a hat, and his winter jacket. Several women wore raincoats over nightgowns, and for a while, those wearing slippers outnumbered those wearing shoes. No one seemed to know what to do. There was talk of saying the rosary, but no one took charge.

Gradually the crowd began to drift, some home to think or to listen to the police radio, some to dress for battle, some to a neighbor's house to talk, some to the Falls Road. When I got to the Falls, a barricade was already in place, and quite a good one, with sections of corrugated iron and scrap lumber piled high. Fifteen yards from the blockade, at the intersection of Clonard Street, about fifty women began saying the rosary. A few knelt on the pavement, but most stood, grouped in a semicircle. Cameramen from American and British networks, having sped over from the Europa hotel a mile and a civilization away, used the rosary formation so smoothly that it appeared they had arranged it. The women's intent had been to hold a religious service, but the cameramen made it a show and seemed to alter the mood of the participants. When the rosary was finished, the women sang a hymn, and they sang very well. For a minute it sounded like Sunday mass. With the last note, however, they let forth a great burst of whistles and lid banging, a harsh and disturbing transition.

In the meantime, a car had been added to the barricade, and for the first time in the eight or ten riots I had witnessed in my time in the city, old men participated—not to a great extent but, as they usually stand back and watch, it seemed notable when they added their strength to help tip the car over. A man of twenty-five, too well-dressed for a riot, pounded a nail into the car's underside, and a steady trickle of petrol flowed out. Milk and soda pop bottles began to arrive from all directions, not in great numbers, not all at once, but steadily, keeping pace with the trickle of gasoline. The actors who gathered at the barricade were entirely different from the cast I had seen at the Divis riot the day before. At Divis, it was child's play. This time it was men of eighteen to thirty, a squad of serious amateurs with no battle plan and no chain of command, but spirited, experienced, and strong.

A stolen van was in the process of being pushed toward the Springfield intersection to form an advanced position when the security forces arrived. A Saracen, one of the army's fourteen-ton personnel carriers, charged the stolen vehicle, rammed it back fifteen yards, retreated, and then charged again, pushing the van back further toward the barricade. The home team began to hurl petrol bombs, bricks, and pieces of pavement. The police began firing plastic bullets from the gun mounts on the side of their Land Rovers. The cameramen scrambled for cover, ending up in a side street between the rioters and the police from which they could film both sides and not be a target of either.

I stood on the other side of the Falls in Dunville Street with residents who watched from their front doors. We could see the lads in balaclava helmets sneak into Dunville Park, intent on flanking the troops and bombarding them from behind the park's iron grille fence. When they made it to their position, however, they found they had no matches, and they cursed each other loudly. A grey-haired woman beside me began moving toward the park to donate a cigarette lighter, but her son pulled her back, saying matches were already on the way.

The matches arrived, the wicks were lit, the bombs were thrown. The sugar and soap powder additives made the flames stick to the roofs of the Saracens, and the spectacle made for great camera footage, but in fact the flames caused little harm. Throwing a molotov at an armored vehicle is a bit like trying to set a cast iron frying pan on fire. The gasoline would ignite, and the flames would burn for a few seconds, and then the Saracen would proceed as before, unfazed by the scalding.

The battle raged for about forty minutes, and then the security forces pulled back, out of range of the petrol bombers, and a lull ensued. I crossed the Falls behind the barricade and made my way toward home via Clonard's back streets, only to find my path blocked by a barricade on the Kashmir. A car blazed away at the mouth of the street, reinforced by metal beer barrels and mounds of scrap. The barricade's architects had already set fire to Campbell Brothers, the glass company next to Mackie's, and seemed much more in command than their comrades on the Falls.

When I arrived, I could see no sign of the opposition, so I decided to risk the ten-yard run from the barricade to Mrs. Barbour's front door.

I made it to the front gate just as a Land Rover pulled up at the intersection. As I put my key in the lock, the police started shooting. I ducked,
then realized they were not aiming in my direction and pushed the door
open and slammed it closed behind me.

For the next two hours, Mrs. Barbour and I sat behind the front room
windows, the lights out, the blinds partially drawn, watching the riot outside. Petrol bombs flew in good number, and a good number of plastic
bullets replied. The security forces made no attempt to take any prisoners. I recognized a few neighbors at the barricade, among them two
members of the defense committee. I wondered about the committee's
strategy. With Sands dying so slowly, surely they could have prepared a
proper barricade if they had intended to seal the district. The haphaz-
ardness of the action indicated it was fighting from the heart, not the
head, that it was not by any means an attempt to set up a no-go area or a
territory controlled by guerrillas.

At 6:00 A.M., the night was gone, and the battle ended. A Saracen
smashed the barricade. Plastic bullets scattered the lads. Foot soldiers
appeared and marched at doublespeed through the glass and debris,
down the Kashmir, then back up, then down again. People huddled in
their homes. A few women stood defiantly in their doorways (a woman's
abuse and defiance is generally tolerated by the troops). One soldier
sang as he trotted; in response to one red-haired mother's obscenities he
yelled, "Give us a kiss."

The army had clearly won the day. The natives had risen, but not
for long.

No one needed to declare a memorial day. Children in west Belfast stayed
home; one school with an enrollment of 400 reported that 14 had shown
up. Stores and offices were open downtown, but in many the clerks outnumbered customers. The city exhaled and assessed the damage of the
night before.

A milkman and his fourteen-year-old son lay dying in a hospital; their
milk truck had crashed after it was stoned by rioters. The loyalist paramilitaries had kept to quarters. The city center had not been disturbed.
The middle and upper class had slept soundly. The Provos had taken no

lives; many believed they would wait until after the funeral to respond militarily. In preparation, every police station in the United Kingdom was put on the alert, and the army's Spearhead battalion, 600 men on permanent standby on the mainland, was brought to the North.

By late afternoon there was a barricade on the Kashmir, manned by children. I recognized a fourteen-year-old from the first aid meeting in the bingo hall. He had been pleased with the effort of the night before ("not bad for a wee little district," he said), and he told me that he and his friends had another car to burn that evening, donated by someone from around the corner who thought he could do well in collecting compensation for its loss. "If your engine is shot," the boy said, "you might as well."

That night was rainy and cold and most of the veterans stayed inside. The army waited until 11:30, when most of the rioters had gone home, and then smashed through the Kashmir blockade. A policeman was shot dead by the INLA in another district, and an INLA man took his own life by mishandling a land mine. Other than that, military activity in the days after Sands's death was light.

Elsewhere there were demonstrations. Hundreds and thousands marched in Paris, Brussels, Athens, the Hague, New York, and Milan. A balloon full of tomato sauce was hurled at the queen, who was visiting Oslo. A British tire company in Toulouse and the British Chamber of Commerce in Milan were bombed. A street in Teheran was named after the dead MP; the street ran alongside the British Embassy.

Editorial writers around the world had widely different reactions. The *New York Times* argued that Mrs. Thatcher's stance had "a core of reason," while *Le Monde* condemned her in a front page editorial. Zurich's *Tagensanzeiger* said Britain had had no choice but to let Sands die, while the *Hindustan Times* in India believed Mrs. Thatcher had "allowed a member of the House of Commons, a colleague in fact, to die of starvation. Never had such an incident occurred in a civilized country."

"How much longer," the *Popular Daily* in Portugal asked, "can Britain retain the inglorious distinction of being the only country in free Europe to hold part of the Continent as a colony?" In South Africa, the black press saw Sands as a martyr and hero, the English papers supported Mrs. Thatcher, and *Die Vaderland*, the Afrikaner afternoon daily, snorted at Sands and Mahatma Gandhi in the same breath. Radio Moscow called the dead MP "a civil rights fighter," while in Poland, Lech Walesa said he grieved for Sands, "a great man who sacrificed his life for his struggle."

Papers in Britain almost without exception supported their government, even the liberal *Guardian*, which said that the prime minister's policy had been correct, her posture disdainful, her remarks insulting. The *Times* said Sands's death had been suicide and that Britain bore no responsibility for it. The *Daily Telegraph* said the government should be admired for its steadfastness. The prime minister was quoted saying that Sands had been "a convicted criminal who chose to take his own life. It was a choice that his organization did not allow to any of their victims."

The funeral was on Thursday, May 7. In an attempt to distract media attention, Ian Paisley held a competing service at city hall for "the innocent victims of IRA terrorism," and about 3,000 people attended. He got some coverage, but nothing by comparison with the Sands ceremony, which was attended by film crews and reporters from all over Europe, from North America, and from Iran, Nigeria, and Japan. After seeing the scaffolding provided for television cameras at the cemetery, one BBC technician said that he hadn't seen the like since the death of Winston Churchill.

In Belfast, the bishop who had wanted no public ceremony did not have his way, and Sands's funeral mass, held at St. Luke's in Twinbrook, was the largest funeral the North had ever seen: 80 to 100 thousand people turned out to pay their respects to the twenty-seven-year-old guerrilla who had killed no one but himself. Hundreds stood in the rain for several hours along the route to Milltown cemetery, and every store, pub, and petrol station in west Belfast was shuttered.

The crowd outside the church was eight deep in some places, and people spoke in whispers when they spoke at all. I stood among them and was relieved of some film by one of the Republican stewards when I shot the IRA's color party on their way in; the steward thought the photo might reveal what house they had come out of. The masked Provisionals stood at attention on the sidewalk, and when the mass ended and the coffin came out, a Sinn Fein executive tacked on a tricolor and the traditional beret and black gloves. Sands's mother, father, sisters, and brother, all looking worn and noble, lined up behind the coffin, along with Sands's eight-year-old son. (As a teenager, before his career in jail began, Sands had married. His wife and child had moved to England after the marriage ended.) The family was followed by three members of the European Parliament (the Euro-MPs from Ireland, Italy, and Belgium), the Iranian ambassador to Sweden, and thousands of mourners from all over the North.

I moved on ahead of the color party. About a mile up the road, the police had sealed off the direct route to Milltown cemetery with a wall made of canvas. The twenty-foot-high structure was an attempt to shield the Protestant residents of the Suffolk housing estate from a sight that might offend them and to shield the mourners from any Protestant abuse. The detour that resulted, however, added at least half an hour to the procession.

I identified myself as a member of the press and was allowed to pass the barrier. Behind the canvas screens were hundreds of policemen, all wearing flak jackets, and a few soldiers. When I was about a quarter of a mile up the hill, I spotted the Reverend Robert Bradford standing on the lawn of the housing estate, watching the cortege pass beneath him. Bradford, the member of the House of Commons representing south Belfast and a practicing minister who had resigned from the Methodist church in 1974, was the man who had called for a ring of steel around the Republican ghetto a few weeks before, and I was surprised to see his interest in Sands's passing. He explained that he was present because the Suffolk estate was in his constituency; whenever his constituents faced a crisis, he said, he felt it was his duty to appear. I asked what he thought of the funeral.

"I'd like to see many more of them," he said. "This is natural justice— the death of Sands—hopefully to be followed by many more occasions in which murderers will lose their lives by their own method or any other."

The Reverend was dismayed by the huge turnout, and said he was coming to doubt whether there was such a thing as a moderate Roman Catholic. As for the continuing crisis in the Maze, he had a solution and was angry that Westminster had not taken him up on it. "Give them all political status," he said. "They are all political criminals, no doubt about that. And if they are prepared to be treated as political prisoners in the full sense of that word, they would be put to death after conviction." The minister explained that under the Treason Act, passed in 1351, last invoked in 1946, anyone attacking the queen or any representative of the queen can be executed.

"If you print that," he said, "you'll get some idiot writing back to you saying, 'But this is 1981, not 1351.' But the greatest laws of the land are the old ones, not the least of which is the Ten Commandments. Thou shalt not kill, for instance."

The Reverend and I and his bodyguard chatted for a few more minutes, and then I moved on. The cortege took three hours to reach the ceme-

tery, and the graveside mood was sad and sometimes angry and sometimes calm. Mrs. Sands cried. Owen Carron called for victory to the
Provisionals. Gerry Adams, the movement's primary spokesman in the
North, said that the IRA would respond in its own time; he asked
the crowd not to walk on the graves as they left the cemetery and not to
desecrate the day by getting into a confrontation with the security
forces. A helicopter, which had hung over St. Luke's throughout the service, hovered so low over the Republican plot that Adams was hard to
hear, but the crowd dispersed peacefully.

Night fell without a riot. The streets were empty. A blast bomb (nails,
gelignite, a tin can, and a fuse) went off near Mrs. Barbour's at about
eleven, and about midnight some of the locals pushed a car up against
Mackie's and then set it on fire, hoping the plant would burn as well.
Mrs. Barbour and I watched the flames from the sitting room for a little
while, wondering if the IRA planned to ambush the soldiers who would
come to deal with the incident. I had had little sleep all week, however,
and I went to bed while the flames were still intense.

It's surprising what you can accept as routine after so short a time.

The North—Catholic and Protestant—heaved a sigh of relief after the
guerrilla's funeral, as if putting him in the ground also buried the problem. The morning after brought the realization that Sands's death was
not the end, but the beginning, that the situation was as unsettled and
explosive as it had been before.

Joe McDonnell, serving the same fourteen years Sands had been
serving, having been captured in the same car and convicted of possession of the same gun, joined the fast to replace his comrade. The arrests
of the H-block activists continued; the committee claimed 180 had been
jailed in five days. Garbage pickup in the ghetto was cancelled; authorities believed the trucks would be hijacked. Bus companies also cancelled
service, and some children had to walk to school through Protestant districts; they were allowed to attend in plainclothes so they would not be
identifiable as Catholics.

After seven weeks without food, Francis Hughes, the second man on
the fast, was blind in one eye and deteriorating quickly. I wondered how
Thatcher would respond. Would she compromise now that the prisoners

had shown they were ready to go the distance? Or would she wait for the world press to go home, for the crisis to become accepted as a normal state of affairs, and then let the Provos and the INLA starve to their hearts' content? Did she think she had weathered the worst with the death of an MP? What would she do about the now vacant seat in Fermanagh–South Tyrone? How would she change the law so the IRA would not win again? Some politicians proposed that a candidate be required to bring his own election petitions to the board of elections, which would eliminate prisoner candidates. But how could you stop Sands's brother from running, or his mother or father or sisters?

I found the Provos also difficult to figure. The government had announced that the IRA had plans to take control of whole sections of Derry and Belfast and to assassinate public officials. For days, everyone waited for some great atrocity. There was instead just the usual—a nail bomb here, sniper fire there, a mortar bomb in Fermanagh. Ten soldiers were injured in the days after the funeral, an escalation of combat from its level during the Sands fast, but there was no grand gesture of vengeance. There were reports that the Provisional leadership, despite pressure from those within the organization who wanted to respond to Thatcher's disdain, had decided there was no need for great violence, that they were winning without it. They had gained far more from peaceful protest—standing in the election and fasting to death—than they could ever have hoped to gain from their military campaign.

Thatcher and Atkins seemed to have no understanding of both this type of combat and the Catholic community. Thatcher and Atkins thought they could turn Catholics with slogans ("a crime is a crime" and "murder is murder") and with claims that the Provos ordered Sands to die and planned to burn the Short Strand. Thatcher thought that she alone had the power to grant political status, but the prisoners had gone over her head, and the world press and foreign governments had overruled the prime minister. Television crews from Nigeria are not in the habit of covering the deaths of Irish gangsters.

The impression left on a generation of Catholic children was immense. The Provos replaced football stars as local heroes. In Dublin and Cork, kids turned up for school in black berets and dark glasses. In Belfast, adolescent girls did calisthenics to H-block chants when the physical education teacher turned her back. An educational welfare officer told me the kids he ran into could rattle off their heroes' statistics—how many days each had gone without food, how long a sentence each was serving, and what he was in for. They knew that Francis Hughes was once considered such a menace that the police had taken the unusual step of printing "Wanted" posters with his picture on them; that Ray McCreesh, the third man on the strike, was very religious and had read the lessons at Mass in the Maze even when he had been two weeks without food; that Patsy O'Hara, the first INLA man on the fast, had been shot in the foot by the army when he was twelve years old; and that Joe McDonnell, Sands's comrade, had a beautiful wife and two children whom he had not seen for almost four years, as he had refused to don the prison uniform even for visits.

The Provos had publicly asked for a peaceful period of mourning, but the teenagers were too wound up for that. They stole and burned and played carelessly. They hijacked and burned a firetruck and a Gas Board vehicle on its way to repair a leak. Firemen responded by imposing a ban on calls to Catholic districts, asking for a pledge of safe conduct in troubled areas. The Provos issued one. "We appeal to young people not to interfere with essential services," said Sinn Fein spokesman Richard McCauley, "and the Fire Service is an essential service."

But the fear and chaos I saw was confined to Catholic districts. An *Irish Times* columnist commented wryly that the rioting was at "an acceptable level." On Saturday afternoon, two days after Sands's funeral, the Lord Mayor staged his annual parade through the city center: fifty floats, eighteen bands, circus ponies, camels, and old King Cole dressed in silken breeches and an ermine robe. "Organizers said the turnout was bigger and better than ever for the show's silver anniversary," the *Belfast Telegraph* reported, "with business and industry forgetting the worries of the recession for the day and supporting the theme of 'our effort, our future.'" It was the recession they worried about, not the hunger strike.

Not more than a few hundred yards from the city center, a whole different world existed. I went down to Divis Flats the night before the parade, hoping to find Frank Shiels at Crazy Joe's. The housing project was a nightmare. The rubbish bins—huge metal containers—had been used for barricades, so there was nowhere to put the garbage (which wasn't being collected anyway) and it was strewn about everywhere. Rats scrambled from heap to heap. A blockade of scrap and dead cars jammed every entrance to the project, and to get inside I had to shoulder my bicycle and pick my way through a dark tunnel alongside a barricade.

I found Frank, and after he locked up the youth club for the night, we carried our bicycles out through the rubble and set off for his neighborhood pub. Shiels lived on the south side of the city, and we rode by City Hall and up past the gas works. Whenever we drew near a spot where Frank thought a Land Rover might be lurking, we dismounted and walked. Frank had no headlight on his bicycle, and he knew the police were capable of treating that as a serious offense. I thought how surprised the world would be, given the media coverage of the hunger strike riots, to see such law and order.

———

At 5:43 P.M. on Tuesday afternoon, May 12, after fifty-nine days without food, Francis Hughes died. He was twenty-five years old, the ninth of ten children in a respectable and prosperous family, a family with no great history of Republican involvement that had been farming in south Derry for 300 years. Francis had joined the IRA at eighteen after he was beaten up by local members of the national guard. By the time he was twenty-one, the constabulary described him as "the most wanted man in the north of Ireland."

Hughes was an explosives expert, and on night missions occasionally wore an army uniform with the word "Ireland" above the pocket. On St. Patrick's Day, 1978, Hughes and a comrade, both in fatigues, came upon five soldiers lying in a field. The troops thought the uniformed duo were allies, members of the national guard. In the gun battle that ensued, the two Republicans killed one soldier and maimed another. Hughes, however, was also wounded. Thirteen hours later, after a massive police and army search, he was found lying in a ditch under a gorse bush, bleeding badly. He spent the next ten months in the hospital. During his interrogation, he refused to eat for seven days, fearing the food was drugged, and his answer even to questions like "Nice day, isn' it?" was that he would have to consult his solicitor. He was eventually given a life sentence for killing the soldier, thirty-four years for two attempted murders, twenty years for causing an explosion, and fifteen years for possession of an explosive.

I heard of his death on the evening news on Tuesday, just five days after Sands's funeral. I was surprised, as the papers had predicted that

he would last through the weekend, and without the vigil I had expected
I felt no sense of climax. I left the house and headed down the Kashmir
toward the laundromat, where a crowd had once again assembled.

At the corner of Clonard Gardens, women again pounded bin lids. Two
children in short pants and kneesocks squatted with them; one child had
a pacifier in his mouth, and he tapped on the pavement with an empty tin
can. The banging ceased after a few minutes, and the women formed a
circle in the middle of the intersection and started the rosary while the
men stood on the corners and watched. In an entry just thirty yards
away, two teenagers began making petrol bombs, and children carrying
shopping bags full of empty milk and soda bottles provided raw material.
While those teenagers had a plan of attack, and I assumed that the IRA
did, my neighbors in the street were unprepared. They finally agreed
that there should be a community meeting at 8:00 in the monastery
parking lot.

The meeting drew forty people, all but four of them women. One of
the Redemptorists stood just thirty yards away, but he was apparently
just out for a chat and had no intention of leading his flock in such a crisis.
The group had little to say. A few got into an argument about whether
this was like 1969, and one who had stayed put through that siege lorded
that fact over others who had fled the district. No one proposed a course
of action until a man with a row of fresh stitches on his brow and an air
of authority walked up and asked those present to leave their entry
doors open.

"That's the IRA talking," a neighbor whispered to me. She claimed the
speaker had been hit by a plastic bullet during the Sands riots and had to
be taken to the Republic to have his wound dressed because he would
have been arrested had he shown up in any hospital north of the border.

After the Provisional left, the meeting fizzled out. Nothing had been
decided. The adolescents at the barricades, the guerrillas, and the security forces would determine what would happen. The rest of us were
powerless, our decisions limited to leaving a back door open or locking
it shut.

When I left the monastery, I discovered a magnificent barricade at the
corner of the Kashmir and Springfield Roads, a barricade made primarily of a long piece of crisscrossed iron bars that looked like the arm of
a wrecking crane, and I wished that I had seen it carried, imagining a
Republican centipede. The corner of Oranmore and Springfield, the dis-

trict's other key intersection, was blocked by a burning car, but it was not well sealed.

When the battle began, the home team had trouble maintaining the two fronts. Petrol bombs flew in good number, but the British did not retreat, and they peppered the mob with plastic bullets. At just about 10:15, the army penetrated the district by skirting the burning auto in Oranmore Street.

I was standing not too far behind the front line, and when the army broke through I turned and ran. I burst into the nearest house, though I had no idea who lived in it, and I was followed by three masked men and two unmasked women. The women were mother and daughter, inhabitants of the house, frightened by the army's charge but not by the presence of four strange men in their living room. The daughter, about eighteen years old, collected the masks from the other three invaders and hid them in the kitchen. Two of the lads washed their hands, perhaps to remove the smell of petrol or the grime from throwing stones, perhaps to thwart forensic investigators. The mother took up a post in her open door as lookout; her age and sex gave her immunity.

A group of soldiers stopped on the corner just outside our refuge. I feared a house to house search, and I imagined the mother shoved back into the house, soldiers pointing rifles at us, and boots pounding on the stairs as the troops ran to check the bedrooms. The three unmasked rioters worked on their alibis. They thought I was safe, as I carried a reporter's notepad and had an American accent.

The soldiers stayed on that corner for a long time, but they raided no houses. Slowly we relaxed. The daughter made tea. One of the lads asked me if I'd heard of Fort Lauderdale, as he was going to visit there soon. He wanted to know what black people were like, and he wondered if he could get American citizenship if he joined the U.S. Army. We talked about Sands's funeral, and one of the trio, recalling the presence of the Iranian diplomat, wondered if the IRA could get a fighter plane from the ayatollah. We joked about seeing it land in the Kashmir Road. The third fugitive was a schoolteacher facing unemployment at the end of his term. He said he was teaching teenage boys, "also with no future," and told a story about a pupil who had recently been arrested. The police searched the kid's house and found dozens of petrol bombs. Working fast to come up with an alibi, the kid claimed he was saving petrol for the day he bought a car.

The army pulled out at about 11:00. The four of us left the house at intervals. The mother told us to come by for tea anytime.

On the following day, the police, citing the Flags and Emblems Act and the emergency provisions legislation, arrested the corpse of Francis Hughes after it was released from the hospital. The constabulary intended to prevent the IRA man's remains from stopping at a church in west Belfast where 2,000 mourners waited, and to that end, the police manhandled the undertakers, commandeered the hearse, and sent the Hughes family in one direction while they and the coffin went in another. The coffin was carried into the Hughes home in the village of Bellaghy about three hours behind schedule.

The government's actions had been so consistently divorced from the reality of life and thought in Catholic districts that no one seemed stunned by the abduction of a corpse, except certainly the Hughes family and the undertakers. Cruelty was becoming the norm. That night I watched the military flood Clonard in the wake of a blast bomb, and I saw two soldiers with their backs to gable walls, surrounded by local women blowing whistles and banging bin lids within inches of the men's faces. I could not stand the noise and I stood thirty yards away. I thought it incredible that neither soldier fired his gun, if only to drive the horde away.

When the troops pulled out, some of my neighbors got the impression that fewer soldiers had left than had arrived, and so speculation began that the army had set up a secret observation post in the district, a not uncommon occurence in Catholic communities. By the time I heard the story, the post was believed to be above the laundromat and plans were afoot to have it petrol bombed. The act would deprive the area of the only washeteria for miles around, and would certainly have been in line with the scorch-your-own-earth policy that had prevailed since Sands's death, but it never came to pass. In the end, all of the windows on the second floor were broken and the rooms were inspected by locals. They found no sign of enemy encampment, and so the building was spared.

At that point, the Protestant community was increasingly distressed with the continuing destruction (though it was not their neighborhoods that were being destroyed) and with the constant attacks on the security

forces with everything from bin lids to Russian rockets. On May 14, the
Irish Times carried the report that Reverend Bradford, the Methodist
MP, had urged the police to shoot petrol bombers with lead bullets instead of plastic. The following day, the UDA posted photos of Sands's
funeral at one of their offices, asking passersby if they recognized anyone in the pictures. Andy Tyrie's armed force had been quiet, but they
indicated that if the security forces did not suppress the rioting, hijacking, and arson soon, the loyalists would take the job on themselves.
Tyrie, however, also called on Thatcher to concede to the five demands,
saying there would be more trouble if concessions weren't made than if
they were. On Friday, May 15, the *Guardian* quoted him saying, "There
are special courts and special legislation, so why can't there be special
prisoners?"

That morning, the newsmen who remained in the North had their
choice of funerals. There was the milkman Eric Guiney, killed by rioters
who stoned his truck, and fourteen-year-old Julie Livingstone, killed
by a soldier who shot her with a plastic bullet. There was Emmanual
McLarnon, an INLA man who had been shot after he fired at soldiers
from a balcony in Divis Flats; Father Buckley had given him the last
rites, and the St. John's Ambulance Corps had rushed him to the hospital.
(According to Buckley, the ambulance was stopped by soldiers who delayed it until McLarnon choked on his own blood.) And finally there was
Francis Hughes, the hunger striker. Most of the press stood with the
65,000 people who watched Hughes funeral in Bellaghy. I stayed home,
weary of the ritual, seeing only more ahead.

I was not alone in that perception. The army called on the family of
hunger striker Ray McCreesh on Monday, May 15, to ask what the funeral arrangements would be. McCreesh was not yet dead.

And so the days passed without negotiation or compromise, while other
lives were ticked off. A twelve-year-old girl carrying a carton of milk and
a forty-five-year-old father of seven were killed by plastic bullets. The
Provisionals killed the first policeman of the season, a twenty-three-
year-old father of a sixteen-month-old daughter, and then blew up five
soldiers on a country road, the army's second worst casualty toll in the
twelve years of war. A Catholic butcher was assassinated in his home in

a mixed district off the Ardoyne, and the killing had all the hallmarks of a sectarian assassination. At that time, Mrs. Barbour had been talking vaguely of moving out of west Belfast, a move her daughters encouraged. The butcher's assassination killed that plan. "See what happens," she said to me, "when you live in an integrated neighborhood?"

Ray McCreesh, the religious hunger striker serving fourteen years for attempted murder, died Thursday, May 21, at 2:11 A.M., after sixty-one days without food. The cardinal sent a telegram to Mrs. Thatcher warning that the government would "face the wrath of the nationalist population" if she continued her rigid stance.

Eighteen hours later, at 11:39 P.M., Patsy O'Hara, the INLA's man on the fast, died also. He was serving eight years for possession of a hand grenade. Both he and McCreesh would be walking the streets today had they been willing to conform to prison rules. Thirty-two masked INLA men escorted O'Hara's coffin to the grave, and stewards at the funeral wore black armbands etched with the word "felon."

In Camlough, in South Armagh, McCreesh's funeral was attended by sixty priests. Cardinal O'Fiaich, also from South Armagh, knew the McCreesh family and told the press, "Ray McCreesh was born in a community which has always openly proclaimed that it is Irish, not British. I have no doubt that he would never have seen the inside of a jail but for the abnormal political situation. Who is entitled to pronounce him a murder or a suicide?"

Ian Paisley felt entitled. The *Belfast Telegraph* quoted him calling McCreesh a suicide and saying that the cardinal's statement was "a good demonstration of Jesuitical hypocrisy and ecclesiastical whitewashing of the most despicable order." The statement, Paisley said, showed that the Catholic Church not only condoned the IRA, but also supported it, and demonstrated what the Ulster Protestant could expect in a Roman Catholic–dominated Ireland.

The riots had a new intensity. In an alley off the Kashmir, I watched a middle-aged neighbor, a man with a job and a family, active in the church, take up stones to throw at the army. The act made no sense. I understood it completely.

A few minutes later, a cry went up to "clear the streets," the warning given to bystanders when the neighborhood guns come out. Two men set up in sniper positions opposite the laundromat. One held an Uzi, the Israeli submachine gun, a weapon I had never seen before. The petrol bombers and the spectators retreated. I ran into a friend's house, a man

I'll call Sean. I was followed by an elderly woman who was on her way home from the monastery chapel. After asking Sean's wife who I was, the old woman said, loud enough that I could hear it, that she had thought I was Special Branch. I could not tell if she was entirely convinced that I wasn't. The snipers opened fire. The army shot back. Bullets drilled into the brick on the corner, where the unemployed men stand in the afternoons.

No one was hit, and the gunmen escaped.

So the unthinkable had happened. In just sixteen days, four hunger strikers had died. Many in the North had thought there would be concessions from the British after Sands, and most certainly after Hughes. McCreesh had told his family that the strike would be settled before his number was up. Now the men in the Maze could have no doubt that the fast meant death, not brinksmanship. I would have thought, therefore, that there would be just one or two men still willing to sign on, to challenge Mrs. Thatcher to a duel. But there weren't one or two—there were eighty. After O'Hara's death, it became apparent that with two-week intervals between fasters, Mrs. Thatcher's common criminals could be dying in the Maze for the rest of 1981 and well into 1982. Within days of the deaths of Hughes, McCreesh, and O'Hara, three Republicans had joined the fast to replace them, and once again, there were four prisoners refusing food.

The month ahead seemed to offer a breathing space. Joe McDonnell, the Provisional who had replaced Sands on the fast, was not expected to die until July, leaving five weeks to work out a settlement. The government, however, seemed to have no ideas, and worse, no will, and the men in the Maze appeared to have no intention of giving up. The Provos, after all, were winning. They had doubled or tripled their support in the ghettoes, contributions were flowing in from home and abroad, and the IRA's international image had never been better.

In Clonard, we felt a sense of relief but not much hope. Anyone who could count realized that if no compromise was reached, another hunger striker would die on or about the Twelfth of July, when Protestants would be on the streets in costume and patriotic fury. And the two communities were more polarized than they had been in years. "Four dead, saves us lead" read the writing on the wall in one Protestant district, and in local elections, Protestants voted in overwhelming numbers for Paisley's hardliners.

"I believe the British handling of the prison crisis will go down as an historic mistake, and I think the reasons why they were able to make such an error lies in the fact that they have treated Catholic paramilitary groups different from Protestant ones," wrote David McKittrick, Belfast bureau chief of the *Irish Times,* in a column in late June.

"In the NIO's analysis, the Loyalist groups are seen as an organic part of the Protestant community. They believe that to act against them means having to take extreme care not to stir up general Protestant resentment. They believe the Loyalist paramilitaries essentially inseparable from Protestants in general.

"They seem to see the Provos, on the other hand, as a distinct group, and one which can be detached from the Catholic community. So in the prison dispute they tackled the Provos head on, making the assumption that the Catholic community, faced with making a stark choice between the government and the prisoners, would favour the government. They were horribly, irrevocably wrong."

That spring, Margaret Thatcher replaced Ian Paisley as the greatest recruiter the IRA had ever known. Seemingly oblivious to her role as the great aggravator, she breezed into Belfast on a surprise visit on Thursday, May 28. She strolled around the demilitarized shopping zone, had lunch at Stormont Castle, talked with government ministers, gave interviews to television reporters, and flew back to London in early evening.

In her wake, she left a furious people. Friday's *Irish Times* reported that the prime minister had said she could not agree with Cardinal O'Fiaich's assessment of the situation, that she could see no evidence that her policy was hardening Catholic attitudes in the North; that the hunger strikes might well be "the last card" in the IRA's campaign; and that she was not prepared "to give political status or special category status to people who are in fact criminals and the enemies of society." She also told a group of forty community leaders at a luncheon that "no one in any responsible position" had urged her to give in to the demands of the hunger strikers, a remark comparable to spitting in the face of the Catholic hierarchy, as both the cardinal and Bishop Daly had called for compromise.

Mr. Atkins added further insult on June 1. In interviews with the BBC, he contended that people were being intimidated into attending the hunger strikers' funerals and that the cardinal had failed to understand "what the hunger strike and the prison protest is really all about." Atkins said that O'Fiaich's appeal for compromise was "wishful thinking," that the prisoners would not settle for anything less than political status.

The British press was also very critical of the Catholic hierarchy at that time. The *Irish News*, the Belfast Catholic daily, was stricken by the short memory of the editors and government ministers who acted as if they had never heard the hierarchy's repeated denunciations of IRA violence, as if they had no idea that the cardinal and Bishop Daly had made every effort to avert the prison crisis. "One is entitled to feel," the *Irish News* editors wrote, "that the English, who bungled their approach to their neighbor for centuries, are doomed to bungle to the very end. They know no more about Catholic Ireland today than they did in the time of Elizabeth I, and their encyclopedic ignorance reappears in every generation."

It might be possible to dismiss the *Irish News'* view as partisan except that it was shared by newspapers throughout Europe. "General European impression ranges from pig-headed Thatcher obstinacy, through scandalous misgovernment, to outright genocide," wrote the chief European correspondent of the *Sunday Times* on May 31. "In other words, it could not be worse."

The correspondent's remarks were published in a *Sunday Times* survey of sixty-four papers in twenty-five countries. Editor after editor told the *Times* that the deaths of the hunger strikers had improved the image of the IRA. In Greece, newspapermen drew parallels between the North and Cyprus: "In the case of Britain," said one editor, "yesterday's terrorists are tomorrow's Prime Ministers." In Italy, the funerals had been crucial in shaping public opinion. "No Red Brigade terrorist," said the *Sunday Times* correspondent, "could make an appearance in public like the IRA men did at the hunger strikers' funerals. For many Italians, the sight of those hooded gunmen bearing forbidden arms parading before television cameras in front of the whole world, relying on the protection of the crowd, meant that the writing was on the wall for the British in Ulster." In Johannesburg, the editor of the Afrikaner paper *Die Transvaler* said, "We share the South African puzzlement that so many people in Britain can roundly condemn things in this country when far worse deeds are being perpetrated in their own country." Overall, the newspapermen surveyed expressed bewilderment that Britain had been able to find an imaginative solution to the problems of Rhodesia, but had failed to achieve anything "in her own backyard." The only friendly responses cited were from a conservative daily in Turkey and from the American press; the *Sunday Times* cited the *Washington Post*'s support of Mrs. Thatcher's handling of the strike and the *New York Times'* belief that the goal of the prisoners was political status, and that such status was not deserved.

At home, Mrs. Thatcher, several Conservative MPs, and the Independent Broadcast Authority (IBA) questioned the media's objectivity. The IBA was upset by a program called "Lying in State," in which television reporters examined their medium's role in spreading propaganda, demonstrating how events were set up for TV cameras by both the government and the guerrillas. The Broadcast Authority refused to allow the program to be shown, objecting to a twenty-second clip of Patsy O'Hara lying in his coffin, surrounded by four masked INLA men. Ten seconds of the segment had already been broadcast several times in a thirty-second promotion of the program, and the commentary that ran over the disputed footage was by no means complimentary to the INLA. The producers of the program refused to cut the O'Hara section, arguing that doing so would only encourage more censorship. As a result, the program has never been shown. (More than fifty television programs on the North have been banned, censored, or delayed since 1959.)

At that point, the Provos were not above a bit of censorship themselves. They too were irritated by the British press coverage, and in late May began papering the walls of west Belfast with a "Don't Buy a British Lie" poster, the word "Lie" spelled out with the logos of the British newspapers. West Belfast newsagents were visited and told not to sell the offending issues. The Provos abandoned their effort after a little less than a fortnight, however, as it proved ineffective. The offending papers were still available in the city center, and many Catholics actually enjoy the British tabloids, though they may not appreciate the papers' views on Ireland.

A few days after the "Lying in State" flap, the government introduced a new Representation of the People Bill containing amendments which would prevent prisoners from standing for Parliament. "The sole purpose of the government's new bill," wrote the *Guardian*'s editors, "is to prevent the electors of one specific constituency from electing as member the candidate whom they otherwise would elect, and that is contrary to the principles of Parliamentary representation as we understand them."

"Certainly in changing the law," the *Irish Times* noted, "the government has left itself open to the charge that it has changed the rules of the game because it does not like the players."

The bill passed its parliamentary hurdles and became law in mid-July. As their candidate for the Fermanagh–South Tyrone seat, Sinn Fein named Owen Carron, the former schoolteacher who had been Sands's election agent and who did not shy away from endorsing the bullet. On August 21, Carron won, gathering 786 more votes than Sands. Once again, it was apparent that in Fermanagh–South Tyrone, Britain was governing without the consent of the governed.

———

After the funerals of McCreesh and O'Hara, a sort of normality returned even to west Belfast. Garbagemen resumed their pickups, and I saw a bus on the Springfield Road on May 28. In June the army entered the district unaccompanied by the clash of bin lids and the screech of whistles. The kids took up joyriding again, and on June 9, a joyrider killed a pedestrian and himself in a high speed crash.

Mrs. Barbour, who had shown a remarkable calm during the May riots, shuddered at what lay ahead. She predicted civil war in six months, and was reluctant to tell the coal man to bring her usual order; it would be such a waste of money, she said, if we got blown up. Her friends, however, assured her that "they" (meaning, I think, the Provos, the security forces, and the loyalists) would never do anything to a house that had an American in it. For a short time I think she hoped I would stay on in the role of good luck charm, and I admit that at times, I would have liked to have stayed, but my money and visa were running out and I had obligations to attend to in Chicago.

In the absence of barricades, the kids in west Belfast grew restless, and the bolder ones continued to hijack and destroy. Adults were increasingly irked. "The Protestant paramilitaries would be foolish to attack the Falls, as our own hooligans are destroying the area street by street," one Catholic wrote to the *Irish News*. "No invasion by any enemy could have inflicted so much material damage or imposed so much hardship and suffering on a people least able to bear it."

In the first week of June, the Provos passed leaflets through west Belfast mail slots warning teenagers that "unnecessary hijackings and burnings of vehicles" would not be tolerated, that "private property, private vehicles, and local businesses are to be exempted from hijacking." The Provos, however, had to do more than issue statements to establish order. In June, they kneecapped two teenagers in the New Lodge; tarred and feathered two adolescents for sexually assaulting a twelve-year-old girl; and shot eighteen-year-old Raymond Devlin, commonly known as "Gangster." Devlin was considered particularly troublesome by the Provos in Andersonstown because he had allegedly been using the IRA's name in his thefts, and so he was shot in both knees, both elbows, and the back. The press and the clergy were loud in their denunciations, saying they could not see how the IRA could plead for humane treatment in the prisons and deal so inhuman a punishment themselves. Among my neighbors I sensed no great sympathy for the wounded youngster. Many, no doubt, were numb.

The air of solidarity in west Belfast began to have an undercurrent of suspicion and fear. The corpse of a Catholic from Lenadoon was found near a rubbish chute in Divis Flats; the IRA said they had killed the man, a well-known H-block activist, because he had turned informer. I heard rumors that a woman had had her head shaved for passing information and that someone on the Springfield Road had been seen giving tea to soldiers and was going to be put out of the district.

In the middle of June, I had tea with friends in one of Clonard's back streets and mentioned that I had toured the border with a retired policeman. I made it clear that I was working on a story about the smuggling of livestock and consumer goods for a Canadian magazine, that the policeman had worked the border in the 1940s, and that he had been retired since 1968. The mood of my hostess was so fragile, however, that she took offense. "Once a policeman, always a policeman," she said. She was worried because I knew of her son's involvement, years earlier, in the IRA, and she passed her suspicion on to her son. The next time I ran into him, we had a drink together and a few good laughs, and he turned to his wife and said, "If John turned out to be a Branchman, do you think you could shoot him?" My friend said he didn't think he could do it, that no matter what he was told, he'd have a hard time seeing me as anything other than John the American. His wife, however, said she was pretty sure that she could pull the trigger, particularly if she was convinced that I had brought harm to her family. I avoided them all after that, a course which seemed wise at the time, but which I now regret.

Back in England, a few politicians seemed to have been profoundly affected by that Irish spring. Most notable among them was James Callaghan, former Labour prime minister, who, as Home Secretary in 1969 had sent the troops onto the streets of Derry and Belfast. In a speech in the House of Commons on July 2, Callaghan said that all policies had failed in the North, even his own, and that it was impossible to win there. The way forward, he said, was to remove the troops and tell the representatives of the people of Northern Ireland that Westminster would offer no more solutions, that the Northerners would have to work the future out for themselves. He foresaw a broadly independent Northern Ireland with ties to both Dublin and London.

Conservatives, however, favored a hard line. One Tory MP called for martial law in the North (many Catholics thought they had been living under martial law for years). An Official Unionist MP from Londonderry proposed that Catholics be given a "golden handshake"—a lump sum of cash if they would leave the province.

Amid the clamor for long-term change, however, there seemed to be little new thought on ending the prison crisis. By the twenty-ninth of June, Joe McDonnell's death seemed imminent. He had gone fifty-one days without food and was vomiting his drinking water. His four predecessors had died seven to fourteen days after reaching that stage.

In west Belfast, the feeling of solidarity was fast giving way to despair. Some wanted the Provos to call off the strike, arguing that they had made their point and would gain nothing from the death of another prisoner. The Provos, however, had not given up hope. They had scored impressive victories in elections to the Dail, the Irish Parliament, on June 11; IRA prisoners had won two seats, and the total vote for H-block candidates was twice as high as anyone had predicted. The Provos thought those victories would force the Dublin government to exert pressure on the British, and in so doing, the Republic would be taking the side of the Provisionals. Mrs. Thatcher needed the Republic's cooperation in the war against the IRA, and some Republicans felt she might compromise if she saw the Irish government being drawn into the fray on the side of the gunmen.

Suddenly, as July began, hope began to eat away at the season's despair. The Irish Commission for Justice and Peace was called out of nowhere by Secretary of State Humphrey Atkins to mediate between the government and the prisoners. The Irish Commission, established in 1968 by the Irish Bishops' Conference, was an organization of clergy and lay people who worked quietly on Third World development and human rights issues. It seemed at first an odd choice; while the Commission was made up of respectable men, the group had nothing of the clout or prestige of others who might have accepted the role—the International Red Cross, for example, or even Cardinal O'Fiaich. The prisoners were skeptical, believing that the Commission was just an arm of the Irish bishops, who had already issued a statement condemning the strike. The Provisionals were won over after Father Oliver Crilly, a Commission representative, met hunger striker Tom McElwee and explained that the group had had nothing to do with the Irish bishops' statement. Crilly, director of the Catholic Communications Institute of Ireland, and McElwee, an IRA man doing twenty years on explosives and bombing charges, were first cousins.

The prisoners, however, still did not trust the government. They suspected that Michael Alison, the North's minister of prisons, was meeting with the Commission only to wipe out the image of intransigence the government had so assiduously acquired, that in the end he might pull out and claim he had been flexible, that it was the Provos who were uncompromising.

Hope spread rapidly, however, in the wake of marathon efforts by the Commission's negotiating team, which included Father Crilly, Rev. Dermot O'Mahony (the auxiliary bishop of Dublin), and SDLP economics spokesman Hugh Logue. The delegates spent eight hours with Alison on Friday, July 3; four hours in the Maze on the fourth; and six hours in the prison on Sunday the fifth. On Saturday and Sunday night, the delegates also met with the prisoners' families and representatives of Sinn Fein and the IRSP.

It was not only those meetings which were encouraging. The government appeared to be recognizing the Provisional's command structure, and therefore the Provisionals, when it allowed the Commission delegates access to Brendan McFarlane, the Provos' commanding officer inside the prison. Furthermore, a senior civil servant from the Northern Ireland Office accompanied the delegates on Saturday's visit to the Maze, an encouraging sign. Alison, Atkins, and Thatcher still wanted to maintain the front they had erected earlier in the strike, so they insisted that although their man had gone into the prison, he had not negotiated with the prisoners. The Commission was willing to play along with the face-saving ploy, and told the press that the delegates were not negotiating, that they were merely transmitting clarifications.

On July 4, the prisoners issued a long statement, characterized by the press as conciliatory, spelling out in detail what they wanted on the five demands. They defined "free association" as freedom to associate with the twenty-five prisoners in their wings, not with their comrades throughout the prison. They said that they were prepared to engage in prison maintenance work, and that "work" should be defined as useful activity, which would include education and arts and crafts. On prison uniforms, they would not compromise, arguing that the current rule, allowing the inmates to wear their own clothes half the time, was illusory. They also said that they had no objection to the privileges they demanded being extended to every prisoner in the Maze.

On Sunday morning, July 5, McDonnell entered his fifty-eighth day without food. Hughes had died on his fifty-ninth day, O'Hara and Mc-Creesh on their sixty-first. McDonnell's mouth was twisted as if he had had a stroke, his lips were covered with sores, and his eyes were vacant. Time was clearly of the essence.

The Commission moved at high speed, running to the Provos, the Irps, and the relatives on Monday afternoon, and to Alison on Monday night. The delegates drew up a list of commitments that had been given them during sixteen hours of talks with Alison, and showed the list to the men in the Maze. The prisoners felt the basis of a resolution was there, and asked that a personal meeting be arranged with an official from the Northern Ireland Office so they would be given clarification of details and confirmation of the British commitment to act according to the spirit and letter of the agreement. The press ran with the news that a deal had been ironed out, that all that remained to be worked out was a guarantee from the British. The Provos believed they had been double-crossed before, and they would not call off the fast without a guarantee.

When the Commission delegates met Alison Monday night, he accepted that the statement they had composed reflected a true picture of what he had indicated except in two respects: he suggested a minor change of phrase in one part, and then said that except for his absolute commitment to concede on clothing reform, his understanding of the sixteen hours of talks was that he had been offering an illustration of possible changes, not a detailed list of specific concessions. The Commissioners rejected that notion and stood by their statement. At the end of the meeting, Alison agreed to send an official to the Maze by mid-morning Tuesday to assure the prisoners of the government's good faith.

At 11:40 A.M. on Tuesday, July 7, the Commissioners were asked to come to Stormont for more talks. The delegates asked if Alison had sent anyone to the prison. Alison had not. The delegates were angry, declined to meet with the government, and called a press conference for 1:00. Just before the meeting with the media, the government called to say that an official was going into the Maze that afternoon. The Commission called off the press conference and waited.

The afternoon passed. No one went to the Maze. At 6:00 P.M. and again at 7:15, the Commissioners told Alison that time was running out. At 8:50, they were told that an official was going in. At 10:00, Alison said that no one would go into the prison that night, but that the delay would be to the prisoners' advantage. He assured the delegates that Joe McDonnell, the upholsterer from Andersonstown and comrade of Bobby Sands, would not die in the meantime.

McDonnell died at 5:11 A.M.

―――――――

The NIO did finally send a man into the Maze. He arrived a few hours after McDonnell's death, and, as the government was still trying to maintain the illusion that they were not talking to the prisoners, the official simply stood next to the prison governor while the governor read the NIO's statement to the hunger strikers. The statement bore no resemblance to the Irish Commission's summary of Alison's assurances. Where Alison had told the Commission that the men would be able to wear their own clothes at all times, for example, the NIO statement now indicated no change in the existing regulations, though it did not rule out further development on the issue.

The prisoners saw nothing new in the government's position, and the Commission delegates, upon receiving a copy of the NIO document, could not control their anger. "We cannot report it as a serious attempt to seek a resolution," they said, and they produced two documents, printed in the *Irish Times* on July 9, which contained a detailed account of the negotiations and outlined the reform proposals which the Commission believed the government had accepted as a "moral obligation." Bishop O'Mahony, the head of the delegation, was quoted in the *Guardian* saying the NIO's delays had been a "significant factor" in McDonnell's death, and the Commission delegates challenged the government to deny their account of the negotiations. The NIO said it would need time to study the Commission's documents, and in a press conference Mr. Alison claimed that he had been misinformed by doctors about how much time McDonnell had left before he died, a claim which seemed preposterous at the time and which Alison himself seemed to contradict later.

To the bulk of Northern Catholics, it appeared "as if a highly respectable body of Catholic clergy and lay people has been deceived, as they believe Cardinal O'Fiaich was before them," wrote reporter Ed Maloney in the *Irish Times*. "As one normally reliable barometer of the Catholic middle ground put it: This didn't do any damage to the extremists, they had been saying all along that this would happen anyway. It was the moderates who stuck their necks out and said that talking to the British was the only way forward, who have suffered. Now they're saying, because they have to, there's only one other language the British really understand."

If the doublecross had occured just a few weeks earlier, Thatcher, Atkins, and Alison would probably have been roundly denounced by opposition members of Parliament and by the world press. The world press, however, was long gone from the North, and the opposition in Parliament was distracted: riots were sweeping the British mainland.

The disturbances had begun on July 3 in a section of Liverpool where 47 percent of young blacks and 43 percent of young whites were unemployed. The attacks on police and property by white and black youths lasted five days and then were replayed in Manchester, London, Brixton, Birmingham, Hull, and Leeds. More than twenty English towns and cities faced varying degrees of mob behavior in the ten days after the Liverpool rising.

A multitude of causes were cited: unemployment; bad housing; the breakdown of family life (Britain had the highest divorce rate in Europe); the disaffection of minorities with the overwhelmingly white police force (in Liverpool there were four blacks on the 5,000 man force); the television coverage of Northern Ireland; and the violence of punk culture. A three-year-old government-sponsored review of British race relations was cited in the *Guardian*: "There are some uncomfortable parallels between the situation of Britain's coloured population and that of Catholics in Northern Ireland. For 50 years British governments condoned discrimination and deprivation in Ulster and in the end Ulster blew up in their face. We believe that not only for reasons of social justice but also to preserve social stability and order in the longer term, more should now be done to deal with the problems of race relations in this country."

With the government encouraging mainland police chiefs to consult the Royal Ulster Constabulary for methods of dealing with the riots, journalists asked William Whitelaw, British Home Secretary, if he would issue plastic bullets to the mainland police. The July 11 *Irish Times* quoted his reply: "I would deeply regret their introduction," he said, "because they are lethal."

To the residents of west Belfast it seemed that ministers at the highest level of government believed it was all right to kill Irish rioters, but not rioters on the mainland.

Back in west Belfast, the morning of McDonnell's death was marked by riots, by the shooting death of a member of the Fianna (the junior IRA), and by the killing of Nora McCabe, a thirty-year-old mother of three. Mrs. McCabe was walking to a shop to buy cigarettes at a time that children and teenagers were throwing stones at RUC vehicles; a policeman shot Mrs. McCabe in the head with a plastic bullet from a distance of about six feet.

Just before seven that evening, a half day after McDonnell had died, our doorbell rang. Mrs. Barbour was sewing in the dining room and did not hear the bell. I was working in the sitting room, and I answered the door, opening it to find two neatly dressed women in their mid-twenties.

"Could we use the phone please?" asked the red-haired woman who stood in front.

"Certainly," I said, and I stepped aside and let them in. Most of the people of Clonard did not have telephones, and a request to use our coinbox model, while not common, was not rare either. The request always came from a neighbor, and although I didn't recognize the women on the doorstep, precedent told me they were all right. The phone was in the foyer, just a few feet inside the door, and after letting them in, I went back to the sitting room, shutting the door behind me so the women would have some privacy and would be spared the noise of my typewriter. I had less than a week left in Belfast and much work to do, and I promptly forgot about the callers in the hall.

A few minutes later, Mrs. Barbour came into the room and abruptly sat in the chair next to my desk. I looked up, still typing as I did, and thought she looked ill. I sensed someone else in the room and turned around. The red-haired woman was just over my shoulder. She was now wearing dark, wrap-around sunglasses, and she was pointing a gun at my head.

"Provisional IRA," she said. "We're taking over the house."

And take over they did. While Mrs. Barbour and I were held in the sitting room, the other woman went upstairs and roused George, a young Catholic from the countryside who had a factory job and was staying with us on weekdays. (George is not his real name.) While the three of us sat in the front room with the gunwoman, her comrade opened the back door to a crew of male volunteers. Their leader, a tall man in his mid-twenties, came in to see us, holding his hand over his face as a mask. He told us we would not be hurt and that we should do as we were told. He was nervous, but firm.

A few minutes later, we were marshaled into the dining room, where an unshaven man wearing a brown winter coat and sunglasses took over guard duty while his colleagues carried out some project behind the closed kitchen door. Before our captors thought to close the dining room drapes, I saw a man scale our yard wall, entering Hardin's, the former hardware store on the corner, now used only for storage. I thought an ambush was being set up, but I had lost my powers of concentration, and I could not draw a mental picture of what might happen, where the sniper's perch would be, or even from which direction the targets would arrive.

There was nothing for us to do, and the gunman among us inhibited conversation, so Mrs. Barbour suggested we watch Coronation Street, the long-running British television serial, and she turned on the set. I struggled to read the newspaper, gave up, tried the television, then tried the newspaper again. I thought that if I could just concentrate on one word, and then the next, and then the next, I could surely proceed through the entire paper. I had a very hard time.

About two hours into the project, the crew in the kitchen handed out cups of tea, and upon hearing that I hadn't had dinner, they also handed out bread, butter, and cheese. The door to the kitchen remained closed. The television blared. The gunman began working a walkie-talkie. "Cookie to Cookie's nest," he said, talking to some command post in the neighborhood. The reply was full of static, and for me indistinguishable.

Without any warning our guard told us to lie on the floor. We scrambled under the table and lay on our stomachs, jammed tight, elbow to elbow. I still had no vision of what was going to happen. The only thing I could imagine that would force us to the floor was incoming fire from the alley.

A minute passed. Something seemed to have gone wrong. The gunman told us to take our seats. A few minutes later, after more communications with his radio, he told us to hit the floor again. I could hear a riot nearby, but no gunshots.

After another minute, the gunman ordered us to rise, but he did so with a tone of defeat. A short time later, he told us that he and his sole remaining comrade were pulling out. "No one has been hurt," he said. "Don't go to the police. If you do, we'll know it." And then he was gone.

After a minute or two had passed, we stood up and examined the kitchen. Nothing seemed amiss, but there were two short pieces of wire there that didn't belong to us. George pulled me aside. From where he had been sitting, he could catch glimpses of the Provisionals' project whenever the kitchen door opened; he told me he thought our visitors had hooked up a bomb, with the power switch in our kitchen, the wires leading over the yard wall, and the explosives in Hardin's shop, and that the setup had apparently failed mechanically. From my bedroom window, we could see that the wires had not been removed, that they had simply been tossed over the yard wall onto the roof of a shed in Hardin's rear. If the wires were still in place, I thought, the explosives probably were also.

I had been invited to a friend's house for dinner that night, and as I explained why I was more than two hours late, various aspects of the Provisionals' plan fell into place. The riot on the Kashmir corner may not have been the spontaneous event it appeared to be. The army's normal procedure was to disperse the mob with plastic bullets, then pull a troop carrier up to the barricade. Soldiers would climb out and fall into position behind the vehicle, waiting the order to charge up the street. As they waited for the order, they would be standing next to the wall of Hardin's shop, and I suspected that on the other side of that wall, the Provos had installed their explosives. I think our captors told us to hit the floor when the soldiers were in place, then pushed the button, and nothing had happened.

The next morning, Thursday, July 9, Mrs. Barbour and I talked over the siege, still not entirely sure what had happened. We were enormously relieved, even giddy at our survival. We did not consider going to the police. I felt an ethical dilemma—to act was to take sides, but not to act seemed to be taking sides as well. Overriding that concern, however, was the feeling that the decision wasn't mine. I had a plane ticket. I could leave in an hour. Mrs. Barbour had been there for decades, and she would be the one most likely to suffer from any retaliation.

It was conceivable that if the police discovered what we knew, we could be charged for withholding information, a charge which can result in six months in jail. That possibility seemed fairly remote, however, as hundreds of other people over the years have been in similar circumstances, unwilling to talk to the police either because they took the Provos at their word and feared punishment, or because they had no faith that the police were a better lot than the neighborhood gunmen, or both.

I thought it conceivable, however, that the police might learn what had taken place without hearing it from us; I did not trust one of Mrs. Barbour's friends, the notorious gossip Mrs. Murphy, who could spread news faster than the radio.

At that point, I figured the Provos would sneak into Hardin's during the day and remove the explosives, if they had not done so already. My immediate concern was for my files in the event of a police visit and search. I had notes from interviews with smugglers of consumer goods, retired IRA men, and kids who had stolen hundreds of automobiles. In some cases I had been careful and had not listed names, but in others I was careless, stupidly assuming I had an immunity that the Provisional bomb squad had just demonstrated I did not have. I resolved to move the files to the other side of the city as soon as I could.

At about 5:00 that afternoon, Mrs. Barbour was cooking dinner when she realized she was low on cigarettes. With a few minutes to spare in the stove operations, she decided to dash out to Early's shop for a pack of Benson and Hedges. She opened the door and was a step or two past it when a tall, thin man entered the footpath. Mrs. Barbour sized him up quickly and asked what he wanted. I heard the commotion from my desk and walked into the foyer. I saw Mrs. Barbour backing up and the thin man advancing. "Was there anyone here last night?" he asked. "Sure there were people here last night," Mrs. Barbour said. "I have boarders." Neither she nor I knew who the man was. Was he a policeman? A soldier in plainclothes? Was this the IRA? Was it, perish the thought, the UVF or UDA?

As this was taking place I saw a woman enter the footpath, turn, and calmly swing the gate shut behind her, as if she had been through that series of motions a thousand times. The series sticks in my mind like a clip from an old movie, and I've run that piece of film over and over and over again. In that innocent motion, there was an explanation.

When I replay the film I know how I should have responded. I should have realized instantly that since this was a male-female team, we were being visited again by the IRA. The Provisionals, knowing women are less likely to be stopped on the street than men, use women to move weapons to take-off points for operations. If I had thought more quickly, I might have guessed that the man would not be armed, that the woman would be carrying the gun, that if I could squeeze past Mrs. Barbour in the foyer and shove the man back out onto the sidewalk, and simultaneously shut the door behind me, Mrs. Barbour and I might have been spared another evening with the Provisionals.

Had I ended up outside the house, tangling with the visitor, I might have been able to deal with all the possibilities. If the man turned out to be a soldier or policeman, my action would have been explainable. If he turned out to be a loyalist, like those who had strolled into a house in the street behind us the previous spring and killed the occupant, we were done for anyway, and he may have been less likely to kill in broad daylight than inside the house. And if the thin man was with the Provos, I could have tried to explain to them afterward why they should not use our house, assuming of course, that they had that in mind and not some threat or punishment.

I did not react instantly, however, and the Provos set up their operation a second time. Some of the personnel who came in from the alley were veterans of the previous night's mission, and they seemed a bit more relaxed, as they knew the lay of the land and their hostages.

I tried to read the paper again, this time with pen in hand, underlining the important information so that when I lost my concentration, I could at least tell which paragraphs I had already read. Two feet from me sat our guard, a man who had either not been present the night before or whom I had not seen, a heavyset fellow wearing gloves and a blue winter jacket with the hood tied tight on his head. As time passed, he toyed with the loading mechanism of his gun, a nervous act repeated over and over. Although he pointed the gun toward the ground as he fidgeted with it, I could see that if his hand slipped and the gun fired, my legs could well be in the path of the bullet. I could almost feel an accidental kneecapping on the way, and I too began to fidget. The unshaven man who had been our guard the previous night was doing kitchen duty, in addition to manning the walkie-talkie.

When the command came to hit the floor, there were again just two men left. The unshaven Provo dashed back and forth between the dining room and the sitting room, where he checked the street. "Cookie to Cookie's nest," he said into his walkie-talkie, "can't you see there's kids there?"

Again there was static, and we could hear only one end of the conversation. There was more dashing back and forth to look out the front window. After a few minutes, we were allowed off the carpet. The two IRA men conferred momentarily in the kitchen, and then we sat in virtual silence for about fifteen minutes. Finally the unshaven man told us that he and his comrade were leaving. "We've decided not to use this house again," he said. "We're sorry for having done this to you, but this is a war, and there is no alternative."

He seemed as relieved as we were. He warned us again not to talk about the incident to anyone, particularly the police, and then he was gone.

The operation had been foiled by children, who had come up behind the troops, either to taunt the soldiers or to see what was happening around the corner. My best guess is that the Provisional on the command end of the walkie-talkie was back up the Kashmir Road in a position from which he could see the Saracen and the soldiers but not the kids behind them. He had told the inside crew to push the button, but our guards, who could see the kids from the front window, called off the operation.

Our visitors left behind a large battery, some wire, and the detonator switch. If the police were to visit us, it would be hard to explain that paraphernalia. I wrapped it in newspaper and buried the bundle midway through the accumulated garbage in the bin. Later that night when I was miles away from the house it occurred to me that my fingerprints were on the battery and the switch, and probably mine alone, as the Provisionals had all worn gloves.

Mrs. Barbour, George, and I all thought it was a good idea to spend the night elsewhere. I recruited a friend with a car to help me move my files, and I stayed at his house that night. When I got back to Mrs. Barbour's Friday morning, I could tell that someone had been back during the night, as the wires from the operation were no longer in sight. I could not tell, however, whether the explosives had been removed, and so I was not much relieved.

The aftermath was as nervewracking as the visits. Too many people knew what had happened—the people I had told, the people Mrs. Barbour had told, the people George had told, and all of the people who had heard it second and third hand. I was worried about the gossip, the explosives, and the possibility that the Provos might pay us a third visit, despite their last assurances. I was suspicious of every young woman who passed on the street whenever I approached the house; if a woman came down the street as I was about to enter the gate, I would wait until she was well past, until I was sure she had no intentions of following me in, before I walked up our footpath. It was no easy proposition convincing Mrs. Barbour that the house was still unsafe, but she finally came around to that point of view. She took her valuables and my cameras to her daughter's house and stayed the night. Before she left, I promised that I'd ask someone in the Provisionals' political wing to find out if the military side had removed the explosives.

I had an interview to do that afternoon, and when I finished, I went to the Falls to find an intermediary. An army patrol pulled me over, and its leader, who had stopped and questioned me the week before, did so again. His questions suggested the army was keeping an eye on my comings and goings.

I could find no one on the Falls. It was raining and cold, a hopeless day, and everyone was at Joe McDonnell's funeral. Pockets of people were drifting back from the cemetery, and I spotted Frank Shiels and some of the kids from the flats among them. Shiels told me the funeral procession had been a nightmare. The Provos had chosen to fire their traditional salute in front of the Busy Bee shopping center, the same spot at which they had fired the salute for Bobby Sands. The firing party was tracked by the army helicopter that hovered overhead, and soldiers on the ground burst into the house where the volunteers were changing clothes. Shooting ensued. Men, women, and children were yelling and screaming, some lying on the pavement for protection, others running into shops and a nearby church. Teenagers began pelting the army with stones, and police and soldiers arrived to reinforce those already in place. Dozens of plastic bullets were fired, and although police denied it, mourners contended that the security forces had fired live rounds at them as well. A local priest described the shooting as indiscriminate.

It was at about that time that I came down with a severe case of paranoia. Since Sands's death I had heard two neighbors question whether I was really the journalist I claimed to be. The army, or at least our local regiment, seemed anxious to see me leave. The Provos had let me know I had no immunity as a reporter, and I was not certain that they were finished with us. I found myself fighting back fear every time there was a knock at the door, and, to top it all off, I realized that Mrs. Barbour was regarding me with suspicion.

On the first night of our siege, when I turned around to discover the phone caller pointing a gun at my head, the first words out of my mouth were, "Oh God, Mrs. Barbour, I'm sorry. I'm so sorry." I was apologizing for letting the women into the house, but Mrs. Barbour had no idea what I was apologizing for. I suspect that when she related the incident to Mrs. Murphy, the malicious gossipmonger had put the thought in her mind that perhaps I was in some way responsible for the IRA's visit. Murphy knew I was friendly with a family that distributed the Provisionals' newspaper and that I had interviewed some local Republicans. Mrs. Barbour wondered, not every hour, but for a minute here and a minute there, if perhaps I had set in motion something that had gone further than I had expected it to.

And she was right to wonder, as I wondered myself. It did not seem possible that the Provisionals would take over the house without knowing who was inside and what the layout was, and their method indicated foreknowledge. Had some friend of mine set us up? The same distrust that Mrs. Barbour directed toward me, I bestowed on my friends.

I stayed that night in the Holy Land, a neighborhood near the university. The house was owned by a friend who was on vacation, and she had left me the key. There was not a noise on the street, not a soldier or policeman in sight. I wondered what was going on back in Clonard, if the house was intact, if there were riots and barricades. In the Holy Land I was alone, I was safe, and I was overwhelmingly bored. I was tempted to go back to the Springfield Road. When I did return on Saturday morning, Mrs. Barbour confessed that while staying at her daughter's, she'd had the same urge.

———

The next day was the Twelfth of July. In Protestant districts, the woodpiles were stacked high and curbs had been painted red, white, and blue, but as the holiday had fallen on Sunday, and as parades and bonfires are not thought to be appropriate on the Lord's Day, the Twelfth was scheduled to be celebrated on the thirteenth.

I visited my chosen intermediary on Sunday afternoon; he told me he had been unable to find out if the bomb was still in Hardin's. Gilles Peress, a Frenchman with the New York photo agency Magnum, had been assigned to take the pictures for an article I was doing for the *New York Times* magazine, and he was scheduled to come by in late afternoon. When I opened the door at the appointed hour, however, I was overcome with a profound dread. Over the shoulder of the stranger who stood before me, I saw a woman walk into our footpath, turn, and shut the gate behind her. "Oh God," I thought, "not again."

A second later I realized it was not a third visit by the Provisionals, and I yelled at the Frenchman for not telling me he was bringing a woman with him. He thought I was perhaps the greatest woman-hater he had ever run into. I apologized over dinner, explained my fear of local women, and Peress's comrade pointed out that I now knew how women felt on the streets of many American cities.

I told the story to Mrs. Barbour that night and she told me she felt something similar. Every young man she passed on the street she suspected of being one of those who had held us captive. "The cheek of you," she said in her mind, "coming into my house, ordering me around." One of her daughters wanted her to move away to a seaside town where there was no trouble, and she gave it considerable thought. She knew she would soon be alone in the house. I was leaving. Frank, the newsagent's assistant, was seldom at home. George, the young man who had been captive with us both nights, would probably look for lodgings in a less hazardous zone. And even without the hunger strike, the trouble around her seemed to be escalating. In the past year we had been visited by burglars, by a weirdly drugged man who crawled up against the front door one night, and by a young skinhead, stabbed in a streetfight, who had passed out on our footpath. I felt guilty to be leaving her.

At about 6:10 Monday morning, July 13, I woke to the sound of bin lids and whistles. No one in the Maze was scheduled to die, so I assumed it was a raid and that house-to-house searches were underway, 6:00 A.M. being the proper hour. I dressed quickly and went downstairs and waited. Five minutes passed and the clatter seemed to be coming closer, but there were no soldiers or policemen in sight. Finally, I went outside.

Martin Hurson, a twenty-five-year-old IRA volunteer, had died after only forty-five days on the fast. He had been expected to live another two weeks, and two men were scheduled to die before him.

I went down to the laundromat corner and watched the women say the rosary again. I couldn't help thinking that it was a terrible day to die, as the Protestants would be on the streets in just two hours for their parade. I saw a group of kids throwing petrol bombs over the peace line wall, and I thought the whole day might be like that: Catholics and Protestants having a go at each other instead of Catholics having a go at the security forces.

I was wrong. No missiles came back from the other side. Instead of charging around west Belfast smashing barricades and shooting rioters, the army and police spent the day on the Orangemen's parade route. And so despite the horrible coincidence of death and parade, the rioting in the ghetto was light. It is difficult to have a war if one side doesn't show.

With Hurson's burial went the last hopes of many that Britain would ever concede. On the day he died, Mrs. Thatcher visited the rioting neighborhoods of Liverpool and said that the previous ten days had been the most worrying of her premiership; she was referring to the English riots, not the deaths in the Maze. At that point, Northern Ireland might as well have been an island in the South Pacific for all the anguish it was registering on the mainland.

Yet the Provos in the Maze remained steadfast; there were reports that volunteers were ready to sign on the strike in such number that the deaths could roll on until June 1982. The prisoners' families, however, were wavering. Each time a hunger striker went into a coma, doctors asked his wife or mother or father if they wanted the man's life to be saved, if they wanted him to be given medical attention. The first six families had all abided by the wishes of the prisoner and had conceded his death, but there were indications that that solidarity might not hold much longer.

There were still new cards being played. The next man up was Kieran Doherty, one of the two IRA prisoners who had won parliamentary seats in the Irish elections a few weeks before. Garret Fitzgerald, the newly elected prime minister of Ireland and no friend of the IRA, was under considerable pressure as a result of Doherty's victory at the polls. The death of a member of the Irish parliament in a British jail could tear relations with Britain to pieces. Fitzgerald's ministers believed that Mrs. Thatcher had been responsible for the delaying tactics that had resulted in Joe McDonnell's death, and there were calls from the electorate to expel the British ambassador. Fitzgerald called for direct negotiations between Britain and the prisoners, for no more intermediaries, and he asked President Reagan to pressure Thatcher to negotiate.

The British, however, were on guard against possible U.S. intervention. They dispatched Mr. Alison, the minister of prisons, to Washington, to assure the Americans that the British were acting in good faith. He was successful: there were no Congressional hearings, and President Reagan refused to intercede.

His statements to Congress and the president, however, must have been far more convincing than what he told the press. On July 11, Sean Cronin, Washington bureau chief of the *Irish Times*, reported that Alison told him that the Irish Commission had been "wildly euphoric and wildly out of perspective" about what he had offered them. Two days later, Cronin added that Alison had compared negotiations with hunger strikers to efforts of governments to distract plane hijackers with the appearance of negotiations while authorities developed plans of attack. Alison, who now admitted that he had only been pretending to negotiate while Joe McDonnell died, was accusing a bishop, a priest, and the SDLP's economics spokesman of lying. No one in Washington or London seemed to see the contradiction.

Back in the North, Cardinal O'Fiaich responded to Mr. Alison's charges, saying he was absolutely certain the Irish Commission was telling the truth, implying, in a not subtle fashion, that Alison spoke with a forked tongue. The *Irish Times* account went on to report the cardinal's plea for direct negotiations. In London, the *Guardian* issued the same call. "The division between the prisoners and the Government is narrow enough to be bridged, and may even be nonexistent," the paper said on July 15. The sticking point was the government's refusal to send in an official to outline the changes in prison regime that the government would agree to. "It is too petty a principle on which to allow more lives—outside the prison as well as inside—to depend. . . . If he is not to be a negotiator, then the Thesaurus can be combed to make him a trustee, a commissary, a proxy, a surrogate, a vice-gerent."

On July 13, the night after Hurson's death, Mrs. Barbour and I had another surprise visitor, this one most welcome. A priest from the monastery called in, and he sat with us for three hours, soothing our nerves with tales of the neighborhood, the Provos, and the clergy. It was only as he was leaving, some time after 10:00 P.M., that I realized his had not been just a social call. He had come because with Hurson's death, he thought there might be a chance that the IRA would repeat their operation of the previous week, and he had intended to be there to prevent it.

I spent the next day packing, as I was to leave the following morning. The photographer Peress came by that night, and I took him down to the flats to meet some of the people I had interviewed. We walked down the Falls, and just as we passed an army patrol, a sniper started shooting. The soldiers, Peress, and I all dove for cover. I found myself in some bushes, huddled next to a young black soldier who had been shot in the arm.

When I got home that night, I was more than ready to leave. Mrs. Barbour told me that my editor from the *Times* had called, and when I called her back, she told me she was changing my article so she could move it to the cover of the magazine, and that I would therefore have to stay on and do four or five days work. I groaned into the phone. In the last seven days, I had been caught in crossfire once and held captive twice; I had slept in three different houses and had my files in hiding; my neighbors had grown more suspicious of me, and I of them; and it was still possible that a quantity of explosives was festering a few yards from my bedroom window. Even if I had thought the phone connection was secure, I knew there was no way I could convey all that and what it meant to an editor at a desk in Manhattan who had just a dim idea of who McDonnell and Hurson and Alison were, and no conception of the claustrophobia and paranoia of the ghetto; of what it is like to have armed men outside your door, stopping and questioning you whenever they please; of what a plastic bullet is or how the law functions or even how cold and wet and miserable Belfast can be in July.

I stayed on. Mrs. Barbour was leaving to visit her daughter on the mainland, and she was pleased to have someone in the house while she was gone. She had come to accept me as an ally again, though in her dark moments, I suspect she still had her doubts.

On Thursday, July 16, Kieran Doherty had gone fifty-six days without food and was given the last rites. On Saturday, there was a major riot in Dublin when 15,000 people marched on the British embassy. I worked through the night on Sunday, July 19, expecting all the while to be interrupted with the news of Doherty's death, but dawn came without the clash of bin lids. Friends drove me to the airport, where I caught the early morning shuttle to London. I boarded a plane to Chicago that afternoon. I thought Doherty might die in the course of the six-hour flight across the ocean, and I realized I was on a plane full of people who had no idea who he was. It had been hard to stay in the North, but in many ways it was harder to leave.

Kieran Doherty did not die that day, that week, or even the week after. He lasted a remarkable seventy-three days and died on Sunday, August 2.

That night, the Provos finally blew up Hardin's shop. They ran the wires not into Mrs. Barbour's kitchen, but into the back yard of a house on the Kashmir. Some of my neighbors later told me that soldiers had been wounded, while others claimed that those tales were just Republican fantasies. When I checked with the police on a subsequent visit, their press spokesman told me that their record book contained no mention of the incident.

Mrs. Barbour was sitting on a chair in the dining room when the explosion occurred, and the next instant she found herself sitting on the floor. Her windows were blown out, her walls were cracked, and the sitting room ceiling fell to the floor. As it was about one in the morning, there were no repairmen to call, and so she went to bed with the wind blowing through the front window. I called her the next day and she told me she had slept very well.

In early September, the INLA, having lost three of its members on the hunger strike, bowed out of the fast completely. Provisional prisoners were willing to carry on, but their families were not, and after the death of Thomas McElwee on August 8, mothers began pulling their sons off the fast at the last minute. On October 3, the Provos abandoned the strike, having lost seven men.

In Clonard and other districts there was great disillusionment, a sense that ten men had died for nothing, that the Provos had held on for far too long, and that the British had won again. Although the IRA's international image had improved immeasurably and contributions from America had also increased, the press generally concluded that the Provos had "lost" the hunger strike.

In the next year, that would prove to be a very short view.

EPILOGUE

IN THE YEARS since the hunger strike, much has happened to the people in this narrative. The two soldiers who ran their Land Rovers over Gary English and Jim Brown in Derry on Easter Sunday, 1981, were brought to court. They were charged not with murder, but with reckless driving, and they were acquitted.

Reverend Robert Bradford, the member of Parliament who told me he was enjoying Bobby Sands's funeral, was assassinated by the IRA on November 14, 1981. Loyalists retaliated; they chose two Catholic men at random and shot them dead.

Gangster Devlin, the teenager who was kneecapped, elbowed, and shot in the back during the hunger strike, was shot dead by the Provisionals on April 22, 1982. The Provos contended that he had not given up his errant ways despite the earlier shooting. The Provisionals have since assassinated several other petty criminals, acts which they previously believed their supporters would not stomach.

Eleanor McClorey, the teacher at Crazy Joe's, left the flats, driven away by the tensions of the job during the hunger strike, and went to work with runaways in Dublin. Frank Shiels also left his post at Crazy Joe's; he moved to England, taking a job as a youth worker at a housing project in Nottingham.

Father Pat Buckley, the Lone Ranger of Divis Flats, was transferred to Kilkeel, a seaside town forty miles from Belfast, and later to Larne, a port north of the capital. Buckley resented the transfer from the flats, which was ordered by Bishop Cahal Daly, and in recent years has become more outspoken, criticizing the Irish Church in newspapers and magazines as timid and weak. In 1985, Bishop Daly relieved him of his post and his salary. Today, Buckley is a priest without portfolio, but he retains a considerable following from his old parish, and is by no means inactive.

Richmond Stokes, the architect who reluctantly designed a brick wall to replace the Cupar Street peace line, did not have to construct the barrier. The Department of the Environment eventually took over the project, and one of their structural engineers, unaware of Stokes's earlier work, designed a wall of white concrete and green metal plate, 300 meters long and a few inches short of twenty feet high. In 1984, the government tore down the derelict rowhouses of Cupar Street, the relics of the time when working-class Catholics and Protestants lived side by side, and replaced them with the concrete and metal structure. The notion of the peace line as a temporary structure vanished in the process.

Tony Meli, who lost an eye and parts of both arms in 1975 when a loyalist left a bomb in his father's fish and chip shop, met further misfortune on May 19, 1982. He was chatting to the girls behind the counter of the Holy Shop, the religious goods store across from Clonard Monastery, when three men wearing ski masks walked in and shot him in both legs.

The Provos' subsequent statement charged Tony with a list of "antisocial activities," including the theft of £1500 from his father's shop, and indicated that the IRA had shot seventeen-year-old Tony with some regret, given his handicaps. When I spoke to Mr. Meli shortly after the shooting, he told me that money had indeed been stolen from the store, but that his son was not responsible. The elder Meli also said he had by no means asked the Provos to deal with the problem. He believed Tony had been shot as a result of longstanding animosity between the Melis and the Provos—a neighborhood feud unconnected with politics.

I visited Tony in the Royal Victoria Hospital two days after he was shot. His bedsheet was elevated so as not to touch his legs, and his swollen feet stuck out the bottom. One tube ran into his neck, and two others drained his lower body. He had resisted the Provisional gunmen, and in the struggle he had been roughed up and his glass eye had been broken, so he had cuts on his face and an empty eyesocket. I couldn't look at him without feeling pain myself.

Before I went in to see Tony I stopped by another ward and visited Sean Stitt. Stitt was the former head of the Divis Demolition Committee, a man who had been a favorite of the foreign press and who had posed for the *National Geographic* with sledgehammer in hand. I had interviewed him in his glory days, and I used to see him helping out at the H-block parades, long before anyone had heard of Bobby Sands. His fortunes and his standing in the flats, however, had declined considerably in the two years that I had known him. In the spring of 1982, he was in the hospital because he too had been kneecapped. The IRA accused him of masquerading as a community worker in the flats, of using that status as a cover for criminal activities that included fencing stolen goods, stealing several hundred pounds from the Divis H-Block Committee, and helping to burn two buses belonging to a youth club. Stitt denied all.

He had been lying in bed for four weeks when I saw him, and he expected to be in the hospital for another six. He told me that the gunmen had told him to lie on the floor of the Divis Community Center, that their first shot had gone through his right leg, hit the hard floor, and then ricocheted back, travelling through his thigh a second time. The femur was destroyed, he told me, and he showed me the steel pin and pulley mechanism by which the leg was then suspended. His left leg also looked thin and weak, but he assured me it was not as bad because the second shot had not been so damaging.

I thought that Stitt might consider starting over, perhaps in some other part of the United Kingdom, as unemployment in the Republic was mounting. When I suggested that course, he told me he couldn't leave. He was barred from the British mainland by an exclusion order, issued under the authority of the Prevention of Terrorism Act. Dishonored, disabled, and barred from escape, he seemed doomed to stay in Belfast.

While the Provos' rough justice continued, so did the legal authority's version. "Protests from the United Kingdom about human rights violations abroad come ill from a government which demands such excessive powers for itself," the London-based National Council for Civil Liberties said in 1981. "The United Kingdom government and the British press and large portions of the British public condemned the Soviet government's 'internal exile' of Sakharov and other dissidents. But a system of internal exile is precisely what the Prevention of Terrorism Act has created for the United Kingdom." The NCCL's protest fell on deaf ears.

More disturbing, however, were the killings of thirty-four men by the security forces in Northern Ireland between October 1982 and March 1986. Those killed were offered little or no chance to surrender; about half were unarmed, and many had no connection to any paramilitary group. A coroner with thirty-three years service resigned because of irregularities in police reports of one incident, and in two cases policemen admitted that their superiors had ordered them to fabricate their accounts. In many of the incidents, it appeared that the security forces had simply executed someone they didn't like, a suspected or known member of a paramilitary group. In October 1985, Amnesty International called for an independent judicial inquiry; the government turned down the request.

In May 1982, the European Parliament voted by a large majority to ban the use of plastic bullets in member countries. The measure was not binding, however, and Britain continued to use the lethal weapon in Northern Ireland. Thus far, the bullets have killed more than a dozen people, six of them children between the ages of ten and fifteen.

When I returned in the spring of 1982, any thoughts Mrs. Barbour had had about leaving the district seemed to have disappeared completely. The ceilings and walls affected by the last summer's bombing had been restored, and the only evidence I could see of the incident was in Hardin's shop next door. Hardin's building was still standing, but the windows and doors were covered with corrugated iron.

The seal, however, was not a good one. I wasn't in the house a fortnight before I began hearing visitors next door, and memories of the previous July began to haunt me. I could not sleep through the night. I would wake up thinking I had heard noises, and I would have to go downstairs to make sure the front door was bolted. Mrs. Barbour tried in vain to get someone to seal the building, calling City Hall, the Department of the Environment, and even the parish priest. I nailed the shop's back door shut, but my handiwork stayed intact for less than a week.

All through May and June I anticipated some disaster. It finally came, but it did not originate from the shop next door. The Provisionals had stored some explosives at Kelly Brothers', a builder's yard on Springfield Avenue, and on June 28, 1982, at 7:30 in the morning, army bomb experts blew the material, and the neighborhood, to pieces.

I woke, felt something in the air, heard the explosion, and saw the window break, the blinds fall, and a cloud of dust float in. I had been up very late the night before, and I was so tired that I gave momentary thought to staying in bed. Mrs. Barbour, however, was up and alarmed, calling to make sure I was all right, and so I struggled into some clothes and went downstairs to inspect the damage.

The door locks had been blown apart and the doors were wide open. The windows in the sitting room were gone, as was one pane in Mrs. Barbour's room and the window in my bedroom. Soot, shaken loose from the chimney, wafted into the sitting room, and a three-foot wedge from a corner of the ceiling was on the floor. The rest of the ceiling stayed put, only to collapse one night, six weeks later, after Mrs. Barbour slammed the front door.

Out on the Springfield, a light rain was falling, a chill was in the air, and there was rubble in the street. Meli's fish and chip shop was cut away like a doll's house; through a two-story hole you could see a chair standing in the second floor bedroom. No one in the district was seriously injured, but nine homes were completely destroyed and ceilings and windows were down and out everywhere.

Mrs. Barbour was unnerved; it was her second bombing in less than a year. She suggested I run across the street to Campbell Brothers to order new glass for the windows. Campbell Brothers was in ruins.

The devastation, the rain, and my own lack of sleep were more than I could stand, and after a half hour of standing around as inactive as everyone else, I went back to bed. Two hours later, I awoke to the sound of Mrs. Barbour sweeping up the glass outside, and I hurriedly joined in the repairs. The sun came out, the road became a hive of activity, and the despondency of early morning gave way to a cheerful reconstruction.

Soldiers were everywhere, but they were relaxed, certain no snipers would venture out in a situation like this. People loaned each other tools, men sawed boards on the public sidewalk, and Mrs. Barbour began to cook soup for a lonely neighbor down the street. By eleven o'clock, representatives from the government's compensation office were going door to door, handing out claim forms and explaining how they should be filled out, and a truckload of hardboard had been trucked in, courtesy of the Housing Executive.

I claimed a piece of hardboard, cut it to the size of the broken pane in Mrs. Barbour's bedroom, and climbed onto the roof over the sitting room window to nail the board in place. As I stood on that high perch, looking at the rubble and the reconstruction, I was completely at ease, a feeling I had never had before in Belfast, and which I have not had since. A great peace had descended on the district. We'd had our trouble, we'd survived, and we all knew the law of averages would spare us from serious calamity for at least a few days, maybe a week. I thought I should get a camera and take some pictures, but I couldn't bring myself to do it, as if doing my real work would somehow spoil the day.

The security forces had one story about the explosion, the Provos another. In the security forces' version, the bomb disposal team arrived on the site in response to a tipoff. They found explosives stored in a van in the builder's yard and towed the vehicle out into the middle of the Springfield Road, believing it was safer to toy with the material in an open area than in the enclosed yard. In the meantime, police and soldiers attempted to evacuate the nearby houses; some people spent the night in church halls, but others refused to leave their homes. The bomb squad's third attempt at controlled detonation resulted in the explosion, which damaged more than 300 homes and resulted in about $5 million in compensation claims. A police superintendent estimated that a thousand pounds of explosives had been blown up, the largest bomb that had ever exploded in Belfast.

The Provos' version of the story was somewhat different. They had indeed stored explosives at Kelly's yard, they said, but it was their homemade co-op mix (a formula that does not become unstable like gelignite), the material was not primed, and there was no command wire or detonator on the premises. The Provos claimed that the army could have carried off the material and disposed of it at their leisure in a safe place, that the bomb squad had blown up the van for the predictable effect it would have on the Provos' relationship with the community: the explosion would suggest that the IRA had no concern for the Catholics they lived among, that they would store their materials wherever they saw fit.

In the end, the incident became just another unexplainable incident. Some in Clonard believed the Provos. Others just chalked it up as an act of God, like a bad wind that had blown through the district. You suffered and you talked about it for awhile and then you went back to your normal life.

Brendan Kelly, the owner of the yard, turned himself in to the police shortly after the explosion. He told them that he had been held for two days by masked gunmen who had demanded the keys to his yard. "I thought my life was in danger," he said, but the police charged him with withholding information. The judge refused to grant bail.

By the end of the week, a few slates on Mrs. Barbour's roof were still missing, and the ceiling in the sitting room had not yet fallen down, but on the whole the house was in good shape. Mrs. Barbour had had the window frames painted just a few weeks before the explosion, and one night when we were both looking out the window she realized that the paint job had been ruined. She told me she would have to call the painters back again, then added that she'd better wait until after August 9, the anniversary of internment, the annual night of bonfires and resistance in Catholic areas. "After the next one," she said, "then I'll get it done."

During the 1981 hunger strike a chorus of diverse voices on the British mainland called for reform in the nation's relationship with the North. "The last great service Britain can do for Northern Ireland is to leave it," the *Sunday Times* proclaimed on August 23, 1981. "The present state of affairs . . . is indefensible. For Britain to pretend anything else any longer is a dereliction of the responsibilities of government." Merlyn Rees, a former Secretary of State for Northern Ireland, called for withdrawal of the guarantee, the promise to Ulster Unionists that the North would be part of the UK as long as a majority wanted it so, the promise that allows Unionists to refuse to share power with Catholics. David Owen, former Labour Foreign Secretary and a leader of the newly formed Social Democrats, proposed that the EEC be asked to work on the problem.

Britain's relationship with Northern Ireland, however, has often been compared to the situation of a man whose roof leaks who considers the problem only when it rains. When I returned to Belfast in the spring of

1982, Britain was fighting Argentina in the Falkland Islands, the hunger strike and the calls for reform were already forgotten, and it took quite a violent storm to catch Britain's attention. On July 20, three weeks after the Springfield Road explosion and a month after Argentina's defeat, there was such a storm. Two bombs exploded in London, killing seven soldiers on a bandstand in Regents Park, and four soldiers and seven horses in Hyde Park.

British outrage was fierce, and was directed not only at the Provos, but at the Irish in general. Tory MPs demanded that the Irish in Britain be forced to carry identity cards. The *Daily Telegraph* called for internment. The Irish embassy, the Irish airline office, the *Irish Times*, and the Irish Tourist Board all received abusive and threatening calls.

Mrs. Thatcher denounced the bombers in the House of Commons, calling them "evil and brutal men who know nothing of democracy." This delighted the Provisionals, who pointed out, in the July 22 issue of the *Republican News*, that if the bombers had grown up in Northern Ireland under British rule, they could not be expected to know anything of democracy. In addressing the charge that the Provos had brutally attacked musicians and horsemen performing ceremonial duties, the editors of the paper asked if the British Army had not attacked the IRA's color guard at Joe McDonnell's funeral, also performing ceremonial duties. Needling Mrs. Thatcher further, the editors went on to quote her justification for the use of force in the South Atlantic war: "You have to be prepared to defend the things in which you believe," she had said three months earlier, "and be prepared to use force if that is the only way to secure the future of liberty and self-determination."

Even the Peace People, by no means friends of the Provos, questioned Mrs. Thatcher's moral posture, calling to mind the Argentine ship the British had torpedoed on May 2, an act that killed 368 men before war was declared between the two nations. "If the sinking of the *General Belgrano*, in international waters, with no state of war existing between the nations involved, is not terrorism, then what is?" asked the editor of the Peace People's newspaper. "If Mrs. Thatcher justified the use of extreme force in order to allow the people of the Falklands to live in the kind of society they want, can the Provos not justify the use of the same methods in the name of the people of Crossmaglen and Ballymurphy?"

The right of self-determination that Mrs. Thatcher wanted to guarantee the Falklanders was not a right that the British had offered to the people of Ireland when they divided the nation in 1921. A majority of the citizens of Ireland at that time were opposed to partition. "The border had no point or meaning except as the largest area which the Protestant tribe could hold against the Catholic," the *Sunday Times* Insight Team reported in 1972. "Protestant supremacy was the only reason why the state existed. As such the state itself was an immoral concept. It therefore had to be maintained from the first by immoral means. . . . For the British, the tragedy was that—through historical obligation and then through sloth and lack of perception—they became involved in the defense of a morally indefensible entity. . . . Nothing was more certain than that Catholics would continue to struggle against the state. They knew the evil in which it had been born and reared, and since evil begets evil, they were prepared to see their own struggle carried on by evil means."

The war in the Falklands lasted seventy-four days. It took the lives of 256 British soldiers and more than 700 Argentines. It cost the British treasury one million pounds for each of the 1,500 British citizens on the islands, and fortifying the islands afterward required two soldiers for every inhabitant. Nonetheless, it was a popular war with the British, and it restored Mrs. Thatcher's popularity. By the time the 1983 Parliamentary elections came around, two years after the death of Bobby Sands, no one on the mainland seemed to remember him. Thatcher's opposition denounced her for her economic policies, while she predicted victory for her party "because of our steadfastness and our perseverance and our rightness." The North was not discussed at all.

The Conservatives were returned to Parliament in overwhelming numbers, and Mrs. Thatcher won a second term as prime minister.

I was not at all surprised when the Provisionals tried to kill her a year later. On October 12, 1984, a bomb went off in the Grand Hotel in Brighton during the annual Conservative Party conference. Five people were killed, thirty were seriously wounded, and Mrs. Thatcher was lucky to escape unharmed.

With the end of the hunger strike, Sinn Fein was finally rid of the albatross of the H-block campaign and it began to concentrate its efforts on social issues. When a child died of gastroenteritis because of poor maintenance of the sewers in the Moyard housing project in west Belfast, Sinn Fein representatives were there lending their voice to the protest. When residents of Turf Lodge were harassed by the police, Sinn Fein publicized their plight. Provisional spokesmen, who previously had talked mostly of military struggle, began to speak of agriculture and unemployment and housing. Where Sinn Fein had formerly been just a propaganda arm of the IRA, in 1982 it seemed that the IRA was just a violent arm of the political party Sinn Fein.

The strategy had stunning results. In October 1982, the government held elections for the Northern Ireland Assembly, a newly created parliament with only advisory powers. Sinn Fein, having learned how powerful elections could be with the Sands's victory, departed from their previous policy of boycotting British elections and nominated candidates. Catholic voters had a clear choice: the SDLP preached nonviolence, while Sinn Fein candidates backed violent means and in some cases had held the gun themselves. When the votes were tallied, one third of the Catholic electorate had backed the party of the gunmen.

"For a decade now," wrote columnist John Healey in the *Irish Times*, "it has been part of the condemnation industry that those who carried out acts of violence, claiming to act on behalf of the Irish people, had no such mandate. The Assembly election has taken that comfortable assertion away from those who champion the political solution. The deeper tragedy is that the British do not see the historical inevitability of it. The Irish see history repeating itself. The British don't."

What the Irish saw was a replay of 1916. The band of rebels who began the Easter Rising by taking over the General Post Office in Dublin were extremists with no mandate from the people of Ireland. After Britain executed fifteen of the ringleaders, however, the rebels were transformed from a violent fringe to popular heroes, and their violence, not legitimate when it occurred, was made legitimate in retrospect. Now, in 1982, in the wake of ten deaths in the Maze, armed republicans had been made legitimate once more.

The 1982 elections proved to be no fluke. Sinn Fein candidates have continued to declare their unambiguous support for armed struggle. Members of the Catholic hierarchy have denounced the party, encouraging their flock to vote SDLP, and Sinn Fein campaign workers have been repeatedly harassed by the police and army. Yet in local and parliamentary elections in the last four years, 35 to 42 percent of the Catholic electorate has voted Sinn Fein.

Britain's creation of ten martyrs in 1981 and the mainland's refusal to pay attention to the problems of the North are not the only reasons why Catholics are demonstrating their support for the IRA's political wing. Some vote for Sinn Fein because its representatives work hard to deliver services to the community. Others vote for the party out of general despair; in many ways, Catholics are worse off today, under direct rule by the British, than they were under the old Unionist regime, and many Catholic voters would argue that the goals of the civil rights movement of 1967 have yet to be realized.

Discrimination in housing has been largely eliminated by the Housing Executive, and the quality of housing has greatly improved in the last ten years, but discrimination in employment has hardly changed. Although Catholics made up about 39 percent of the population in the 1981 census, a Fair Employment Agency investigation in 1983 found that the proportion of Catholics at the highest levels of the civil service was 8 percent, down from 8.4 percent a decade earlier. An FEA investigation of the Northern Ireland Electricity Service in 1982 found that it was "a Protestant preserve," with Catholics making up 4 percent of senior management and 10 percent of the engineering staff. A 1984 FEA report on the Northern Ireland Fire Service found that although Catholics represented 33 percent of the applicants for full-time employment, they got only 12 percent of the jobs.

The civil rights demonstrators of 1967 wanted to see the B-Specials disbanded and the Special Powers Act repealed. The B-Specials are gone, but they have been replaced by a sectarian militia—the Ulster Defense Regiment—which is 97 percent Protestant. The Special Powers Act has been replaced by two pieces of emergency legislation which were called "draconian" and "unpalatable to a democratic society" by the two Cabinet ministers who presented them to Parliament. The civil rights activists' demand for one-man, one-vote was granted, but when Catholics elected Mr. Sands to Parliament, Britain changed the rules, and when Catholics elected Sinn Fein leaders Gerry Adams, Martin McGuinness, and Danny Morrison to the Assembly in 1982, the British sent the trio exclusion orders, banning them from the mainland, preventing them from attending a scheduled session with London city councilmen who wanted to hear Sinn Fein's case.

The North today has the highest infant mortality, the highest unemployment, the lowest wages, the lowest standard of living, and the lowest life expectancy in the United Kingdom. It has more than double the per capita prison population of the mainland. The industrial landscape is so bleak (more than one out of four men is out of work, and in Catholic Strabane, the figure is one out of two) that the development authorities cannot convince even British companies to invest; British corporations will invest in the Republic, but not in the North. In December 1982, the *Sunday Times* reported that experts were divided on the North's economic crisis: some believed it could take twenty years to solve its problems, while others believed the problems were beyond solution.

All of this helped feed Sinn Fein, and Sinn Fein's growth ultimately alarmed the British and was in part the impetus for the Anglo-Irish Agreement. The agreement, signed by Mrs. Thatcher and Garret FitzGerald in November 1985, conceded to the Republic an advisory role in the management of the North. The pact was historic in that Britain finally recognized that the Republic had an interest in the North, but the role awarded to the Republic was largely symbolic, and the treaty was not by any means a solution to the problems of Northern Ireland. In its first year, the agreement did not change the lives of Northern Catholics at all. Protestants, however, reacted violently to the signing of the accord, burning policemen out of their homes, pummelling the Northern Ireland Secretary at Belfast City Hall, shutting off electricity supplies, and rioting on numerous occasions. The risen loyalists succeeded in intimidating the British government; various reforms in the court system were postponed, for example, due to the upheaval on the streets.

―――――

While the world finds the problem in the North complex, a teenager in Clonard or Ballymurphy sees it as elementary. He knows he will have no work, or if he does have it, it will not reflect his intelligence or pay him enough to escape the ghetto. He finds himself regarded not as a citizen, but as a suspect, and at some point in his young life he will probably have a confrontation with the army or the police that will convince him that those forces are not his protectors. He will probably get little guidance from his parish priest, except perhaps at election time, and it is unlikely that he will reach adulthood knowing a single neighbor who is active in the SDLP. Given his natural desire for dignity and his conviction that the system is unjust, it comes as no surprise when he assumes the role of the violent man or his auxiliary.

"Before the unreasonable or the unyielding, even moderation has to resort to violence to be heard," the reporters of Thames Television wrote in their book, *The Troubles*. "However unpalatable, the fact is that violence, and often only violence, has been effective in achieving progress in Ireland."

The British government and even some segments of the British press, however, seem to have a hard time understanding this, and they speak of the conflict as a war against the barbarians. The headlines "Monsters" and "These Evil Bastards" have been employed by tabloids after IRA atrocities, and in a televised Christmas message in 1982, Mrs. Thatcher claimed the army was "fighting the forces of darkness" in the North. The logical conclusion to this line of thought is that the IRA is not a symptom but the cause of problems in the North, that repressive laws and extra-legal police behavior will pacify, not enrage the natives, and that the IRA's defeat will bring peace to the North. With that end in mind, the British proclaim the Provisionals' impending demise every few years. In 1972, the Provos' command structure was "greatly weakened." In 1976, the IRA was "reeling." In 1977 and 1978, the IRA was "finished," "degenerating into Chicago type gangsters," and being squeezed "like . . . toothpaste." In 1981, the Provos played "their last card."

James Prior, Secretary of State for Northern Ireland from 1981 to 1984, visited Washington in the wake of Sinn Fein's first electoral victories. According to reports in the *Belfast Telegraph*, he "stressed that there was good news emerging from Northern Ireland. He said there was a greater degree of security and a return to normality with the Grand Opera House in Belfast and city cinemas full." The paper also reported that Prior told a Westminster Committee on Industry and Trade, that the government had to do more to "project a more realistic image of Northern Ireland," to show "the high degree of normality in everyday life."

And that normality is indeed there. The bread is in the shops. The milk is on the doorstep. The police outside City Hall carry automatic weapons, but you hardly notice it after a while. Unless you know where to look, and unless you care to look there, it is easy to believe that it is not a society in a state of suppressed war, but a society at peace which is plagued by a few "godfathers of violence" who will soon be sorted out by the police, the army, or the Diplock courts.

It has not been difficult to sell the British view to Americans, in large part, I think, because Northern Ireland is largely ignored by the American press. No American newspaper or television network has a bureau in Belfast. The violence and brutality of the IRA are easy to portray by reporters who drop in for a quick visit in the wake of some atrocity, but the cruelty of the society that drives men to take up arms is more subtle and requires some time to understand. As a result, the barbarian view of the IRA prevails in the United States, and there is little protest when the Reagan administration denies visas to Sinn Fein representatives when they attempt to visit and explain their viewpoint.

This limited and unrealistic coverage of the North is particularly sad, as it prevents Americans from learning the North's lessons, and there is much to be learned there about emergency legislation, police behavior, segregation, and the way a nation with noble intentions can generate such resistance among people they believe they are protecting. A study of Northern Ireland might cause Americans to pause and reflect about their own ghettoes, to wonder what could happen in a land where, in 1985, 40 percent of black teenagers were out of work, or perhaps even to think about Puerto Rico, a colony of high unemployment, a separate national identity, and a violent fringe that studies the tactics of the IRA.

How long can the British wage this peace in the North? Can the citizens of England, Scotland, and Wales stomach it for four or five more decades, until Catholics, with their higher birth rate, outnumber Protestants and vote their way out? (And not all demographers believe that new majority will come to exist.) It would mean more dead cavalrymen in Hyde Park, another dead Mountbatten or two or six, a continuing series of embarassing political postures like internal exile or internment (they matter little, as the whole world is not watching), hundreds more dead in the North (they matter little, they're only Irish), and a continuing drain on the British economy. Can this go on for two more generations? Yes, that seems possible.

I am reminded of the re-enactment of the Battle of the Boyne at Scarva in 1980, and the words of King William as he conquered King James for the thirty-sixth time in thirty-six years. "We've been doing it so long," he said, "that we don't need any practice."

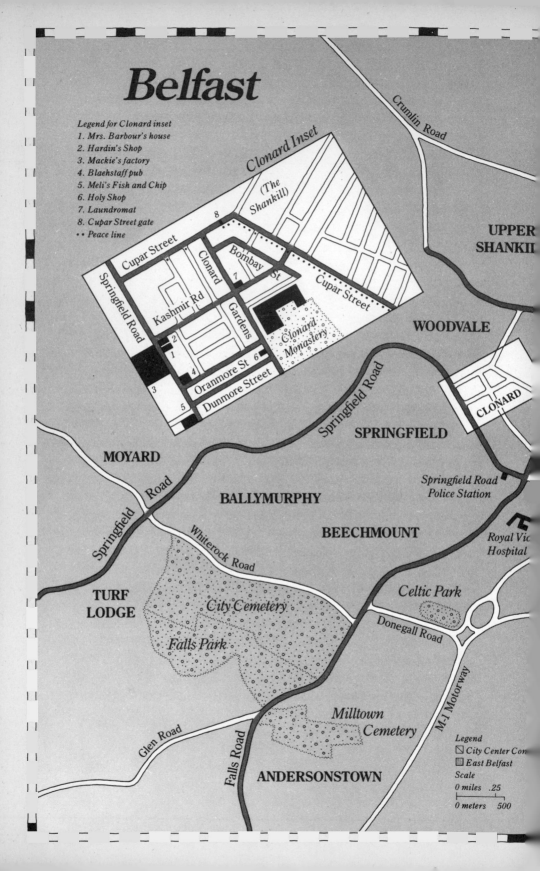

Belfast

Legend for Clonard inset
1. Mrs. Barbour's house
2. Hardin's Shop
3. Mackie's factory
4. Blaehstaff pub
5. Meli's Fish and Chip
6. Holy Shop
7. Laundromat
8. Cupar Street gate
•• Peace line

Clonard Inset

(The Shankill)

Cupar Street
Clonard
Bombay St
Cupar Street
Springfield Road
Kashmir Rd
Gardens
Clonard Monastery
Oranmore St
Dunmore Street

Crumlin Road

UPPER SHANKII

WOODVALE

CLONARD

SPRINGFIELD

Springfield Road

MOYARD

Springfield Road

BALLYMURPHY

Springfield Road Police Station

BEECHMOUNT

Whiterock Road

Royal Vic Hospital

TURF LODGE

City Cemetery

Celtic Park

Falls Park

Donegall Road

Milltown Cemetery

M-1 Motorway

Glen Road

Falls Road

ANDERSONSTOWN

Legend
◹ City Center Con
◩ East Belfast
Scale
0 miles .25
0 meters 500

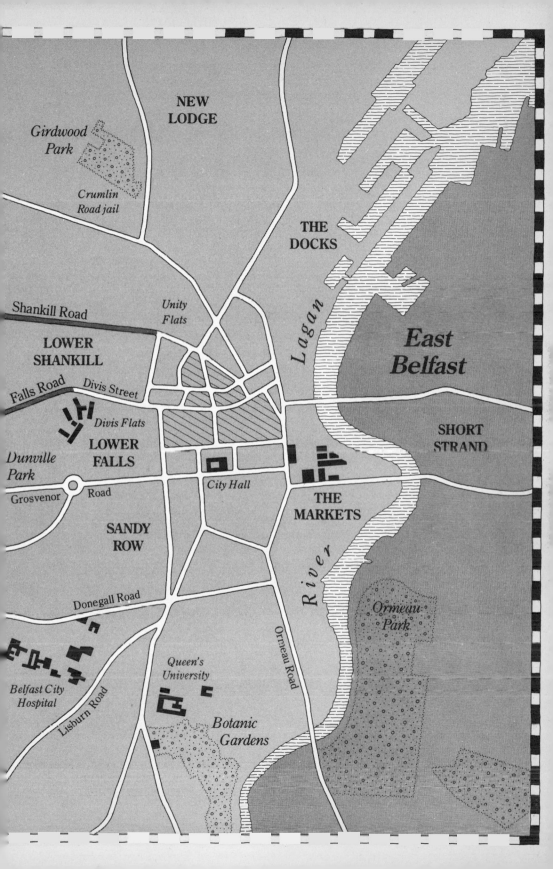